THE WORLD'S WORST CRIMES

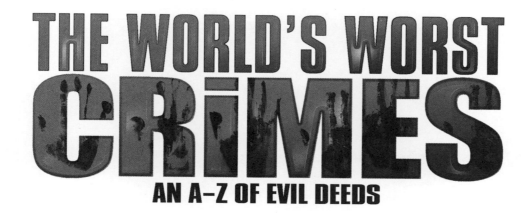

THE WORLD'S WORST CRIMES

AN A–Z OF EVIL DEEDS

CHARLOTTE GREIG with PAUL ROLAND, NATHAN CONSTANTINE and JO DURDEN SMITH

Capella

This edition published in 2008 by Arcturus Publishing Limited
26/27 Bickels Yard, 151–153 Bermondsey Street,
London SE1 3HA

Copyright © 2007 Arcturus Publishing Limited

ISBN: 978-1-84193-827-1

Printed in Singapore

CONTENTS

INTRODUCTION

The motives that drive people to commit the most ghastly and hideous crimes are many and varied, and so are the criminals. There is an undeniable and compelling interest in these crimes and the people who carry them out. We may not care to admit it, even to ourselves, but evil has its attractions – even if it is only to act as a warning to others.

Some people will kill for money, having no real sense of right or wrong to show them that a handful of cash is not worth a human life. John Haigh tried to claim bizarre motives for his murders in a bid to get a verdict of insanity, but he undoubtedly killed for cash benefit. Belle Gunnes likewise murdered for profit, working her way through an unknown number of husbands and lovers to gain their money.

Others kill out of pride or to show their fellow criminals that they are worthy of respect. Many a gang member has killed, sometimes more than once, simply so that he would fit in. The true gang bosses, of course, keep themselves carefully removed from any actual crimes. Al Capone was famously convicted of tax evasion after police failed to find any evidence

to link him directly with the many crimes that his gang carried out on his orders. Dutch Schultz was similarly careful, but this did not save him from being murdered by his fellow gangsters when he got too arrogant.

A few crimes spring from simple amoral arrogance. Nathan Leopold and Richard Loeb killed because they were bored and wanted to see if they could outfox the police.

Sex has long been a prime motive in killing. Jealous rage or lust has been enough to turn some men into killers. More disturbing perverted urges have driven others. Peter Kürten roamed Germany in the 1930s killing for pleasure with ever-increasing ferocity. Kenneth Bianchi and Angelo Buono found fame as the Hillside Stranglers in 1970s California as they raped and butchered a succession of women. Some find the most unlikely accomplices. Sex killer Paul Bernardo had the help of his attractive girlfriend Karla Homolka, even when her own sister became a victim.

Some get a taste for murder and kill for many reasons. Charles Ng and Leonard Lake killed men for money, women for sexual kicks and children if they got in the way. They did away

with about 25 people in 14 months.

The most prolific serial killer of all was Dr Harold Shipman who snuffed out the lives of hundreds of his patients. Disturbingly, nobody really knows why.

Few of those who have perpetrated the most horrific crimes would fit the general image of evil come to life. Some are quiet, others gregarious. Some are charming, others rude. Only their heartless devotion to killing, mayhem and crime links them together.

Doubt hangs over the convictions of some. Albert DeSalvo was convicted of the Boston Strangler murders. Although he was undoubtedly a perverted sex offender, some think he was no killer, but had been framed by the real culprit. Doubt of another kind hovers over John Dillinger: many think that it was another gangster who died in a hail of police bullets in 1934 and that he got away.

No doubt hangs over the fact that there are evil men and women among us. Many make mistakes and are caught. Others are still active. They kill, rob and maim, but they are not caught. They are out there still.

THE ACID BATH MURDERS

Arguably Britain's worst serial killer since Jack the Ripper, John George Haigh the 'Acid Bath Murderer' remains something of an enigma. Was he a calculating swindler who murdered for profit? Did he deliberately portray himself as a crazed lunatic who needed to drink human blood so that he could plead insanity? Or was he indeed a modern-day vampire?

John Haigh was born on 24 July 1909 in Stamford, Yorkshire, in the north of England. Soon after his birth, his parents, John Robert and Emily, moved to Outwood, near the larger town of Wakefield. They were both members of the Plymouth Brethren, an ultra-puritanical Christian sect, with a hellfire ideology based on sin and punishment.

BACKGROUND

The family seems to have been settled enough, but religion dominated Haigh's childhood. His father often showed him a scar that he said was a punishment from God for committing a sin. The young Haigh at first lived in fear of receiving such a mark himself, but when he did sin and received no such mark, he began to develop the profound cynicism that would characterize his adult life.

On leaving school, Haigh worked briefly as a car mechanic. Although he loved cars, he had a lifelong aversion to dirt (later he would habitually wear gloves to avoid contamination). He soon left the job and worked briefly as a clerk before finding a career in which he was able to exploit an already well-developed ability to embellish the truth: he became an advertising copywriter. He did well at the job and bought himself a flash Alfa Romeo car. But before long he was sacked after some money went missing.

In 1934 he met and married Beatrice Hammer. Four months later he was convicted of fraud for a scam involving hire-purchase agreements, and sent to prison. While he was there, Beatrice gave birth to a child who she immediately gave up for adoption. On his release, Haigh left Beatrice and then simply ignored her, acting as if he had never been married.

Prison seemed to have shocked Haigh back on to the straight and narrow. He started a dry-cleaning company that prospered until his partner in the business died in a motorcycle accident, and business began to decline with the coming of war. Haigh then moved to London where he worked in an amusement arcade, owned by a man

◄ John Haigh arrives for his trial which shocked post-war Britain

named Donald McSwann. A year later, he struck out on his own with a scam that resulted in him being sent to prison again, this time for four years. In prison he talked a lot to his fellow inmates about committing the perfect crime. An imperfect understanding of the law allowed him to develop the notion that if the police could not find a body, then the killer could not be convicted of murder. He decided that the best way to effect this would be to dissolve a body in acid. He experimented in the prison workshops, managing to dissolve a mouse in acid.

LIFE AFTER PRISON

Once back in the community, he put his plan into action. He met up with McSwann, luring him to a workshop that he was renting. Haigh then killed him and, with some difficulty, dumped his body into a large barrel of acid that he had prepared for the purpose. The plan worked perfectly and Haigh was able to

him to sell off their substantial estate. For the next three years he lived off the money he had received. Thanks to his gambling habit, however, the money ran out and he had to look around for new victims.

He found a couple called Archie and Rosalie Henderson, who met the same fate as the McSwanns and once again Haigh managed to get his hands on their estate. However, it took him less than a year to get through their money. By February 1949 he was unable to pay the bill at the hotel he was living in, a place called the Onslow Court, popular with rich widows. He persuaded one of the widows, Olivia Durand-Deacon, that he had a business plan she might be interested in. She agreed to come with him to his new workshop, located next to a small factory in Surrey, just outside London. Once there he shot her in the head, removed her jewellery and fur coat, and dumped her in an acid bath.

Within two days a friend of Mrs Durand-Deacon alerted the police and mentioned that she had been planning to meet Haigh. Haigh claimed that she had never arrived at the meeting, but his manner was suspicious and they decided to investigate further.

They learned of his workshop in Surrey and obtained a search warrant. They found several clues to suggest that

tip the last sludgy remains of his friend down a drain. McSwann's parents were suspicious but Haigh managed to fob them off with the story that McSwann had fled to Scotland to avoid being drafted to fight in the war.

When the war ended and McSwann failed to return, his parents became more suspicious. Haigh took drastic action. He lured the parents to the workshop and murdered them both, just as he had killed their son. He then forged letters to enable

Mrs Durand-Deacon had been there, and then obtained evidence from a local shopkeeper, who identified Haigh as the man who had sold him the widow's jewellery. They duly brought Haigh in for questioning.

THE DEFENCE

Once in custody, Haigh boasted that Mrs Durand-Deacon would never be found because he had dissolved her in acid, believing that without her body they would be unable to charge him. In fact, once the police went back and dredged through the hideous sludge in the bottom of the acid bath, they found several pieces of human bone and part of Durand-Deacon's dentures.

The game was clearly up for Haigh, who now switched his tactics. Clearly aiming to plead insanity, he confessed to the murders of the McSwanns and the Hendersons, as well as three other murders of unidentified victims. He claimed that the motives were not financial but that he was tormented by dreams that dated back to his religious childhood. These dreams apparently gave him an unquenchable thirst for human blood – that he sucked up through a drinking straw. It was generally believed that he had added a confession to the three mystery victims because the motivation for the murders of his actual victims was so clearly financial.

The defence found a psychiatrist to attest to Haigh's insanity, but the jury was not convinced, and he was found guilty of murder and sentenced to death by hanging. The sentence was carried out at Wandsworth Prison, London, on 6 August 1949.

ALL IN THE FAMILY

From the age of 9 until he was 32, Charles Manson, who was born illegitimate, spent almost all of his life in institutions, though he did spend enough time on the outside to be sent down for armed robbery (at 13), homosexual rape (at 17) and car stealing, fraud and pimping (at 23). In prison for this last set of offences, he became, by an odd coincidence, the protégé of another killer, Alvin Karpis of the notorious Barker Gang, who taught him the guitar well enough for him to be able to boast later:

'I could be bigger than the Beatles.'

In a way of course, Manson was. For, let out of prison in 1967, the year of 'the summer of love,' he became the most hated and vilified figure in America, a symbol of everything that had gone wrong in the 60s.

Emerging from San Pedro prison with little more than a beard, a guitar and a line in mystic hocus-pocus, Manson was soon playing hippie Jesus on the streets of nearby Haight-Ashbury to a group of adoring disciples – most of them middle-class drop-outs who lived on a diet of hallucinogenic drugs and acted out their fantasies in sex orgies. It wasn't long, though, before he decided his ambitions were too big for San Francisco. So he took his 'Family' south, picking up new acolytes on the way, and settled in the grounds of the Spiral Staircase club in Los Angeles, where he began to attract the attention of the wilder fringes of the Hollywood party scene: musicians, agents and actors looking for kicks or black magic – or the next big thing.

Manson's vision, though, by this time was becoming darker, more apocalyptic; and by the time he moved the 'Family' to the Spahn Movie Ranch 30 miles from the city, he was no longer interested in merely sex, drugs and adoration. He believed that there would soon be a nuclear day of reckoning, called Helter Skelter. He drew up a death list of people he envied or wanted revenge on ('pigs' like Warren Beattie and Julie Christie); and he became obsessed with the idea of a dune-buggy-riding army of survivalists which would escape into the Mojave Desert.

To set up this army – and its transport – he, of course, needed money. So, like a latter-day Fagin, he set his 'Family' to crime: drug-dealing, theft, robbery, credit-card fraud, prostitution and eventually murder. First, a drug-dealer, a bit-part actor and a musician were killed on his orders; and then, when some of his

'Family' were arrested on other charges, he announced Helter Skelter day.

That night, August 8th 1969, four of his demented disciples invaded the house of movie director Roman Polanski and murdered five people, including his pregnant wife Sharon Tate. Before they left, they used Tate's blood to daub the word PIG on the front door.

When he later heard the names of the victims, Manson – who'd chosen the house only because one of the people on his death-list had once lived there – was delighted. As Hollywood panicked, he led the next murderous raid himself, selecting a house for no other reason than that it was next-door to someone he disliked. This time a forty-four-year old

▼ *Theoretically, Manson could have become eligible for parole in 2005*

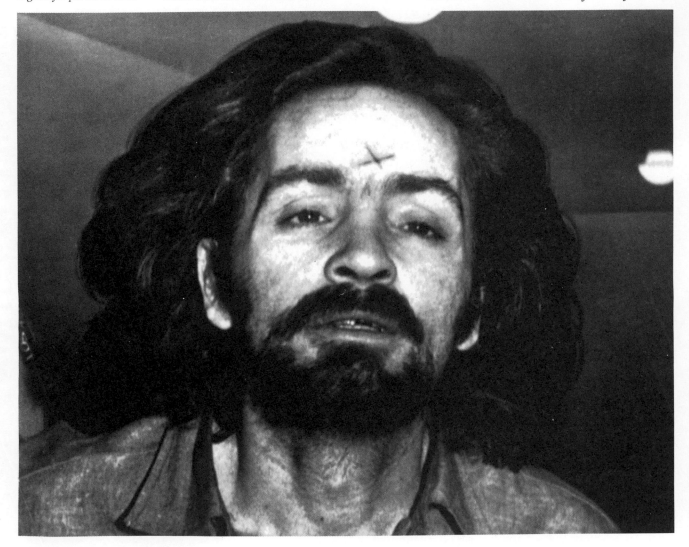

Members of Manson's 'Family' — all were spared the death penalty

supermarket president called Leno LaBianca and his wife Rosemary were stabbed in a frenzy, and their blood used to write DEATH TO PIGS, RISE and HEALTER (sic) SKELTER on the walls. The word WAR was carved onto Mr LaBianca's stomach.

The two cases of multiple murder were investigated by different law-enforcement agencies and at first no connections were made. Manson and members of the 'Family' were arrested, but on other charges, and were eventually released. But then one of Manson's female acolytes told a cell-mate that she'd been involved in the murders. Manson and members of the 'Family,' two of whom later turned state's evidence, were picked up.

The trial of Manson and three of his female acolytes — others were tried elsewhere — lasted nine months, and was not without sensation. When Manson appeared in the dock one day with a cross carved with a razor-blade onto his forehead, the three girls soon burned the same mark onto theirs. On another occasion 5-foot 2-inches tall Manson jumped 10 feet across the counsel table to attack the trial judge, who afterwards took to carrying a revolver in court under his robes.

In the end all four were sentenced to death, but were spared execution when the California Supreme Court voted to abolish the death penalty in 1972. When last heard of, Manson was working as a chapel caretaker in Vacaville Prison in southern California. Theoretically, he became eligible for parole in 2005, when he was 71.

BEER BARON OF THE BRONX

Born in a different time and place, Dutch Schultz was one of those men who might have aspired to greatness. He had brains and vision, plus a definite streak of ruthlessness. However, as he was born into grinding poverty in the Bronx at the beginning of the twentieth century, it is not altogether surprising that he put these attributes to work in the services of organized crime.

BEER BARON OF THE BRONX

Like many other mobsters of his generation – from Al Capone to Lucky Luciano to Meyer Lansky – it was Prohibition that made Schultz his fortune. Known for a time as 'The Beer Baron of the Bronx', Schultz became one of the most powerful and feared men in New York, before his violent life finally led to a violent death.

Dutch Schultz was born Arthur Simon Flegenheimer on 6 August 1902 in the Bronx, New York. His parents were both German Jews and his mother Emma, in particular, tried to pass religious values on to her son. She was successful only to a limited extent. Schulz did take an interest in religion, but not a consistent one. He described himself at various times as Jewish, Protestant and Catholic. As he grew up, he joined one of the street gangs that ruled the streets of the Bronx. When Schultz was fourteen, his father abandoned the family, and young Arthur decided to adopt the criminal life. He started doing jobs for a local mobster, Marcel Poffo. In 1919, when he was seventeen, he was caught burgling an apartment and received his one and only prison sentence.

As often happens, prison only served to turn the young Arthur from apprentice hoodlum to fully fledged criminal. When he came out he had a new name, 'Dutch' Schultz, and a reputation as a hard man. Prohibition had come in the previous year and it was becoming clear that there was big money to be made now that alcohol was illegal. Schultz worked his way up, starting as a hired muscle protecting deliveries, then driving a beer truck, then working in a speakeasy run by a gangster named Joey Noe, a childhood friend. Noe saw Schultz's potential and made him a partner in their bootlegging business. The duo bought their own delivery trucks and gradually forced all the other speakeasy owners in the Bronx to buy their beer from them. Anyone who refused was treated with extreme brutality.

WAR IN GANGLAND

Once they had taken over the business in the Bronx, they turned their attention to Manhattan and stated delivering to speakeasies across the Upper East Side. This soon brought the gang into conflict with 'Legs' Diamond, the mobster who dominated the Manhattan scene. On 15 October 1928, Diamond's men ambushed Joey Noe outside the Chateau Madrid nightclub, shooting him dead. War had been declared; mob money man Arnold Rothstein was shot dead two weeks later. Schultz's main gunman, Bo Weinberg, eventually shot Diamond dead, but not for another three years.

The next threat to Schultz came from within his own organization. In 1931, a gunman named Vincent Coll set himself up as a rival. Angry over an unpaid loan, Schultz brought matters to a head by assassinating Coll's brother. Coll responded by killing four of Schultz's men and hijacking his beer lorries. Schultz refused to stand for this and, after several near misses, he finally had Coll shot dead in a drugstore in February 1932.

EASING IN ON THE NUMBERS RACKET

By now it was clear that the great Prohibition experiment was coming to an end. Schultz was smart enough to

look for another lucrative scam. His attention alighted on the numbers racket, a popular form of gambling particularly prevalent in New York's black communities. Organized crime had paid little attention to the numbers because the individual stakes were generally

Although he had the face of an 'ordinary Joe', mobster Dutch Schultz was anything but

▶ *There was more than just a fly in his soup when Dutch was killed – by order of the Mob – in a Newark chop house*

very small. Schultz, however, realized that if all the different small-scale outfits could be brought together, the total daily take would actually be sizable. With a characteristic mixture of diplomacy and ruthless violence, Schultz proceeded to take over the Harlem lottery.

Soon afterwards, Schultz alighted on another scheme: systematically intimidating the restaurants of New York into paying a weekly amount of protection money – disguised as voluntary membership dues paid to a front organization called the Metropolitan Restaurant & Cafeteria Owners Association. This was run for Schultz by a hood named Jules Martin. Schultz appeared to be riding higher than ever as Prohibition drew to a close, helped by his links to the city's corrupt mayor.

THE LAW CLOSES IN

Nemesis, however, was just around the corner in the shape of Special Prosecutor Thomas E. Dewey, who was determined to nail Schultz. His chosen weapon was the one that had been so effective against Al Capone in Chicago: tax evasion charges. Rather than catch a gangster red-handed, all the prosecution needed to do was prove that he had received substantial earnings and that he had paid no taxes on them.

Thus, on 25 January 1933, Dutch Schulz was indicted for tax evasion. His immediate response was to go on the run. For more than a year, he avoided the law and carried on running his businesses. Finally, however, he grew tired of running and, in November 1934, he gave himself up for trial.

While out on bail, Schultz discovered that Jules Martin had been skimming money from the restaurant shakedowns. Schultz invited his own lawyer and Martin to a meeting. When Martin admitted skimming, Schultz shocked the lawyer by immediately shooting Martin in the head, killing him instantly.

VIOLENT DEATH

Soon after this incident, Schultz's trial began. The first jury was unable to come to an agreement. A retrial was ordered and, much to Dewey's fury, the jury this time acquitted Schulz. When Dewey started preparing new charges. Schultz decided to put out a hit on Dewey. Fellow mob bosses, including Lucky Luciano, decided it would be very bad for business to have Dewey murdered. Instead, they put out their own hit on Schultz. On 23 October 1935, Schultz and three of his men were shot dead in the Palace Chop House in Newark, New Jersey. Thus ended the career of one of the mob's most formidable gangsters.

THE BELTWAY SHOOTINGS

For three weeks in October 2002, John Allen Muhammad, a black ex-US army sergeant, and John Malvo, a Jamaican teenager Muhammad had adopted as his son, brought terror to the area surrounding Washington DC. Known to the media as the 'Beltway Sniper', Muhammad and Malvo killed at least fourteen people and wounded at least five more before they were finally captured. Muhammad was definitely the dominant partner in the killings but his motivation remains obscure. Some believe that, as a convert to Islam, Muhammad may have been carrying out a deliberate terror attack on Washington. By contrast, his ex-wife, Mildred, believes it was part of an elaborate, if crazy, plot to kill her and gain custody of his three children.

EXPERT MARKSMAN

John Muhammad was born John Allen Williams in Louisiana on 30 December 1960. His mother died when he was young and his father was absent, so his grandfather and aunt raised him. Muhammad became a excellent football player, marrying his high-school sweet-heart Carol Williams in 1982. He enlisted in the army in 1985, training as a mechanic and combat engineer. He was transferred to Germany in 1990, fought in the Gulf War in 1991, returned to the United States the following year, and was given an honourable discharge from the army, as a sergeant, in 1994. Unconfirmed reports suggest that his discharge was connected with a grenade attack that Muhammad was accused of carrying out on his fellow soldiers. He did not receive specific sniper training while in the army, but qualified as an expert with the M-16 rifle, a civilian version of which – the Bushmaster .223 – would be the weapon he had when he was finally arrested.

CONVERSION TO ISLAM

After leaving the army, Muhammad settled in Tacoma, in Washington state. By now he was living with his third wife, Mildred, and their three children. Muhammad worked as a car mechanic and started a martial arts school. He converted to the Nation of Islam, changing his name to Muhammad.

At his stage, Muhammad appears to have been a well-respected member of the community. Then things started to go wrong. Soon, he was locked in a bitter custody battle with Mildred. He took the children and fled to Antigua in the Caribbean. There he tried to establish himself as a businessman but ended up helping people to obtain false papers for entry into the US. One of those he helped was a teenage boy called Lee Malvo, originally from Jamaica. When things failed to work out in Antigua, Muhammad returned to Washington state with his three children plus Malvo, whom he claimed was his stepson. Muhammad moved to the town of Bellingham, close to the Canadian border, and attempted to register his children in school there. At this point investigators tracked him down and returned his three children to their mother, who promptly left the state and went into hiding in Maryland. Muhammad and Malvo, now calling himself John as well, stayed in Bellingham for a while. They lived in a homeless shelter but Muhammad seemed to have enough money to take regular flights around the States. During this period, the pair carried out their first murder: they intended to kill a friend of Mildred's in Tacoma, but accidentally shot the woman's niece instead.

In the late summer of 2001, Muhammad and Malvo took a trip down to Louisiana, where Muhammad visited his relatives. He claimed to be doing well, to have a family and business in the Virgin Islands, but his big talk was belied by the fact he had not washed or cut his hair. His relatives were worried about

◄ *Jamaican youth Lee Malvo fell under the spell of the older John Muhammad*

him, as well they might have been. After leaving Louisiana, Muhammad and Malvo bought a car, a blue 1990 Chevrolet Caprice. As they roamed around the States they are suspected to have committed a whole series of robberies and shootings: three in Maryland, one in Alabama and one in Louisiana. Another murder, in Atlanta, is suspected to be their work as well.

By the end of September, the duo may have killed as many as nine times. At first, the murders seemed to be part and parcel of robberies. However, they increasingly seemed to have been carried out for their own sake.

Then came the events of October 2002. On the evening of 2 October, a fifty-five-year-old man was shot and killed in the parking lot of a grocery store in Wheaton, Maryland. The next day, five more people were shot and killed as they went about their business; one mowing a lawn, one mailing a package, one crossing a street, two filling their cars with gas — none of them with any inkling that their next breath would be their last.

RANDOM VICTIMS

Panic was immediate. What could be more terrifying than a sniper — few people imagined there were two of them — hiding out and taking pot shots at passers-by, deciding on a whim whose life to take, and whose to spare.

The next shooting was of a woman in Spotsylvania, Virginia. She survived, but it was now becoming clear that the sniper was circling the Washington suburbs, keeping close to the Beltway, the ring road that surrounds the city. Three more days passed without a shooting, then the duo shot a thirteen-year-old boy outside his school in Bowie, Maryland, leaving a Tarot card at the scene.

The following day, Baltimore police stopped a vehicle driving erratically. The driver identified himself as John Muhammad; John Malvo was also in the car. However, a background check indicated that Muhammad had no outstanding warrants, and — tragically, as it turned out — he was allowed to carry

on. Over the next ten days the pair killed three more times.

STATE OF EMERGENCY

The whole area was now in a state of emergency; people were afraid to go shopping or to fill their cars with gas.

The day after the last killing — a bus driver in Aspen Hill on 22 October — the authorities, acting on a phone tip, searched a house in Tacoma, where Malvo and Muhammad had once lived. Neighbours had complained in January that Muhammad routinely used his backyard for target practice. The authorities issued a nationwide alert for the blue Chevrolet Caprice, and it was announced that an arrest warrant had been issued for Muhammad.

Finally, on 24 October, the vehicle was spotted by a motorist at a rest stop. Washington police soon surrounded the car and found Muhammad and Malvo sleeping inside. They arrested both of them and found that the car had been modified for use as a sniper's hideout. They also found a .223-calibre Bushmaster XM15 rifle in the car.

At trial both Muhammad and Malvo were found guilty of murder. On 9 March 2004, Muhammad was sentenced to death, while Malvo received a sentence of life imprisonment. At time of writing, Muhammad is planning an appeal.

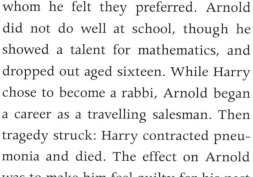

THE BIG BANKROLL

Arnold 'The Brain' Rothstein masterminded the transformation of the New York criminal underworld into a series of highly efficient organized crime syndicates, operating gambling, prostitution, bootlegging and narcotics operations on a grand scale. He is remembered today for his alleged involvement in the Black Sox scandal of 1919, in which it was rumoured that the Chicago baseball team was paid to lose an important match in the World Series. However, his involvement was never verified. He finally met his end in 1928, when he was shot, apparently in a drunken brawl, after failing to pay a gambling debt. Although Rothstein was not a violent man, his business dealings brought him into close contact with many cold-blooded killers, and it was his connections with these men that ultimately brought about his demise.

'THE BIG BANKROLL'

Rothstein was the son of a wealthy New York Jewish businessman, Abraham Rothstein. As a child, he felt unloved by his parents, and was extremely jealous of his older brother Harry, whom he felt they preferred. Arnold did not do well at school, though he showed a talent for mathematics, and dropped out aged sixteen. While Harry chose to become a rabbi, Arnold began a career as a travelling salesman. Then tragedy struck: Harry contracted pneumonia and died. The effect on Arnold was to make him feel guilty for his past jealousy of his brother, and somehow responsible for his death. He attempted to improve family relations by returning home, working in his father's factory and resuming his religious faith, but his father continued to reject him, so he gave up trying to please his parents and moved on.

Rothstein now began to use his mathematical skills in the pursuit of gambling. He started to play pool, poker and craps for money. He also bet on boxing fights, elections, baseball games and horse races. In addition, he booked bets for other people and lent money at high interest rates. In order to impress his colleagues and customers, he began to carry a large wad of money around with him, thus earning the nickname 'The Big Bankroll'. He soon gained a reputation as a cautious, intelligent gambler and began to make a lot of money, which he invested in legitimate businesses such as shops and car dealerships.

▶ *Rothstein — relying on his brains rather than hired brawn, he was a particularly successful, 'white-collar' criminal mastermind*

A LIFE OF LUXURY

One of those whom Rothstein impressed was Carolyn Greene, a young actress. When the couple decided to marry, Rothstein took her home to meet his parents. Abraham asked Carolyn if she would change her faith to become Jewish but she refused. As a result, the Rothstein parents stayed away from the couple's wedding; apparently, when Abraham heard news of it, he recited the Jewish prayer of the dead, the Kaddish, for his son.

The newly married Arnold promised his wife that he would earn as much money as he could to keep her in luxury. She knew of her husband's gambling interests, but later claimed not to have discussed any details of them with him. Over the next few years, Rothstein set up several gambling clubs, enhancing his reputation as one of the best pool players in the city. The clubs attracted wealthy customers who pitted their skills against Rothstein's, both at pool and at cards. As well as running the clubs, Rothstein conducted his many other business ventures from his 'office' at Lindy's Restaurant on the corner of Broadway and 49th Street, often standing on the street outside to collect money, surrounded by his bodyguards.

GODFATHER OF THE MAFIA

By 1913, Rothstein had become one of the most powerful figures in New York, with friends in high places as well as low. His polite manner, his formidable intelligence and, of course, his tolerance towards all kinds of immoral activities made him a central conduit between the corrupt politicians of Tammany Hall and the ruthless mobsters of the criminal world. On the one hand, he received protection from Tammany Hall boss Charles F. Murphy and his advisor Tom Foley; on the other, he was in league with mob bosses such as Lucky Luciano, Meyer Lansky and Bugsy Siegel. Such was his standing in the crime world that he became known by many nicknames, including 'The Brain', 'The Fixer' and 'Mr Big'. As well as his gambling interests, he ran a real estate enterprise, a bail bond business and a racing stables. He amassed a fortune, and expanded his interests in and around the New York area. Today, Rothstein is credited with consolidating organized crime into what later became known as the Mafia.

As well as betting on horse races and baseball games, Rothstein was also rumoured to 'fix' them. The most sensational of these rumours hit the headlines in 1919, during the World Series, when members of the Chicago White Sox team agreed to lose the game to the Cincinnati team for payment. In 1921, eight of the men were convicted of fraud and were banned from playing baseball again professionally. Rothstein was also called to testify in the case, but was acquitted due to lack of evidence. To this day, it is still unclear exactly what his involvement was in the scandal.

THE DAY OF RECKONING

Despite his links with the criminal underworld, Rothstein always seemed to keep his hands clean and emerge unscathed from any scandal. Up until the day of his death, he was never convicted of any criminal activity. However, in 1928, his luck ran out. He took part in a high-stakes game of poker that lasted several days. In the end, he lost a total of over three hundred thousand dollars and, in the weeks that ensued, did not pay off his debts. The host of the game, George McManus, eventually called him to a meeting in a hotel room to settle the matter. Rothstein was then somehow shot in the abdomen. McManus was arrested but later acquitted due to lack of evidence. The shot proved fatal when Rothstein died several days later. Thus, the kingpin of the New York underworld was finally brought down by a dispute over a game of cards.

THE BIRMINGHAM CHURCH BOMBING

On 15 September 1963, one of the most significant racially motivated terrorist attacks ever to take place in the United States occurred at the 16th Street Baptist Church, Birmingham, during a service. On that quiet Sunday morning, nineteen sticks of dynamite, secretly planted by Ku Klux Klan members in the church's basement, detonated with a huge blast. Four teenage girls – Denise McNair, Carole Robertson, Addie Mae Collins and Cynthia Wesley – were killed, and twenty-two more of the congregation injured.

The bombing had been intended to intimidate the black people of Birmingham, who at the time were the subject of constant racist attacks, so much so that the city was becoming known as 'Bombingham'. But this proved to be one bomb too many. The people of Birmingham and America as a whole, both black and white, were outraged by this unprovoked assault on a peaceful group of citizens at prayer, and their calls for justice helped to foster the burgeoning civil rights movement of the day.

When the case came to trial, the authorities, under segregationist governor George Wallace, let the bombers off lightly, in true Southern style. However, resentment against the injustice of the incident continued to simmer, until many years later the case was reopened and the culprits finally brought to book.

◀ *Aftershock: Alabama State Troopers arrive in Birmingham to assist local officers at the scene of the church bombing which killed four girls and left twenty-two members of the congregation injured*

The Birmingham church bombing eventually became one of the most renowned cold cases in United States legal history. As the mother of one of the victims, by that time aged eighty-two and in a wheelchair, commented when justice was done more than three decades after the event:

'I'm very happy that justice finally came down today. I didn't know whether it would come in my lifetime.'

RULE OF HATE

In the mid 1960s, the Ku Klux Klan was continuing its rule of hate in the South. It was a secret society dedicated to the

SIX CHILDREN DEAD!
WHEN WILL YOU ACT !?!
...SS PROTE... ...1.22ND 3P.
U.S. COURT... ...QUARE

THEY WON'T DIE IN VAIN !

▲ *Thousands gathered in New York to protest against the Birmingham church bombing. Among those on the platform are James Baldwin, Medgar Evers, and Thomas Kilgore Jr*

eradication and intimidation of black people, and its members had infiltrated the top echelons of the police and judiciary. Ordinary citizens were terrified of the Klan, which often took reprisals against white people as well as black, in response to what they saw as fraternizing with the enemy. In the city of Birmingham, which had a large black population, there were constant attacks

28

on black leaders, and the perpetrators of these crimes were left unpunished, or given ludicrously lenient fines or prison sentences. By 1963, the situation had got completely out of hand.

On 15 September 1963, the congregation of the Bethel Baptist Church on 16th Street, Birmingham, assembled for Sunday worship. A group of eighty teenage girls went down to the basement with their teacher for a Sunday school class. At 10.22, the church exploded: walls collapsed, windows were blown out, and the air was filled with dust. Some survivors managed to crawl out of the rubble, but others could not move. When the rescue operation began, the mangled bodies of the four dead girls were recovered. The remnants of dynamite sticks were found under a flight of stairs leading to the basement.

A SCENE OF CARNAGE

The bombing provoked national outrage; even Governor Wallace condemned the crime. The FBI came under intense pressure to find the culprits and a reward was advertised for information leading to the culprits. Just fifteen days after the event, three men were arrested: Robert Chambliss, John Wesley Hall, and Charles Cagle. Known as a virulent racist and member of the Ku Klux Klan, 'Dynamite Bob' Chambliss had been observed on the day of the bombing standing stock-still watching the scene of carnage, while others around him rushed to help the victims. Chambliss was on friendly terms with the local police force, and was widely considered to have immunity from police prosecution as a result.

To the dismay of the nation, the racist Southern courts gave the men only six-month suspended jail sentences, and fined them a thousand dollars each. The Klan were jubilant. But public pressure continued to mount, and the FBI continued their investigations, concluding that the bombing was the work of four men, all members of the same Klan group. Their names were Robert Chambliss, Thomas Blanton Jnr, Bobby Frank Cherry and Herman Frank Cash.

FBI COVER-UP

The FBI assembled a mass of evidence against these men, but FBI boss J. Edgar Hoover suppressed the information, fearing that a prosecution would fan the flames of the civil rights movement. Hoover was obsessed with destroying the reputation of Martin Luther King, whom he regarded as a Communist agent, and knew that the truth about the Birmingham bombing would help the civil rights leader's case. However, there were others who were more concerned that justice should be done. In 1970, the new Attorney General of Alabama, William J. Baxley, was elected, and made it his business to get to the bottom of the case, which had shocked him deeply as he was growing up.

Baxley put a great deal of effort into investigating the case, but after a few years became convinced that the only way it would be solved would be to reopen the suppressed FBI files. He threatened the FBI with exposure for withholding the information, and in 1976, the bureau finally allowed him access to the files. The following year,

▼ *A protest by numbers: Dr Martin Luther King is followed by the Reverend Fred Shuttlesworth, left, and Ralph Abernathy as they attend funeral services for the four girls killed in the bombing*

Robert Chambliss was brought to trial, and his niece, Elizabeth Cobbs, testified against him, along with others. Chambliss received a sentence of life imprisonment, and died in 1985, still swearing to the very end that he was innocent.

Baxley had made himself too unpopular to win an election as governor of the state. Once he was out of power, the case grew colder and colder. However, fifteen years later, in 1997 it was finally reopened. The FBI were continuing to block the investigation, but new evidence had apparently come to light – Herman Frank Cash, one of the original suspects, had died, but Thomas Blanton and Bobby Frank Cherry were tracked down – Cherry living in a beaten-up trailer in Texas. The pair were arrested for murder.

MURDER BOASTS

Blanton's trial in 2001, over thirty years after the event, attracted national attention. The FBI had planted a bug in his apartment, and, on the tape, he was heard talking about bombing the church. He was found guilty of murder and sentenced to life imprisonment. The case against Cherry took longer to bring to court, because his lawyers alleged that he was mentally unfit to be tried. However, eventually, the trial took place in 2002. His ex-wife and granddaughter testified against him, and secret FBI tapes revealed

that he boasted about bombing the church. Like Blanton, he was convicted of murder and sentenced to life imprisonment. He died in prison two years later.

Thus it was that the perpetrators of the Birmingham church bombing were finally brought to justice in one of the oldest, coldest cases in United States legal history. In his oration at the girls' funeral, Dr Martin Luther King had said: 'God has a way of wringing good out of evil'. Decades after their death – and King's assassination too – with the power of the Ku Klux Klan diminished in the South, many felt that his words had finally come true.

▲ *Dr Martin Luther King, dressed in black robes, conducts a solemn church service for the four young African-American girls killed in the Birmingham church bombing*

THE BITCH OF BUCHENWALD

In 1950, when the 'Bitch of Buchenwald' Ilse Koch was finally tried for mass-murder in a German court, she protested that she had no knowledge at all of what had gone on in the concentration-camp outside Weimar. Despite the evidence of dozens of ex-inmates, she insisted:

'I was merely a housewife. I was busy raising my children. I never saw anything that was against humanity!'

As hundreds of people gathered outside the court shouted 'Kill her! Kill her!' she was sentenced to life imprisonment.

Ilse Koch was born in Dresden, and by the age of 17 she was a voluptuous blue-eyed blonde: the very model of Aryan womanhood – and every potential storm-trooper's wet dream. Enrolling in the Nazi Youth Party, she went to work in a bookshop that sold party literature and under-the-counter pornography; and she was soon having a string of affairs with SS men. Then, though, she came to the attention of SS and Gestapo chief Heinrich Himmler, who selected her as the perfect mate for his then top aide, the brutish Karl Koch. Shortly after the wedding, when Koch was appointed commander of Buchenwald, she was installed in a villa near the camp, given two children, and then more or less forgotten by her husband, who was too busy staging multiple sex-orgies in Weimar to care.

Perhaps in revenge, Ilse began mounting orgies of her own, taking five or six of her husband's officers into her bed at a time. She was perverse, sexually insatiable – and it wasn't long after the beginning of the war that she started turning her attention to the mostly Jewish prisoners at the camp.

She first sunbathed nude outside the wire to tantalise them; then started greeting their trucks and transport trains semi-naked, fondling her breasts and shouting obscenties. If any of the incoming prisoners looked up at her, they were beaten senseless; and on one occasion, about which she filled out a report, two were clubbed to death and one had his face ground into the earth until he suffocated. All were executed, she wrote blithely, for ogling her.

She encouraged the guards to use the prisoners for target practice; and often took part herself. She scouted out good-looking soldiers seconded to the camp and offered them mass-orgies with her. Then, finally – perhaps jaded with mere sex – she started to collect trophies.

One day, by chance, she saw two tattooed prisoners working without their shirts. She ordered them to be killed immediately and their skins prepared and brought to her. She soon became obsessed with the possibilities of human skin, particularly if tattooed. She had lampshades made from the skin of selected prisoners for her living room, even a pair of gloves. Not content with this, she also started to experiment with prisoners' severed heads, having them shrunk down by the dozen to grapefruit size to decorate her dining-room.

She was tried as a war criminal at Nuremberg after the war by an American military court, and sentenced to life in prison, but two years later she was

▲ *Ilse Koch, otherwise known as the Bitch of Buchenwald*

▶Koch at the time of her trial. She eventually died in prison in 1971

released, on the grounds that a crime by one German against others could not properly be considered a war crime. By the time she appeared in a German court in Augsburg, she was a bloated, raddled figure who blamed everything on her husband — who had conveniently been executed by the Nazis for embezzlement years before. She staged an epileptic fit in court, and when she heard its final judgment in her prison cell, she merely laughed. She died in prison in 1971.

THE BLACK WIDOW KILLINGS

Belle Gunness can lay serious claim to being the first female serial killer of modern times. She was the archetypal black widow killer, a woman who repeatedly attracted husbands and other suitors, and promptly murdered them for their money. While others, like Nannie Doss, were relatively timid murderers who would wait years for the chance to poison their latest husband, Belle was happy to despatch most of her suitors almost immediately and, if they did not care to take a drop of cyanide, she was quite willing to terminate their prospects with the blow from an axe or hammer. After all, at a strongly built 280 pounds, there were not too many men able to overpower her.

Belle Gunness may also have a second claim to fame. There are very few serial killers who have succeeded in evading the law even after being identified. The Hungarian Bela Kiss was one; Norwegian-born Belle Gunness was another.

Belle Gunness was born Brynhild Paulsdatter Storset on 11 November 1859 in the Norwegian fishing village of Selbu. Her parents had a small farm there and Belle's father also moonlighted as a conjuror. Allegedly Belle, in her youth, would appear alongside him as a tightrope walker and it is certainly true to say that she walked a tightrope for the rest of her life.

FOSTER MOTHER

In 1883 her older sister, Anna, who had emigrated to Chicago, invited Belle to join her in the United States. Belle jumped at the chance of a new life and soon arrived in Chicago. The following year she married a fellow immigrant, Mads Sorenson. They lived together happily enough for the next decade or so. They failed to conceive children but instead fostered three girls: Jennie, Myrtle and Lucy. The only dramas to strike these hard-working immigrants were the regular fires that dogged their businesses. Twice their houses burnt down and, in 1897, a confectionery store they ran also succumbed to fire. Thankfully, each time they were well insured.

Insurance also served Belle well when, on 30 July 1900, Mads Sorenson died suddenly at home, suffering from what was officially listed as heart failure, but strangely showing all the symptoms of strychnine poisoning. Amazingly enough, he died on the day that one life insurance policy elapsed and another one started, so his

▶ *Belle Gunness was a heartless killer whose ultimate fate remains shrouded in mystery.*

grieving widow was able to claim on both policies.

GRIEVING WIDOW

With her $8,500 windfall, Belle decided to start a new life. She moved her family to the rural town of La Porte, Indiana, a place popular with Scandinavian immigrants, and soon married again, this time to Peter Gunness, a fellow Norwegian. Sadly, this marriage was not to last as long as her first. In 1903 Peter died in a tragic accident after a sausage grinder allegedly fell on his head. If some observed that it looked as if a hammer blow might have caused the head wound, the grieving – and pregnant – widow's

tears were enough to quieten them. Once again there was an insurance payment, this time for $4,000.

Belle never married again, though not, it appears, for want of trying. She placed regular advertisements in the Norwegian language press' lonely hearts columns. Describing herself as a comely widow, she advertised for men ready to support their amorous advances with a solid cash investment in their future lives together. She received many replies and several of these suitors actually arrived in La Porte, cash or bankbooks in hand. They would be seen for a day or two, tell their loved ones they were preparing to marry a rich widow and then they would disappear.

They were not the only people around Belle to disappear. Her foster daughter Jennie also vanished – Belle told neighbours that she had gone to a finishing school in California. Farmhands seemed to go missing on the Gunness farm on a regular basis. As far as the community as a whole was concerned, however, Belle Gunness was a model citizen who had had some very bad luck.

This view seemed to be compounded once and for all when, on 28 April 1908, Belle's house caught fire. Fire-fighters were unable to stop the blaze in time and the bodies of two of Belle's three children were found in the rubble, along with an adult female body assumed to be that of Belle herself – though identification was difficult as the body had been decapitated. The beheaded body was clear evidence that this was no accident but murder. The police immediately arrested an obvious suspect, local handyman Ray Lamphere, who had had an on/off relationship with Belle, but had lately fallen out with her and threatened to burn her house down.

That might have been the end of the matter if investigators had not continued digging around the site, looking for the corpse's missing head. They did not find the head but they did find fourteen other corpses buried around the farm, mostly in the hog pen. Among those they were able to identify were two handymen, foster daughter Jennie and five of the hopeful suitors. The remainder were mostly presumed to be other unidentified suitors.

NO ORDINARY WIDOW

It was horribly clear that Belle Gunness was no ordinary widow but a vicious serial killer. More alarm bells rang when it was discovered that some of the bodies recovered from the fire had cyanide in their stomachs. Rumours immediately began to spread that the adult female corpse was not Belle. These were partially quashed a couple of weeks later, when her dental bridge and two teeth (looking suspiciously untouched by fire) were found in the rubble. Some accepted this as definitive evidence that Belle was dead. Others saw it as simply a final act of subterfuge.

The prosecution of Ray Lamphere went ahead, but the jury expressed its doubts as to whether Belle was really dead by finding the handyman guilty only of arson and not of murder.

Sightings of Belle Gunness began almost immediately and continued in the ensuing years. Most of them were obviously wrong, and to this day, the true story of the United State's first known female serial killer remains shrouded in mystery.

THE BLOOD OF INNOCENTS

When Countess Elizabeth Bathory, aged 15, married Count Nadasdy in around 1576, it was an alliance between two of the greatest dynasties in Hungary. For Nadasdy, the master of Castle Csejthe in the Carpathians, came from a line of warriors, and Elizabeth's family was even more distinguished: It had produced generals and governors, high princes and cardinals – her cousin was the country's Prime Minister. Long after they've been forgotten, though, she will be remembered. For she was an alchemist, a bather in blood – and one of the models for Bram Stoker's Dracula.

Elizabeth was beautiful, voluptuous, savage – a fine match for her twenty-one-year-old husband, the so-called 'Black Warrior.' But he was forever off campaigning, and she remained childless. More and more, then, she gave in to the constant cajolings of her old nurse, Ilona Joo, who was a black witch, a satanist. She began to surround herself with alchemists and sorcerers; and when she conceived – she eventually had four children – she may have been finally convinced of their efficacy. For when her husband died, when she was about 41, she surrendered to the black arts completely.

There had long been rumors around the castle of lesbian orgies, of the kidnappings of young peasant women, of flagellation, of torture. But one day after her husband's death, Elizabeth Bathory slapped the face of a servant girl and drew blood; and she noticed that, where it had fallen on her hand, the skin seemed to grow smoother and more supple. She was soon convinced that bathing in and drinking the blood of young virgins would keep her young forever. Her entourage of witches and magicians – who were now calling for human sacrifice to make their magic work – agreed enthusiastically.

Elizabeth and her cronies, then, began scouring the countryside for children and young girls, who were either lured to the castle or kidnapped. They were then hung in chains in the dungeons, fattened and milked for their blood before being tortured to death and their bones used in alchemical experiments. The countess, it was said later, kept some of them alive to lick the blood from her body when she emerged from her baths, but had them, in turn brutally killed if they either failed to arouse her or showed the slightest signs of displeasure.

Peasant girls, however, failed to stay the signs of ageing; and after five years, Elizabeth decided to set up an academy for young noblewomen. Now she bathed in blue blood, the blood of her own class. But this time, inevitably, news of her depravities reached the royal court; and her cousin, the Prime Minister, was forced to investigate. A surprise raid on the castle found the Countess in mid-orgy; bodies lying strewn, drained of blood; and dozens of girls and young women – some flayed and vein-milked, some fattened like Strasburg geese awaiting their turn – in the dungeons.

Elizabeth's grisly entourage was taken into custody and then tortured to obtain confessions. At the subsequent trial for the murder of the eighty victims who were actually found dead at the castle, her old nurse, Ilona Joo, and one of the Countess's procurers of young girls were sentenced to be burned at the stake after having their fingers torn out; many of the rest were beheaded. The Countess, who as an aristocrat could not be arrested or executed, was given a separate hearing in her absence at which she was accused of murdering more than 600 women and children. She was then bricked up in a room in her castle, with holes left for ventilation and food. Still relatively young and youthful, she was

never seen alive again. She is presumed to have died – since the food was from then on left uneaten – four years later, on 21 August 1614.

▲ *Countess Bathory pursued a grisly beauty regime*

BORN UNDER A BAD SIGN

Everything was against Aileen Wuornos, right from the beginning. Her father deserted her mother before she was born; and her mother ran off from Rochester, Michigan, not long afterwards, leaving her and her elder brother in charge of her grandparents, both of whom were drunks. Her grandfather beat both his wife and them; allowed no friends in the house; and wouldn't even let them open the curtains. Malnourished and unable to concentrate in school, the children took to lighting fires with firelighters for amusement, and at the age of six, Aileen's face was badly burned, scarred for life. By the time she reached puberty, she was already putting out to boys for food and drink, uppers, anything she could get. At thirteen she was raped by a friend of her grandparents. At fourteen, she was pregnant – and the child, she said, could have been anybody's: the rapist's, her grandfather's, even her brother's. The baby, a son, was put up for adoption almost immediately after birth.

Then, when her grandmother died of cancer in 1971, she and her brother were thrown out of their grandfather's house and became wards of court. She dropped out of school and took up prostitution, while her brother robbed stores to feed an increasing drugs habit. Soon after her grandfather committed suicide in 1976, her brother died of throat cancer. He was only 21, a year older than she.

As if all this wasn't enough, even her own genes seemed to be against her. For, quite apart from the cancers, the drinking and the suicide, the father she never met turned out to be a paranoid schizophrenic and a convicted paedophile. After spending time in mental hospitals for sodomising children as young as ten, he hanged himself in a prison cell.

She had a couple of chances to go straight, it's true. She was picked up while hitch-hiking by an older man, who became besotted with her and married her; and she also got $10,000 from a life-insurance policy her brother had taken out. But the husband she abused and beat; and she used the insurance money to buy a fancy car, which she promptly crashed. So she was soon back on the road as a hitchhiking hooker, hanging out with bikers, and getting regularly arrested: for cheque forgery, breaches of the peace, car-theft, gun-theft and holding up a convenience store. For the latter, she did a year in jail, and when she came out, she tried to commit suicide.

Then, though, in 1986, Aileen, by now known as Lee, met twenty-two-year-old Tyria 'Ty' Moore in a Daytona Beach gay bar; and she turned out to be the love of her life – all the love that she'd never had. They rented an apartment together; they worked at motels and bars while Aileen turned tricks on the side. Her looks, though, weren't getting any better – and at some point Aileen decided that Ty shouldn't have to work any more: She, after all, was Ty's 'husband.' That's when she started to kill.

Beginning at the end of 1989, there was a string of deaths that soon had police baffled. All were men; some were found naked; and they'd all been killed by the same small-calibre gun. They included a trucker, a rodeo worker, a heavy-machine-operator, even a child-abuse investigator. And a sixty-year-old missionary had disappeared.

There was only one clue to the killer's identity. The missionary's car was involved in an accident and two women seen walking away. The police released sketches to the press; and Ty and Lee were identified. Lee had also pawned the possessions of many of her victims, and she'd left her finger- or thumb-prints – as per Florida law – on the pawn-shop receipts. It was only a matter of time.

There was one final betrayal. Ty, to save herself, went to the Florida police; and then, via a taped call to Aileen, persuaded her to confess. She did, but she said that her victims had beaten and raped her. She wasn't believed. She was condemned to death, even though her defence presented her as terminally damaged, with a personality disorder.

Almost immediately, her story was told in a made-for-TV movie. Feminist writers defended her; an Aileen Wuornos Defence Group was set up. However, in 1999, she admitted that the claims about beatings and rape had been entirely made up. But she also said that the police had delayed five months before arresting her, because they were negotiating a movie deal with Hollywood producers desperate for the real-life story of a female serial killer. In his 2003 documentary *The Selling of a Serial Killer*, Nick Broomfield claims that there was a meeting to discuss rights to the police investigation a month before she was arrested.

On Death Row, Wuornos seems to have had a religious conversion. She said:

'I believe I am totally saved and forgiven by Jesus Christ'

— and added that there were angels waiting for her on the other side. She was executed in late 2002.

THE BOSTON STRANGLINGS

Albert DeSalvo was oversexed, everyone agreed. His lawyer, F. Lee Bailey, wrote that he was,

'without doubt, the victim of one of the most crushing sexual drives that psychiatric science has ever encountered.'

His wife said he demanded sex up to a dozen times a day. If it hadn't been for this monumental sexual appetite of his, everything might have gone well for Boston handyman DeSalvo. For he was, to all appearances, a clean-living individual.

But the need for sex kept getting him into trouble. In Germany, it was the officers' wives. And in Boston, after he'd been honourably discharged and had moved back home, it was all the gullible pretty women who wanted to be models.

In 1958, Albert DeSalvo began to be known in police circles as the 'Measuring Man.' Posing as a talent scout for a modelling agency, he had started smooth-talking women into having their measurements taken. He would touch them, whenever and wherever he could. Then he'd leave, saying that the agency would soon be in touch.

He was finally caught in March 1960, when he was convicted as a burglar. The police thought that the 'Measuring Man' act was a device for entering apartments and houses he intended later to rob.

When he got out of prison, after serving an eleven-month term, DeSalvos' wife, as her own form of punishment, denied him all sexual contact. So DeSalvo was forced to take on a new identity, this time that of the 'Green Man'. The 'Green Man' got his name from the green trousers he liked to wear when talking his way or breaking into women's houses. He'd strip some of his victims at knifepoint and then kiss them all over; others he would tie up and rape. He boasted of having 'had' six women in a single morning.

In 1962, another and yet more sinister character appeared on the scene, one that was to terrorize Boston for eighteen months: The Boston Strangler. In June of that year, the naked body of a middle-aged woman was found in her apartment, clubbed, raped and strangled. Her legs had been spreadeagled and the cord from her housecoat had been wound round her neck, then tied beneath her chin in a bow. The necktie, the bow and the spreadeagling were all to become, as the months dragged on, horrifyingly familiar.

Two weeks later, the Strangler struck twice. Both victims were women in their sixties. Two more were murdered in August 1962, one 75, one 67. Then, in December, he struck once more – and from then on no woman in Boston felt safe, for she was only 25. Sophie Clark was strangled and raped, and her body carried all the marks of the Strangler.

The killings went on, with increasing violence, until January 1964. There was no particular pattern, apart from the spreadeagling, the bow, the ligature. The youngest victim was 19, the oldest 69. As the number of dead mounted up, panic increasingly gripped the city. But Albert DeSalvo was never even interviewed.

Then, the killings stopped. After January 1964 the Strangler seemed to disappear – even though the 'Green Man' was still at work. For that autumn a young married student gave a description of the 'Green Man' that tallied with that of the 'Measuring Man,' and DeSalvo was arrested. DeSalvo was sent to Bridgewater mental hospital for routine observation.

It was at Bridgewater that the controversy that still surrounds DeSalvo began. A fellow prisoner called George Nassar, who'd been arrested for murder, claimed that DeSalvo told him details of the crimes of the Boston Strangler. Nassar told his lawyer, F. Lee Bailey. In a deal engineered by Bailey, DeSalvo stood trial only for the 'Green Man' offences. He was sentenced to life imprisonment; and is said to have confessed in detail to the Boston Strangler's crimes in 1965.

Even so there remain some doubts. For DeSalvo as the 'Measuring Man' and the 'Green Man' invariably chose younger women. Witnesses who'd actually seen the Strangler failed to identify him. So could the Boston Strangler have really been George Nassar, who'd somehow fed DeSalvo details of the crimes in Bridgewater and then persuaded him to confess? We shall never know. For DeSalvo was stabbed to death in Walpole State Prison in 1975. The inmate who knifed him through the heart was never identified.

▼ *Alberto DeSalvo became known as the Measuring Man*

43

THE JACKAL STRIKES

Ilich Ramirez Sanchez, better known as Carlos the Jackal, was once one of the most feared terrorists in the world. During his career of crime, which spanned the 1970s and 1980s, he committed a horrifying series of brutal terrorist attacks across Europe. Most disturbingly, as his trail of carnage increased, he seemed to show that he was no longer fighting for a cause, but was simply enjoying the violence and revelling in his notoriety. He was eventually handed over to the French authorities and imprisoned for life. Today, several cases are still pending against him, and he has yet to be tried for the majority of the crimes he committed.

Sanchez was born in 1949 in Caracas, Venezuela, the son of a millionaire Marxist lawyer who named his three sons Vladimir, Ilich and Lenin. The young Ilich travelled around the world, picking up skills as a linguist on the way. He later used these as a cover for his activities, posing as a language teacher. As he grew up, he also became involved in youth communist activities. In 1966 his parents divorced, and he moved to London with his mother and brothers.

A BULLET IN THE HEAD

Sanchez went on to study in the Soviet Union, at the Patrice Lumumba University there, where he came into contact with the Communist Party. His interest was in the problems of the Middle East and, at the beginning of the 1970s, he was sent to Amman, Jordan, to train as a guerrilla fighter for the Popular Front for the Liberation of Palestine (PFLP). At this time, he began to use his nickname 'Carlos'. 'The Jackal' was added later, when a copy of the spy thriller *The Day of the Jackal* was found at one of his hide-outs.

After his spell in the Middle East, he returned to London. There, possibly under orders from the PFLP, he performed his first terrorist act. He shot and wounded British businessman Edward Seiff, head of the chain store Marks and Spencer and a major figure in Jewish life. Carlos called on Seiff's house and forced his way in with a gun; it was only by sheer luck that the bullet he put into Seiff's head did not kill the man. During this time, Carlos bombed an Israeli bank, the Hapoalim Bank, in London.

BOMB ATTACKS

Carlos then went on to make a series of bomb attacks in France. He bombed the

◄ Carlos the Jackal – a terrorist with a political motivation, or a cruel psychopath killing for the joy of it?

premises of newspaper buildings accused of being pro-Israeli, often making warning calls and arranging for the bombs to be detonated at night, 'to limit casualties', as he said. However, his subsequent attacks in France showed different patterns, and some caused a great deal of damage. In 1982, one person was killed and sixty-three were injured when a car bomb exploded in the centre of Paris.

His most notorious attack was in 1975, at an Organization of Petroleum

◀ *The shocking chaos of the aftermath of an explosion that killed one person and wounded sixty-three – the rue Marbeuf bomb attack, Paris, April 1982, carried out by the Jackal*

Exporting Countries (OPEC) meeting in Vienna, when he led a team of terrorists who seized over sixty hostages and killed three people. Carlos and his men stormed the meeting, and then demanded that a statement they had written be read out and transmitted by radio all over the Middle East. The terrorists left with their hostages, including ministers from eleven OPEC states. After negotiations with the Austrian government, the hostages were released and the terrorists granted asylum.

From this point, it became clear that Carlos was enjoying his notoriety. The Palestinian groups that had supported him now withdrew their backing. However, Carlos continued to mount terrorist attacks across Europe. Dozens of people were killed and hundreds injured in these attacks.

THE KILLER PLAYBOY

During this time, Carlos was harboured by radical Arab regimes in Iraq, Libya, Syria, Yemen and Lebanon. He was protected by the governments of these countries from the agencies that were trying to hunt him down: the CIA, Interpol and French intelligence. As his career continued, it became clear that he was now also acting as a mercenary for these regimes, carrying out attacks at their behest for money. He is thought to have amassed a fortune through this work, and acquired a reputation as a playboy who enjoyed the high life.

In 1982, he and a terrorist group attacked a nuclear reactor in France, but the attempt failed. Two members of the group were arrested, including Carlos' wife Magdalena Kopp, who was connected to the Bader-Meinhof gang in Germany. Carlos wrote to the police asking them to release the pair, and then went on to launch a series of bombings, including one on a passenger train in France, killing five people and injuring dozens more. Despite this attempt to intimidate the authorities, the terrorists were convicted, and Kopp was sentenced to six years' imprisonment. Once she had served her term, she was set free to rejoin Carlos.

BROUGHT TO JUSTICE

By now it was becoming clear that the Soviet bloc countries were not supporting Carlos' activities any longer. He was also being kept at arm's length by the radical Arab countries. Eventually, Carlos found a home in Syria, but even here he was allowed to remain only on condition that he stop his terrorist activities.

When Iraq invaded Kuwait in 1990, it was rumoured that Saddam Hussein was going to approach Carlos to make terrorist

strikes on the United States. Syria expelled Carlos, and he went underground, taking shelter in various Middle Eastern countries. He found his way to the Sudan, which had become a focus for terrorists such as Osama bin Laden. However, his playboy way of life did not sit at all well with the religious fundamentalism of the Islamic sheikh who offered him protection. The sheikh arranged for him to be handed over to the French authorities.

The arrest took place in Khartoum, the capital city of Sudan, in 1994. Carlos was immediately transferred to mainland France and, after three years of solitary confinement, was tried for three murders – from among the scores that he had committed.

Carlos was sentenced to life imprisonment. He staged a short hunger strike, but no one took very much notice, and today he continues to serve out his sentence.

▲ *The Jackal had a stash of weapons with him when the police arrested him in Khartoum, Sudan*

A CASE WITHOUT A CORPSE

Forensic science is not simply a matter of running trace evidence through high-tech apparatus and printing out the perpetrator's ID after the database has produced a match. Even the most sophisticated equipment can only analyze the evidence. It takes a tenacious, imaginative and highly motivated CSI to gather all the elements, interpret the evidence and make a case. The following account is a good example of the lengths that forensic scientists must now go to and the attention to detail they need to secure a conviction.

Just before Christmas 1986, the police received a call from Keith Mayo, a private investigator, who said he was concerned that his client, flight attendant Helle Crafts, had gone missing from her home in Connecticut. When questioned, her husband Richard claimed that she had stormed out after an argument and that he had no idea of her whereabouts. Neither had her colleagues, but without a body there was nothing much the police could do except conduct a routine missing persons enquiry. Until, that is, a snowplough driver remembered seeing a man fitting Richard Crafts' description operating a wood chipping machine by a river at 3.30am in the midst of a blizzard. The inference was clear. Crafts had dismembered his wife's body and shredded it into compost. If he had tipped the contents into the river the current would have distributed the remains across the state and no amount of circumstantial evidence would be enough to convict him.

Fortunately the coroner in charge of the case, Henry C. Lee, possessed local knowledge and told the police precisely which spot on the river to search as body parts had been washed up there in earlier cases. Sure enough, they pulled a chain saw from the water and were able to match it to the chipper and the truck that Crafts had rented. But even this proved only that Craft had discarded a rented saw in a river. It did not prove conclusively that he had mulched his wife's remains.

A GRUESOME TASK

So for nearly a month investigators scoured the location where Craft had been seen using the shredder during the snow storm and brought back a small mountain of wood chippings and human tissue to Lee's laboratory. There the team sifted through the debris, putting plant material to one side and human hair, tooth fragments and tissue in another.

Each hair had to be analyzed to see if it was animal or human and, if it was human, which race and gender it belonged to. Hair that had been pulled had to be separated from hair that had been shed naturally and then those that had been torn out had to be matched to a specific part of the body. Hair that had been cut had to be subjected to further examination to see if it had been cut cleanly by scissors or ragged by a shredder. After separating body fragments from the wood chippings, Lee and his team were left with just a few ounces of body parts, a fingernail, a dental crown, a bone fragment and pieces of plastic bag in which the body parts had been transported to the site.

Tooth fragments proved sufficient to positively identify the rest of the remains as belonging to the missing woman and when Dr Lee identified a bone fragment as part of the skull it proved conclusively that Mrs Crafts was dead. Moreover, the

▲ *An observant snowplough driver's actions helped convict Helle Crafts' killer*

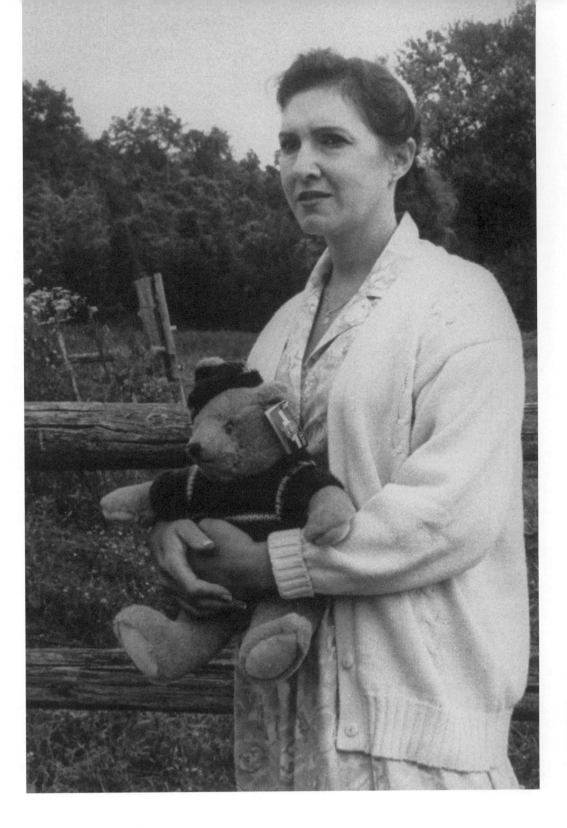

▶ *Flight attendant Helle Crafts who went missing in 1986*

◀ *Private investigator Keith Mayo was hired by Helle Crafts before she disappeared when she discovered that her husband had had a series of extra-marital affairs*

tissue on the chainsaw matched tissue found at the site; hair taken from Mrs Crafts' hairbrush was matched with hair recovered from the chippings and, if that wasn't enough, a sliver of nail polish was analyzed with a sample obtained from a bottle at the Crafts' house and found to be identical.

But the final flourish in Henry Lee's exemplary investigation was his decision to consult R. Bruce Hoadley, a forensic tree expert. By examining the chippings found at the river and those taken from the hire truck, Hoadley was able to state that they were from the same tree and that both chippings showed the distinctive cut marks made by the chipper that Crafts had hired.

If Richard Crafts had entertained hopes of evading arrest and prosecution for murder, he had seriously underestimated the dedication and dogged persistence of the forensic investigators on his case, who had spent almost three years putting their evidence together.

When his case came to trial in 1989, Richard Crafts' defence was systematically demolished by Dr Lee and his team of expert witnesses. Crafts was found guilty and sentenced to 50 years in prison.

THE CHICAGO CULT KILLINGS

That one lone killer might abduct, rape, torture and kill a string of young women is horrifying enough. That four men should get together to carry out such crimes as a team almost beggars belief. That, however, is exactly what Robin Gecht, Edward Spreitzer and the Kokoraleis brothers, Andrew and Thomas, did. Known as the 'Chicago Rippers', they were responsible for at least seven and conceivably as many as eighteen murders of women, all of them carried out with dreadful savagery and without any apparent motive, beyond the basest of sadistic urges.

The first murder to be carried out by the gang was that of twenty-eight-year-old Linda Sutton. On 23 May 1981, she was abducted. Ten days later her body was found in a field, in the Villa Park area of the city, not far from an establishment called the Rip Van Winkle motel. Sutton's body had been mutilated and her left breast amputated. This was evidently the work of a sexual sadist but, as yet, the police had no clues to go on.

It was almost a year before the Rippers struck again. On 15 May 1982 they abducted another young woman, Lorraine Borowski, as she was about to open up the realtor's office in which she worked. This time, however, it was five months before the body was discovered in a cemetery in Villa Park.

By this time, the Rippers had struck several more times. On 29 May, they abducted Shui Mak from Hanover Park, a little way to the north of Villa Park. Her body was not found for four months. Two weeks after the abduction of Shui Mak, a prostitute known as Angel York was picked up by a man in a van, who handcuffed her and slashed her breast before throwing her out, still alive.

MORE BREAST AMPUTATIONS

York's description of her attacker failed to produce any leads, and two months passed before the Rippers struck again. On 28 August 1982 the body of Sandra Delaware, a prostitute, was discovered by the Chicago River. She had been stabbed and strangled and her left breast amputated. On 8 September thirty-year-old Rose Davis was found in an alley, having suffered almost identical injuries to Delaware. On 11 September, Carole Pappas, whose husband was a pitcher for the Chicago Cubs, vanished, never to be seen again.

A month later, the killers committed their last crime, one that was to prove to be their downfall. Their victim, a prostitute named Beverley Washington, was found by a railway track on 6 December. In addition to other injuries, her left breast had been cut off and her right breast severely slashed. Amazingly, she was still alive and was able to offer a description of her attacker and the van he had used to abduct her.

CULT

This description led the police to Robin Gecht, a twenty-eight-year old carpenter. Gecht, as a teenager, had been accused of molesting his sister and had a long-term interest in satanism. At first, police had to release Gecht for lack of evidence, but after investigating further, they discovered that the previous year he had rented a room at a motel along with three friends – each of them with adjoining rooms. The hotel manager said they had held loud parties and appeared to be involved in some kind of cult. Detectives then traced the other men, the Kokoraleis brothers, and Edward Spreitzer, a man of subnormal intelligence.

SATANIC CHAPEL

Under interrogation, Thomas Kokoraleis confessed that he and the others had taken women back to Gecht's place, to what Gecht called a 'satanic chapel'. There they had raped and tortured them,

cutting off their breasts with a wire garrotte. He further alleged that they would eat parts of the severed breasts as a kind of sacrament, and that Gecht would masturbate into the breasts before putting them into a box. Kokoraleis claimed that he once saw fifteen breasts in the box.

Police arrested the three men and Gecht. They searched Gecht's apartment and found the satanic chapel. Both Kokoraleis bothers confessed, as did Spreitzer. Gecht, however, protested his innocence. After a series of trials, Andrew Kokoraleis was convicted of murder and put to death in 1999. Thomas Kokoraleis was convicted of murder and sentenced to life imprisonment. Edward Spreitzer was sentenced to death but had his sentence changed to life imprisonment. In the absence of evidence linking him to the crimes, Robin Gecht was convicted only of the rape and attempted murder of Beverley Washington. He was sentenced to a 120 years in prison, where he continues to maintain his innocence.

▲ *Non-descript faces for crimes that were anything but: it is, perhaps, unsurprising that the Chicago Rippers were difficult to find*

CODE OF HONOUR

Carmine Galante's Mafia nickname was 'Lillo' – for the little cigars he constantly smoked. He was short, fat, bald – and immensely violent; and when he came out of federal prison in 1978 he had two ambitions: to make money – by taking over the immensely lucrative New York heroin trade; and to become the ultimate man of respect: the Boss of All Bosses.

Galante grew up in East Harlem, New York, the son of Sicilian immigrants; and he was to remain at heart a Sicilian, out of tune with the pliable Italian-Americans who gradually took over the Mafia – and were willing to keep a low profile for the sake of business. He was a man of vendettas; he lived by the gun and the code of honour; and as such he became in the early days a trusted member of the Bonanno family.

In 1957, he travelled as consigliere to his boss Joe Bonanno to the Palermo summit of Sicilian and American Mafia leaders, organised by 'Lucky' Luciano. He then organised the American end of the so-called 'Montreal Connection,' by which perhaps 60 per cent of all America's heroin illegally crossed the border from Canada. But when the 'Connection' was rolled up by the FBI and its Canadian counterpart, and he himself was imprisoned, all he could do was watch, powerless, from behind bars as boss 'Joe Bananas' became increasingly eccentric and his family was forced to yield power to others. Once out of prison, he wanted revenge.

His timing was spot on. For Carlo Gambino, the most powerful of the New York dons, had recently died; and the newly elected boss of the Bonanno family, Phil Rastelli, was himself behind bars – and stood aside when Galante hit the streets. He'd also planned well. For he'd gathered around himself a large group of old-country Sicilian hit-men who had no allegiance to anyone but himself – and to the Mafia code he believed in. They quickly muscled and killed their way to control of the heroin business.

Equally quickly, though, they and their boss became a 'business problem' to the New York Commission, especially to one member, Paul 'Big Paulie' Castellano, who, in the absence of any real leadership in the Bonanno family, had taken over many of its interests. No one, though, wanted a bullying throwback, a 'Moustache Pete' from the past, to rock the boat. So the Commission ordered Galante's assassination – and the job was

*◀ Carmine Galante,
the cigar smoking king
of violence*

handed, as per custom, to a member of his own family, underboss Salvatore Catalano.

On 13 July 1979, as Galante was enjoying an after-dinner cigar with two friends on the patio of Joe and Mary's Italian Restaurant in Brooklyn, three men wearing ski-masks and shotguns walked in through the back door. Galante was dead so fast, his cigar was still in his mouth as he hit the patio floor. The traditional .45 bullet was then fired into his left eye; and his guests were finished off by his own trusted bodyguards – who then calmly walked out with his killers.

That same day, at a meeting in prison, Phil Rastelli was reconfirmed as head of the Bonanno family, and Mafia bosses met in a social club in New York's Little Italy to celebrate. But Galante later came back to haunt them. For as the result of wiretaps installed during the investigation into the so-called 'Pizza Connection,' Salvatore Catalano and the members of the New York Commission were eventually charged with his murder.

THE COLOMBIAN CONNECTION

During the 1970s and 1980s, the illegal drugs industry expanded massively in size. What had once been a very marginal industry, selling only to those on the fringes of society, now became a multi-billion dollar business selling to everyone from bankers and politicians to suburban teenagers. The drug at the heart of this expansion was cocaine. The marijuana industry remained relatively small, due to the ease of growing and preparing the product. Cocaine, however, is the product of a particular climate and needs a larger scale production system to process it.

The prime sources of the coca leaf are in South America. For years, cocaine had been manufactured in small quantities and sold at a high price. During the 1970s, however, demand began to build and a few criminal masterminds in South America saw that there were huge profits to be made if they began to control not just the growing, but also the refinement, distribution and sale of cocaine on a much larger scale. Chief among these criminals was a Colombian called Pablo Escobar, who in little more than a decade would become the first of the billionaire drug dealers.

THE MEDELLIN CARTEL

Escobar was born on a small farm in Rionegra, near Medellin in Colombia, on 12 January 1949. In his teens he gravitated towards petty crime. He stole gravestones, of all the unlikely commodities, for resale. He also helped steal cars. Before long, he became involved with a small Mafia-run cocaine-producing operation, and then developed his own small business. He soon became aware that this was a business with an almost limitless market. He approached other cocaine growers in the Medellin area and offered to pay them double what they were receiving for their crop from the Mafia, who were their main buyers. They agreed. He used friends and relatives to take the drugs into the United States and establish distribution networks.

Escobar's business grew with extraordinary speed. His business plan mimicked that of legitimate multinational companies. There were a whole host of separate cocaine operations – franchises if you like – all manufacturing and distributing cocaine, and all wired into a network that was organized by Escobar to give him a handsome share of their profits. The organization was known as the Medellin cartel, with Escobar its CEO.

To ensure his continued dominance in a competitive and murderous world – a big business regulated not by law but by machine guns – Escobar used an individual mixture of extreme brutality and surprising philanthropy.

THE COLOMBIAN NECKTIE

Escobar himself was a hands-on leader who carried out many murders himself. He was even credited with inventing the 'Colombian necktie' – this referred to his predilection for cutting his victims' throats, then pulling their tongues through the open wound. At the same time as terrorizing his enemies, Escobar ploughed a lot of his ill-gotten money into social improvements. He built sports facilities and new housing, and even created Colombia's first ever welfare programme

▲ *Escobar took on the Mafia and won, building a huge cocaine-based empire in little more than a decade. He is shown here attending a soccer game in 1983, in Medellin, where he sponsored a team* in his home town. These charitable acts made him an enormously popular figure in Medellin. He was even elected to a seat in Congress in 1982. A useful side effect was that his popularity made it very difficult for rival cartels to assassinate him.

His political career did not last long, but his criminal career continued to flourish. The US appetite for cocaine continued to grow, entirely unaffected by Nancy Reagan's 'Just Say No' campaign. By the late 1980s, Forbes magazine ranked Escobar as the seventh richest man in the world, worth over three billion dollars.

ASSASSINATION ATTEMPTS

By 1989, however, the US started to put extreme pressure on the Colombian government to clamp down on the cocaine moguls; the billions at stake also meant that there were other criminal gangs – in particular the Cali cartel – determined to murder Escobar and take his business.

After several near-miss assassination attempts, Escobar decided on a novel survival plan.

In 1990 he turned himself in to the government and agreed to plead guilty to a relatively minor drug-dealing charge for which he would receive an agreed sentence of nine years. What Escobar was able to demand in return for this is remarkable.

Firstly, he received a guarantee that he would not be extradited to the United States as the US government wanted.

The second and perhaps more astonishing condition was that he would build his own private prison in which to serve his time. The prison itself, nicknamed the 'Cathedral', was a luxurious fortified abode designed less to imprison Escobar than to keep his enemies out.

WALKING OUT OF JAIL

After a year, Escobar was growing very tired of his imprisonment. At the same time, he was worried that changes in the government might change his terms of imprisonment, and his erstwhile minions were taking advantage of his absence to siphon off huge amounts of money. So in 1991, he went back to running his organization from a succession of safe houses.

Escobar had been right to fear the change in government policy. For the first time, the authorities began to make serious attempts to put an end to his reign. On 2 December 1993, he was trapped in a Medellin apartment block by the secret police, who killed him during a rooftop gun battle.

However, his legacy remained: the worldwide trafficking of cocaine continued to expand at full speed.

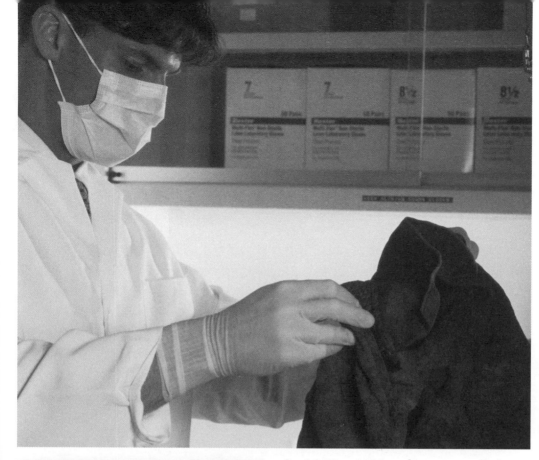

◀ *Storing DNA profiles: people who have committed crimes in earlier years now stand a very good chance of being linked to their past if they offend again, thanks to DNA evidence*

THE CRACK HOUSE MURDERS

One of the most shocking multiple murders to occur in the 1990s was that of five black women, who were stabbed to death in a crack house in the north-east area of Oklahoma City. The murders occurred in 1992, but it was not until five years later that the authorities caught up with the perpetrator, who had managed to steer clear of the law, evading all responsibility for such a terrible crime up until that time.

On 16 May 1992, police were called to a crack house to find a horrifying scene. It was one of carnage: five women lay dead, butchered by an unknown assailant. They were all found naked, lying in pools of blood; and four of the victims were also found to have been sexually assaulted. The victims were 47-year-old Phyllis Adams, 35-year-old Sandra Thompson, 37-year-old Carolyn Watson, 30-year-old LaShawn Evans, and 34-year-old Fransill Roberts.

BUTCHERED IN A CRACK HOUSE

Samples of blood were taken from some of the women's clothing, including two

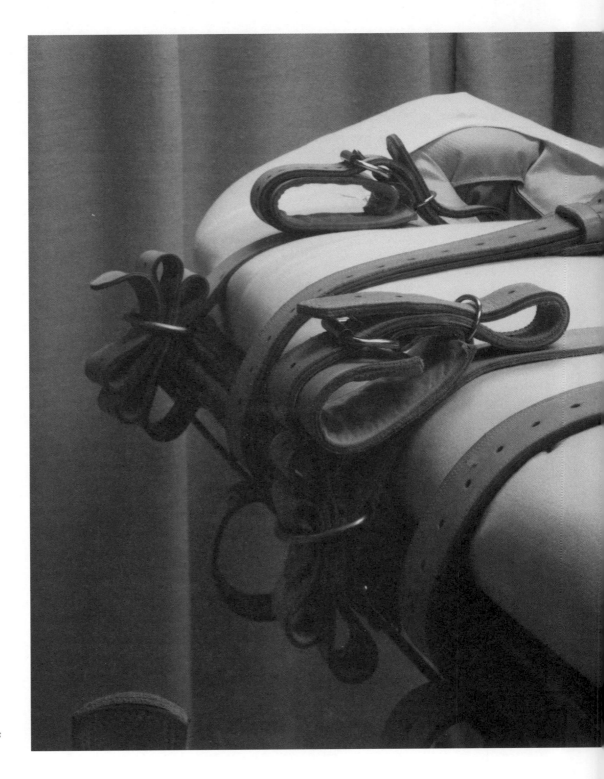

▶Guilty: Danny Keith Hooks received five separate death sentences for the murders

shirts and a jacket, as well as a bloody handprint that was found on a curtain. However, the murder investigation launched at the time yielded no results, and no suspect was named. The multiple murders shocked the local community, and the police were criticized for failing to find the killer. The National Association for the Advancement of Colored People (NAACP) accused the law enforcement agencies of racism, saying they were not making enough effort to find the culprit because the victims were black and were frequenting a crack house. The house was known as a place where penniless drug addicts, mostly women, came to sell sex in return for drugs. Many commentators from the black community felt that because of the house's bad reputation, very little was being done to bring the killer of these women to justice.

It was not until five years later that police ran the DNA profile of Danny Keith Hooks into their computer database. Hooks had been picked up on a charge of rape. To their surprise, it matched the samples taken from the scene of the crime at the crack house. The evidence was compelling, and Hooks was soon brought to trial and charged with the five murders.

At the trial, Hooks claimed that the bloody handprint on the curtain was the result of a cut on his hand that he had sustained from riding his bicycle. He admitted that he had smoked crack at the house earlier that day with the five women, and that he had had sex with two of them. However, he said that he had then decided to leave the house and it was only when he returned later that he had found the dead bodies.

During the trial, Hooks testified that he was innocent. He repeated the story told to police that he had smoked cocaine and had sex with the women during his first visit and later found the bodies in a bedroom, as well as describing the finger allegedly cut when he fell off his bicycle.

'It's a plausible explanation,' said defense attorney Irven Box, who ridiculed the idea that one man could have controlled five 'streetwise women.' He called the idea 'baloney.'

But prosecutor Brad Miller called Hooks' testimony 'high-gear silliness' and impossible. He listed some 16 problems with Hooks' account, including where Hooks' blood was found.

Miller pointed out Hooks had no explanation for why he would return to the house since he claimed he'd spent all his money the first visit. Prosecution witnesses, including one of Hooks' former co-workers, said Hooks had talked before of his desire to have orgies.

The prosecution alleged that to the contrary, Hooks had killed the women in a frenzy of violence. He was a crack addict who had become mentally unstable as a result of his addiction. The prosecution suggested that he had tried to force the women into a sex orgy with him. When Adams, who he knew, tried to flee he had stabbed her some 10 times after cornering her in a closet.

'Once it went bad, everybody had to go. He wasn't going to leave any witnesses,' Miller said.

DEATH PENALTY

Jurors were heard arguing – shouting at times – as they began deliberations. At the end of the first day, the jurors reported they were split 10-2 after six hours of discussion. On the second day of deliberations they spent eight hours arguing.

What held their deliberation up was the fact that it was hard to understand how five women could have been killed – apparently easily – by one man, but in the end they decided that that was what had happened. They therefore returned a verdict of guilty. On hearing the verdict, Hooks showed no reaction. He was convicted of five counts of first-degree murder and sentenced to death. Commenting on the death penalty for Hooks, the daughter of victim Phyllis Adams, Barbara Booker, said 'I don't think he deserves to live because those women did not have a choice'.

THE CRIME OF THE CENTURY

It was called at the time the Crime of the Century, a 'superman' murder. But in reality the 1924 killing of Bobbie Franks by two young University of Chicago students, Nathan Leopold and Richard Loeb, was both senseless and lazy. Far from being the 'perfect' murder, a secret demonstration of how much 'better' and 'less bourgeois' they were than their friends and relatives, it only proved that even intellectuals can be supremely cack-handed.

Fourteen-year old Bobbie, the son of a millionaire, was abducted outside his school on 21 May 1924; and soon afterwards his mother received a call saying that he'd been kidnapped and that a ransom note would arrive through the post. The next day it came, demanding $10,000. But before anything could be done, the police found a body that matched Bobbie's description. It had been discovered by maintenance men — strangled and with a fractured skull — in a culvert near the railway. Nearby lay a pair of horn-rimmed spectacles.

It took only a week for the spectacles to be traced to a rich nineteen-year-old law

student and amateur ornithologist called Nathan Leopold. Leopold immediately agreed that they were indeed his, and he claimed that he must have dropped them while bird-watching in the area some time before. But the spectacles showed no sign of having been left outside for long; and when Leopold was asked what he'd been doing on the afternoon of May 21st, all he could come up with was that he'd been with his friend, fellow-student Richard Loeb, and two girls called Mae and Edna. Loeb soon corroborated this, but neither man could give any sort of description by which the two girls could be traced. Besides, Leopold's typewriter, when tested, was found to be exactly the same

▲ *Leopold and Loeb thought they had committed the 'crime of the century'. They were wrong*

▶ *Leopold and Loeb were jailed for life, despite the best efforts of their lawyer, Clarence Darrow*

model as the one which had written the ransom note.

It was, oddly, Richard Loeb — easily the more assured and dominant of the two men — who first confessed under questioning. But he was soon followed by Leopold, whose younger brother, it turned out, had been a friend of Bobbie Franks. The fourteen-year-old had been chosen as their victim, it transpired, not because of any particular enmity, but for a much simpler reason: he'd be easy to get into their car.

Two months after the killing, defended by famous lawyer Clarence Darrow, they came to trial. Darrow did his best, claiming that both his clients were mentally ill, either paranoiac (in Leopold's case) or schizophrenic (in Loeb's). This defence probably saved their lives, but there could be no doubt of their guilt. They were imprisoned for life for Bobbie's murder, and given a further ninety-nine years' sentence for his kidnapping.

Twelve years later, Loeb was killed by a fellow-inmate. But Leopold, who'd been throughout his term a model prisoner, was finally released in 1958. He moved to Puerto Rico, got married, and died in 1971 at the age of 66.

THE CUSTOM-BUILT DUNGEON

As individuals, Leonard Lake and Charles Ng were both unsavoury characters. Together, they were a deadly combination. In the space of little over a year, they killed, tortured and raped at least twelve and perhaps as many as twenty-five people, including men, women and two baby boys. The men were mostly killed for money; the women, for sexual thrills; and the babies simply for being in the way.

INTEREST IN GUNS

Leonard Lake was a fat old hippie obsessed with survivalism. Charles Ng was a young ex-marine from Hong Kong, with an addiction to stealing. What brought the two of them together initially was an interest in guns.

The sexual enslavement of women had long been a fantasy of the older of the two men, Leonard Lake. Lake was born in San Francisco on 20 July 1946. His parents by all accounts had a dreadful relationship and, when Lake was six, his mother left, leaving him with his grandmother. As a child, Lake collected mice and enjoyed killing them by dissolving them in chemicals (a technique he would later use

▲ *Leonard Lake –
custom-built a dungeon
in the woods*

to help dispose of his human victims). In his teens, he sexually abused his sisters.

At eighteen, Lake joined the US Marines and made the rank of sergeant. He served two tours in Vietnam as a radar operator. Following a spell in Da Nang, he suffered a delusional breakdown and was sent home before being discharged in

67

▶ *Charles Ng – shoplifting was to be his downfall*

1971. He was already married by this time, but his wife left him because he was violent and sexually perverted.

Lake became part of the hippie lifestyle centred around San Francisco. He also became increasingly obsessed with the idea of an impending nuclear holocaust, and for eight years lived in a hippie commune near Ukiah, in northern California. There he met a woman named Claralyn Balazs, or 'Cricket', as he nicknamed her. A twenty-five-year-old teacher's aide when he met her, Balazs became deeply involved in Lake's fantasies. She starred in the pornographic videos he began to make, the latest manifestation of his sexual obsession. His other obsession was with guns – part of his survivalist paranoia – and through a magazine advert he placed in 1981, he met Charles Ng.

ARSONIST

Born in Hong Kong, Ng, or 'Charlie' as Lake called him, was a disruptive child, obsessed with martial arts and setting fires. His parents sent him to an English private school in an effort to straighten him out, but he was expelled for stealing. Next, he went to California where he attended college for a single semester before dropping out. Soon after that he was involved in a hit-and-run car crash and to avoid the consequences he signed up for the US Marines, fraudulently claiming to be a US national. It was at this time that he met Lake. They came up with a plan to sell guns that Ng would steal from a marine arsenal. However, Ng was caught stealing the guns and was sentenced to three years in prison.

When he was released in 1985, he immediately contacted Lake, who invited him to his new place, a remote cabin near Wilseyville, California, that he was

renting from Balazs. He had custom-built a dungeon next to the cabin ready for his friend Charlie to come up and have fun. It is thought that by then Lake had already murdered his brother Donald and his friend and best man Charles Gunnar, in order to steal their money and, in Gunnar's case, his identity.

Over the next year Lake and Ng indulged themselves in an orgy of killing, rape and torture. Their victims included their rural neighbours, Lonnie Bond, his girlfriend Brenda O'Connor plus their baby son Lonnie Jr, and another young family, Harvey and Deborah Dubs and their young son Sean. In both cases the men and babies were killed quickly, while the women were kept alive for Ng and Lake's perverse sport. They would rape and torture the women – Lake filming the whole awful business – before putting them to death. Other victims included workmates of Ng's; relatives and friends who came looking for Bond and O'Connor; and two gay men.

The career of evil might have gone on a lot longer if it had not been for Ng's addiction to stealing. On 2 June 1985, Ng was spotted shoplifting a vice from a San Francisco hardware store, probably for use as a torture implement. Ng ran away from the scene. Lake then appeared and tried to pay for the vice. By then, however, the police had arrived. Officer

Daniel Wright discovered that Lake's car's number plates were registered to another vehicle, and that Lake's ID, in the name of Scott Stapley, was suspicious. When Wright found a gun with a silencer in the trunk of the car, he arrested Lake. Once in custody, Lake asked for a pen, paper and a glass of water. He then wrote a note to Balazs, and quickly swallowed the cyanide pills he had sewn in to his clothes. After revealing his true identity and that of Ng, he went into convulsions from cyanide poisoning and died four days later.

KILOS OF BONE

Further investigation soon led the police to the Wilseyville ranch. Ng was nowhere to be seen. However, they found Scott Stapley's truck and Lonnie Bond's Honda there and, behind the cabin, they found the dungeon. Officers noticed a human foot poking through the earth, and proceeded to unearth 18 kilograms of burned and smashed human bone fragments, relating to at least a dozen bodies. (A month or so later, less than a mile away, they were to find the bodies of Scott Stapley and Lonnie Bond, stuffed into sleeping bags and buried.) They also came across a hand-drawn 'treasure' map that led them to two five-gallon pails buried in the earth. One contained envelopes with names and victim IDs suggesting that the full body count might be as high as twenty-five. In the other pail, police found Lake's handwritten journals for 1983 and 1984, and two videotapes that showed the horrific torture of two of their victims. If there was any doubt that the missing Ng was as heavily involved as Lake, it was dispelled by these tapes, that showed Ng right there with Lake, even telling one of the victims, Brenda O'Connor: 'You can cry and stuff, like the rest of them, but it won't do any good. We are pretty – ha, ha – cold-hearted, so to speak.'

Ng, meanwhile, was on the run. He had flown to Detroit and crossed the border into Canada where he was eventually arrested. In a Canadian prison, he began an epic legal battle against extradition back to the United States on the grounds that Canada did not have the death penalty, and thus to send him back to the US would be in breach of his human rights. It was not until 1991 that he finally lost this battle and was shipped back to the States. Even that was not the end of the story. Ng stretched out pretrial proceedings for seven years at the cost to the state of $10 million. Finally, in May 1999, Ng was convicted of murder and sentenced to death. To no one's surprise, Ng appealed against the verdict. At the time this book went to press he was on death row in San Quentin prison awaiting the outcome of the appeal.

DARK DARK FANTASIES

On the surface, Paul Bernardo and Karla Homolka seemed the most unlikely of serial killers. They were a middle-class young Canadian couple, both good looking and fair-haired. However, these ostensibly model citizens conspired together in the rape, torture and murder of at least three young women, including Karla's own sister, Tammy. At her trial, Karla blamed all the crimes on her abusive husband Paul. Subsequent evidence showed that she herself was deeply implicated. However, it is probably true to say that without Bernado, Homolka would never have killed – while Bernardo almost certainly would have done, whether or not he had had a lover to aid and abet him.

ABUSIVE FATHER

Paul Bernardo was born in the well-to-do Toronto suburb of Scarborough in August 1964, the third child of accountant Kenneth Bernardo and home-maker Marilyn. At least that is what Paul believed when he was growing up; it was only when he was sixteen that his mother revealed him to be the offspring of an affair she had had. By this time, it was abundantly clear that all was not well in the seemingly respectable Bernardo household. Kenneth was physically abusive to his wife and sexually abusive to his daughter; meanwhile, Marilyn had become grossly overweight and remained virtually housebound.

Nevertheless, up to that point Paul appeared to be a happy, well-adjusted child, who enjoyed his involvement in scouting activities. It was only when he became a young man that he revealed a darker side to his nature. He was good-looking, charming and, not surprisingly, popular with women. However, his sexual appetites turned out to be anything but charming. He would beat up the women he went out with, tie them up and force them to have anal sex. This behaviour carried on through his time at the University of Toronto, a period during which he also developed a money-making sideline in smuggling cigarettes into the US. After leaving college, he got a job as an accountant at Price Waterhouse. Not long afterwards, in October 1987, he met Karla Homolka at a Toronto pet convention.

Karla Homolka was born on 4 May 1970 in Port Credit, Ontario, the daughter of Dorothy and Karel Homolka. She had two sisters, Lori and Tammy. Like Bernardo's, this was a middle-class family,

▲ *Paul Barnardo had a close escape early in his criminal career that left him free to kil!*

but in this case it seemed to be a genuinely happy one. Karla was a popular girl who attended Sir Winston Churchill High School and then became a veterinary assistant, working at an animal hospital, which was where she met Paul Bernardo.

DARK FANTASIES

Unlike most of his previous girlfriends, Karla was not repulsed by her new boyfriend's sexual sadism. Instead, she joined in enthusiastically, encouraging him to go ever further into his dark fantasies. Before long, this meant going out and finding women to rape. Over the next few years, Bernardo carried out well over a dozen rapes around the Scarborough area. How far Homolka was involved is not entirely clear, though one victim reported seeing a woman lurking behind the rapist, filming the event.

The police took a long time to deal with the case. In 1990, they finally released a photo-fit sketch that produced an immediate identification of Paul

Bernardo. A blood test was taken from Bernardo, revealing that he had the same blood group as the rapist. Further tests were called for. Unbelievably, it took the police laboratory three years to carry out detailed tests, which proved conclusively that Bernardo was the 'Scarborough Rapist'. By that time, however, he was also a murderer.

As time went on, raping strangers was no longer enough for Bernardo. He developed a fantasy about raping Karla's fifteen-year-old sister Tammy. Once again, Karla was a willing accomplice. She decided to drug Tammy, using anaesthetics stolen from the veterinary clinic where she worked. On 24 December 1990, Karla got Tammy drunk and administered a drug called Halothane to her. Both Paul and Karla then raped Tammy and videotaped the entire episode. They did not initially intend to kill Tammy but the anaesthetic caused her to choke on her own vomit, and she died on her way to hospital. The official cause of death was suffocation. Karla's grieving parents put the tragedy down to an accident, caused by Tammy having drunk too much.

MARRIAGE OF MINDS
Karla grieved briefly but was soon engrossed in planning her wedding that summer. A few weeks beforehand, she lured one of her friends, a teenager named Jane, round to the house and gave her the same treatment she had doled out to her sister. This time, though, Jane survived the experience, awaking from her

▼ *The presence of Karla Homolka may have allayed the suspicions of victims*

drugged sleep confused and sore, but unaware that she had been raped by both Karla and Paul. This lapse of memory undoubtedly saved her life.

The couple's next victim, fourteen-year-old Leslie Mahaffy, was not so lucky. Paul abducted her on 15 July 1991 and the couple raped and tortured the girl over a twenty-four hour period, filming the event, before Paul finally killed her. Her body was found soon afterwards, dismembered and encased in cement on Lake Gibson. The same day that Mahaffy's body was found, Paul and Karla were married in a lavish affair at Niagara.

Four months later, on 30 November 1991, fourteen-year-old Terri Anderson disappeared. She may well have been murdered by Bernardo and Homolka, but the case remains unproven. Their final victim was seventeen-year-old Kristen French, abducted from a church parking lot on 16 April 1992. This time, the couple kept their victim alive for three days, raping and torturing her. They finally murdered her when they realized they were due to attend an Easter dinner at Karla's parents house.

This was the last murder the couple committed. By the summer of 1992, Bernardo had started to take out his rage on Homolka and in January 1993 she left him. The following month, the police lab finally ran the test on Bernardo's blood sample and discovered that he was the Scarborough Rapist. As Bernardo's name had also come up in the investigations into the murders of Mahaffey and French, the police finally put the whole case together. Homolka successfully painted herself as just another victim of the dominating Bernardo, and agreed a plea bargain whereby she would plead guilty of manslaughter and receive a twelve-year prison sentence in return for testifying against Bernardo.

WILLING PARTNER

Homolka's trial duly began in June 1993. She once again played the abused wife and received the agreed sentence. However, two years later, when Bernardo's trial began and the prosecution revealed the new evidence of Bernardo's videotapes, the judge and jury were able to see, in all too graphic detail, how willing a partner Homolka had been in the rape and torture of Mahaffey and French. Bernardo did his best to put the blame back on to Homolka, but the videotapes were utterly damning, and he received a life sentence in prison. Homolka, however, was released from prison in July 2005 and went to live in Montreal under supervisory conditions imposed on her by a judge.

THE DEATH OF JFK

In the United States, the Mafia, perhaps, has never aimed quite so high. But it should be remembered that in the 1960 election, which brought President John Kennedy into office, the outcome in the end was decided by a few hundred thousand votes and that the Democratic majority in Cook County, Illinois was finally key. Cook County, Illinois just happens to have been Al Capone's old stamping-ground, as Kennedy's father Joe, who'd been a bootlegger

▲ *John Kennedy's possible links with the Mafia have long been the subject of whispered discussion*

75

and had associated with the Italian Mafia, knew well; and Mafia boss Sam Giancana – who shared at least one lover with President Kennedy – later boasted of having swung the election there for Joe's son as a favour. Giancana and the Mafia were also involved in American-sponsored attempts to kill Fidel Castro of Cuba and several of the conspiracy theories surrounding the assassination of the President in November 1963 claim that he was killed at the behest of the American Mafia because he refused to return the favour it had done him. Indeed, by allowing his brother, Attorney-General Robert Kennedy, to investigate the Teamsters Union and Jimmy Hoffa, he'd made matters much worse.

We will probably never know the truth of any of this. But then that's in the nature of our knowledge of the Cosa Nostra. It exists in the shadows, and only very occasionally does it come out into the light, through the confessions of *pentiti*, via wiretaps, at trials. The rest is silence, discretion. As Tommaso Buscetta, the highest-ranked of all the *pentiti*, said:

'In my ambience no-one asks direct questions, but your interlocutor, when

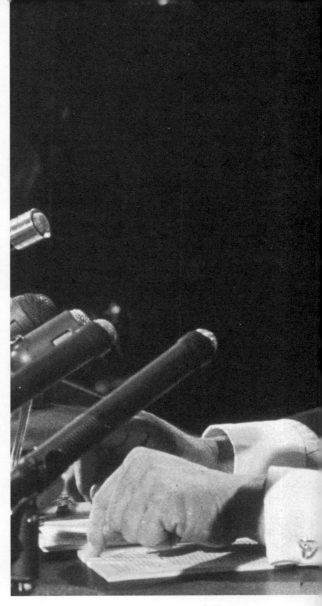

he considers it necessary, makes you understand, with a nod of the head, with a smile. . . even simply by his silence.'

Added to this is the fact that the family bosses and the members of the New York and Sicilian Commissions are far, far removed from the actual

commitment of any crime. They live at the top of a pyramid: outwardly respectable businessmen – sometimes, it is true, with no visible source of income, but sometimes with an income that, on the surface at any rate, seems quite legitimate. Rosario Spatola in Sicily, for example, had made millions of dollars from construction alone. He was said to be the fifth-highest payer of taxes in the whole of Italy.

Silence, remoteness, wisdom, power: were – and are – the watchwords that govern the behaviour of the senior ranks of Cosa Nostra. They were – and are – the law: a law that was regularly broken, however, by the head of one of New York's five families: Joe Bananas.

WANTED

JOHN HERBERT DILLINGER

On June 23, 1934, HOMER S. CUMMINGS, Attorney General of the United States, under the authority vested in him by an Act of Congress approved June 6, 1934, offered a reward of

$10,000.00

for the capture of John Herbert Dillinger or a reward of

$5,000.00

for information leading to the arrest of John Herbert Dillinger.

DESCRIPTION

Age, 32 years; Height, 5 feet 7-1/8 inches; Weight, 153 pounds; Build, medium; Hair, medium chestnut; Eyes, grey; Complexion, medium; Occupation, machinist; Marks and scars, 1/2 inch scar back left hand, scar middle upper lip, brown mole between eyebrows.

All claims to any of the aforesaid rewards and all questions and disputes that may arise as among claimants to the foregoing rewards shall be passed upon by the Attorney General and his decisions shall be final and conclusive. The right is reserved to divide and allocate portions of any of said rewards as between several claimants. No part of the aforesaid rewards shall be paid to any official or employee of the Department of Justice.

If you are in possession of any information concerning the whereabouts of John Herbert Dillinger, communicate immediately by telephone or telegraph collect to the nearest office of the Division of Investigation, United States Department of Justice, the local addresses of which are set forth on the reverse side of this notice.

JOHN EDGAR HOOVER, DIRECTOR,
DIVISION OF INVESTIGATION

▶ *Dillinger became the FBI's Public Enemy No1*

DEATH OR GLORY

There was something desperate, death-or-glory, about John Dillinger. For his big-time career as America's most wanted criminal lasted, in fact, little more than a year. He came out of prison in May 1933 after a nine-year stretch, and by July the following year he was dead, gunned down outside a cinema in Chicago. In that short space of time he robbed untold numbers of banks, broke into police armouries, escaped from prison twice, and survived at least six different shoot-outs. If he hadn't existed, J. Edgar Hoover's Federal Bureau of Investigation – which made its reputation out of his death – would have had to invent him.

John Herbert Dillinger was born into a religious Indianapolis Quaker family in 1902, and moved with it to Mooresville, Indiana eighteen years later. In 1923, after an unhappy love-affair, he joined the navy. But he deserted soon after, married a local girl and then, in September 1924, was sent down for nine years for assault while attempting to rob a grocer. He seems to have come out of prison nine years later as a man with a mission. For within a month, he'd robbed an Illinois factory official; and within two, he'd com-

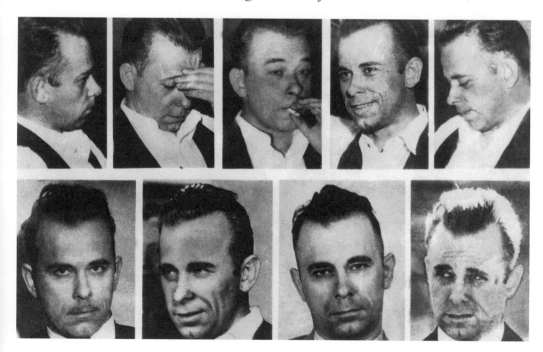

◄ *Dillinger was one of the most photographed criminals in US history*

mitted his first bank robbery. At this point he gathered a gang together, among them 'Baby Face Nelson' Gillis, and together they went on a spree, robbing banks all over the Midwestern states and killing anyone who stood in their way.

There were occasional hiccups. In July 1933, Dillinger was arrested for his part in a Bluffton, Ohio bank heist. But three of the gang posed as prison officials and soon got him out – the spree went on. They moved from rural banks to the big city: they robbed the First National Bank in East Chicago, and escaped with $20,000, killing a policeman on the way. And though Dillinger was again arrested – this time in Tucson, Arizona for possession of stolen banknotes and guns – this did little to cramp his style: legend has it that he carved himself a wooden gun, held up officials with it and bluffed his way out the joint.

The only other thing he did wrong on this occasion was to steal a car from a sheriff and drive it across the state line. This was enough to involve J. Edgar Hoover's Feds, who then played him up to the newspapers as a deranged killer even as they tried to track him down. Dillinger, in fact, had a reputation as a courteous man, particularly to women and children. So he resented the publicity, and did his best to avoid it. He tried to disguise himself via facial surgery – and he even had his finger ends shaved off to evade fingerprint identification.

In April 1934, a tip-off led the government men – or G-men, as George 'Machine Gun' Kelly seems to have been the first to call them – to a hide-out at a lodge in Little Bohemia, Wisconsin. The Feds, though, shot at the wrong car during a night-time raid, and Dillinger escaped, leaving a dead G-man behind him. Gradually, however, the net closed in. Rewards for Dillinger's arrest were by now on offer from several states, and there'd even been a special appropriation voted by Congress to add to the pot.

In July 1934, then, a friend of Dillinger's, a brothel-keeper called Anna Sage, came to claim it; and on the 22nd, by previous arrangement, she went with him to the Biograph Cinema in Chicago.

As they came out after the show, a half-hearted attempt was made to arrest him. He resisted and was shot dead. J. Edgar Hoover, who was on hand to grab the limelight cast by his Public Enemy Number One, later described Dillinger

'as a cheap, boastful, selfish, tight-fisted plug-ugly.'

It's worth remembering that it was this same J. Edgar Hoover who announced that the Mafia – a much more difficult target than Dillinger – simply did not exist in America.

◄ *Dillinger survived six shootouts before the one that finally killed him*

With a total of over 200 suspected murders to his name, Harold Shipman is the most prolific serial killer of modern times. His grisly tally of victims puts him well ahead of Pedro Lopez, the 'monster of the Andes', who was convicted of fifty-seven murders in 1980. Lopez claimed to have killed many more, but the exact number of deaths was never verified. Until Shipman's crimes came to light, Lopez had the dubious distinction of topping the serial killer league; at present, however, it is a British family doctor, rather than a penniless Colombian vagrant, who has become the world's number one murderer.

MOTHER'S FAVOURITE

The sorry tale begins in 1946, when Harold Frederick Shipman was born into a working-class family in Nottingham. Known as Fred, the boy had an unusual childhood. He had a brother and sister, but it was clear that he was his mother's favourite. She felt that Fred was destined for great things, and taught him that he was superior to his contemporaries, even though he was not especially clever and had to work hard to achieve academic success. During his schooldays, he formed few friendships with other children, a situation that was exacerbated when his mother became seriously ill with lung cancer. The young Shipman took on the role of carer to his mother, spending time with her after school waiting for visits from the family doctor, who would inject her with morphine to relieve her from pain. It is possible that the stress of this experience during his formative years may have pushed him into mental illness, causing him to re-enact the role of carer and doctor in the macabre fashion that he later did.

By the time Shipman was seventeen, his mother had died of cancer, after a long and painful illness. He enrolled at medical school, despite having to resit his entry exams. Although he was good at sport, he made little effort to make friends. However, at this time he met and married his future wife Primrose; the pair went on to have four children, as Shipman began his career as a doctor in general practice. To many, he seemed kind and pleasant, but colleagues complained of his superior attitude and rudeness. Then he began to suffer from blackouts, which he attributed to epilepsy. However, disturbing evidence emerged that he was in fact taking large amounts of pethidine, on the pretext of prescribing

◀ *Harold Shipman's kindly manner made him popular, even with those he would later kill*

the drug to patients. He was dismissed from the practice but, surprisingly, within two years he was once again working as a doctor, this time in a different town.

PILLAR OF THE COMMUNITY

In his new job, the hard-working Shipman soon earned the respect of his colleagues and patients. However, it was during his time at Hyde, over a twenty-four-year period, that he is estimated to have killed at least 236 patients. His status as a pillar of the community, not to mention his kindly bedside manner, for many years masked the fact that the death toll among Shipman's patients was astoundingly high.

Over the years a number of people, including relatives of the deceased and local undertakers, had raised concerns about the deaths of Shipman's patients.

Many patients died suddenly, often with no previous record of terminal illness; and they were usually found sitting in a chair, fully clothed, rather than in bed. The police had been alerted and had examined the doctor's records, but nothing was found. It later became clear that Shipman had falsified patient records, but at this stage the doctor's calm air of authority was still protecting him against closer scrutiny.

Then Shipman made a fateful mistake. In 1998 Kathleen Grundy, a healthy, active eighty-one-year-old ex-mayor with a reputation for community service, died suddenly at home. Shipman was called and pronounced her dead; he also said that a post-mortem was unnecessary, since he had paid her a visit shortly before her death. When her funeral was over, her daughter Angela Woodruff received a badly typed copy of Mrs Grundy's will leaving Shipman a large sum of money. A solicitor herself, Mrs Woodruff knew immediately that this was a fake. She contacted the police, who took the unusual step of exhuming Mrs Grundy's body. They found that she had been administered a lethal dose of morphine.

Surprisingly, in murdering Mrs Grundy, Shipman had made little effort to cover his tracks: either to forge the will carefully or to kill his victim with a less easily traceable drug. Whether this was through sheer arrogance and stupidity, or through a latent desire to be discovered, no one knows. However, once the true nature of Mrs Grundy's death was uncovered, more graves were opened, and more murders came to light.

During his trial, Shipman showed no remorse for the fifteen murders he was accused of. There were known to be others, but these alone were more than enough to ensure a life sentence. He was contemptuous of the police and the court, and continued to protest his innocence to the end. He was convicted of the murders and imprisoned. Four years later, without warning, he hanged himself in his prison cell.

Today, the case of Harold Shipman remains mystifying: there was no sexual motive in his killings and, until the end, no profit motive. His murders did not fit the usual pattern of a serial killer. In most cases, his victims seem to have died in comfort, at peace. It may be, as several commentators have pointed out, that he enjoyed the sense of having control over life and death, and that over the years he became addicted to this sense of power.

What is clear is that, in finally taking his own life, Harold Shipman ensured ultimate control: that no one would ever fully understand why he did what he did.

DOCTOR DOUBLE CROSS

When 33-year-old Ohio paramedic Michelle Baker became pregnant, her live-in lover, soft-spoken and charming medical resident Maynard Muntzing, seemed genuinely delighted and offered to celebrate with a dream wedding on a tropical island paradise. But unbeknown to Michelle, Dr Muntzing secretly entertained hopes of being reunited with his former lover Tammy Erwin, and saw the baby as a hindrance to his love life. Nevertheless the couple flew to the island as planned, where Muntzing invented an excuse for postponing the ceremony. Michelle then began to suffer severe cramps and some light bleeding which she attributed to food poisoning or a local bug. On her return to Ohio she consulted her own doctor, who reassured her that nothing was amiss.

Michelle was initially delighted when Muntzing purchased a luxury home in which to raise his new family. But the cramps and bleeding continued, causing the expectant mother considerable anxiety. She then happened to hear a record request on her local radio station for a listener named Maynard whose voice was eerily familiar. Maynard was supposedly on vacation in Columbus at the time! Her curiosity aroused, Michelle drove to Tammy's home where she found her fiancé and his ex-girlfriend together.

A confrontation ensued, but Michelle was persuaded that the amorous doctor was committed to her and the baby and that his affection for Tammy was in the past. However, the nausea, cramps and bleeding continued, forcing Michelle to conclude she was being poisoned. She managed to smuggle a drink Maynard had made her to the police, whereupon it was proven to contain cytotec, a drug used to treat stomach ulcers which was expressly forbidden for pregnant women since it was likely to cause an abortion. But as detectives pointed out, there was no proof that Dr Muntzing had put it there; Michelle could have put it in her own drink to discredit her two-timing lover.

It was only when Michelle returned with a video she had made showing Dr Muntzing putting something in her drink that the police were forced to test her story. They too set up a secret camera in her kitchen which they monitored from the garage and thus they were witness to Muntzing mixing one of his mysterious cocktails while Michelle was out of the room.

▶ *Michelle Baker who was poisoned by her live-in lover*

They immediately rushed into the house and arrested Muntzing. The drink was analyzed and found to contain yet more cytotec. More vials of the drug were found in his car. Muntzing was charged with the attempted murder of an unborn baby, but the case never came to court. Unfortunately the poisoning had affected Michelle's health and just weeks before the trial she gave birth to a stillborn child.

Maynard cut a deal and spent five years in jail in addition to losing his medical license. His sentence might have been longer and he might still be there today had it not been for the fact that no cytotec was found in the placenta after the birth and Michelle's failing health meant that she was not able to take the witness stand during what might have been a lengthy trial.

DOUBLE HOMICIDE

The case of Linda Leon and Esteban Martinez is a shocking one. It was a double homicide, in which the couple were tortured and murdered in front of their young children. The aftermath was no less shocking: Leon and Martinez made their living as drug dealers, which meant that few in their circle were willing to come forward with information. Nobody seemed to care very much about the fate of a couple of drug dealers, even where their children were involved.

It was not until a determined detective named Wendell Stradford picked up the case that the investigation began to move. He believed that, however the victims earned their money, the perpetrators of the crime needed to be brought to justice. Leon and Martinez had been brutally murdered in the most horrific way, and their young children callously left alone with their mutilated, bleeding bodies. By the time Stradford began work, the case had been on the files of the New York City Police Department for a long time, and had gone completely cold, but he was determined to catch up with the culprits.

STABBED IN THE EAR

It was in the run-up to Christmas of 1996 that a 911 operator received a call from a six-year-old boy telling her that someone had killed his mother and father. At first, he was too upset to give the address, but the operator was eventually able to wheedle it out of him, and police officers were immediately sent there. Once at the apartment, they found a scene that was as heartbreaking as it was appalling: the dead parents were lying on the floor, bound with duct tape, their bodies covered in blood, with the children trying to nestle in against them.

When the officers spoke to the children, little by little the story began to emerge: that their mother Linda Leon, twenty-three, and their father, Esteban Martinez, twenty-nine, had had a visit from four people, two men and two women. While the women had sat with the children, the men had taken their parents to another room, and repeatedly stabbed them before shooting them dead.

JUST ANOTHER STATISTIC

Although this was a double homicide, and the evidence showed that the perpetrators had been sadistic killers, the case was allowed to go cold. The annual rate of homicides in New York City is high, especially among those involved in drug dealing. Leon and Martinez soon became just another statistic on the files of a crime-ridden city, despite the fact that murderers were still on the loose and out there somewhere, waiting to torture and kill the next drug dealers that crossed them.

It was not until 1998 that the case reached the Cold Case Squad at New York City's Police Department and some action began to be taken. Detectives found out that the Drug Enforcement Agency had been on the tail of Martinez, who was a cocaine dealer, and thought that he had probably been killed by members of a Colombian drug cartel. The investigation into this dragged on until Detective Wendell Stradford noticed that the name Robert Mitchell kept cropping up. He noticed that one of the children had

◀ *Detective Wendell Stradford (centre) noticed one particular name that kept cropping up in the cold case file; that of the person who was to become the chief suspect of the case*

referred to a 'Tio Rob', Uncle Rob, who often visited the house. Stradford tracked down Mitchell, and an associate named Tavon Blackmon. When Blackmon was picked up by police, he admitted that he knew Mitchell. According to his story, Mitchell had boasted to him that he had 'smoked' a guy and his wife in New York. He had gone round to their apartment with his girlfriend Keisha Washington, her twin brother Kevin, and Kevin's girlfriend Nisey. They had stolen a kilo and a half of cocaine and crack from Martinez, and had also made off with thousands of dollars, which Mitchell had used to buy himself an expensive new car.

In 2001, the detectives on the case managed to track down Keisha Washington, who by now had split up with Mitchell and was living in Baltimore. Under the guise of helping her to find Mitchell and gain child support from him, they interviewed her. She spoke of a terrible incident that had estranged her from her brother Kevin, 'Something I can never make up for', as she called it. Now a born-again Christian, Washington was attempting to make a new start in life, away from Mitchell and his influence.

SCREAMS AND GUNSHOTS

Washington gave detectives enough information to know that they were, at last, on the right track. They interviewed her again, and found out more. She told them how Mitchell had persuaded her to visit Esteban Martinez and his family, saying that Martinez was causing him to lose money. Her role was to look after the children while Mitchell discussed the matter with Martinez. They met up with Kevin and Nisey, and all went over to the apartment, where she and Nisey sat on the bed in the children's bedroom watching television with them. The children constantly asked for their parents and cried when Robert and Kevin came in, roughly told them to shut up, and searched for money.

Then the real nightmare started, as the children began to hear their mother screaming. Kevin was stabbing her in the ear, trying to get her to say where the drugs and money were hidden. Next there were gunshots, and the children became frantic. The women held them down, covering their mouths, and waited until the men were ready to go. The four adults left, leaving the children running out of the room, screaming and crying, with their dead parents lying on the floor.

After this interview, the police let Keisha Washington go, but only after taking fingerprints from her. They later found that her fingerprints matched those lifted from a soda can at the scene of the crime. They also managed to identify the fourth suspect in the killing: 'Nisey' was Denise Henderson, a thirty-four-year-old woman from Baltimore.

AN UGLY KNIFE

The police now concentrated their efforts on tracking down Kevin Washington. When the police caught up with him, he tried to blame the murders on Robert

Mitchell, claiming that Mitchell had only said they were going to rob the couple, take the drugs and the money, and then leave. However, according to him, when they got to the apartment, Robert pulled a gun on Esteban. Kevin then admitted that the women bound Linda and Esteban with duct tape, and that he had tried to cut Linda's neck with what he called 'a wood knife'. However, it had a serrated edge and would not cut – as one of the children had described it, 'that bad man had a ugly knife'. This, Washington seemed to feel, was some kind of defence for his behaviour. He then reported that Mitchell had shot both Esteban and Linda dead. After that, the four had set off back to Maryland, where Mitchell had disposed of the gun in an empty lot.

SHOPPING FOR CHRISTMAS

Police now had enough evidence to arrest Kevin Washington and charge him with second-degree murder and robbery. While he was awaiting trial, they went after Denise Henderson, who gave them more information. She described how they had all put gloves on as they went up the stairs to the Martinez apartment. This seemed to point quite clearly to the fact that the crime was premeditated. When they got inside the apartment, she and Keisha were told to wait in the bedroom with the children. The women rifled through Linda's belongings, trying to placate the children as they did so. There were sounds of screaming and gunshots from the next room, and then the men ran in and told them all to leave. When Henderson left, she saw a body on the floor, but just jumped over it on the way out.

The police arrested and charged Keisha Washington and Denise Henderson. Along with Kevin Washington, they now had three of the four murderers. But Mitchell proved harder to get hold of. In the end, the police had to conduct night-time raids on the house of his mother and his girlfriend in an effort to catch him, but he was not there on either occasion. In the end, it was only by pretending that they had come to protect Mitchell's family from violent drug runners that they managed to find out where he was, in an apartment on the other side of town. When they raided the apartment, they found Mitchell cowering under a bed wearing nothing but his underpants.

'UNCLE' ROBERT

Mitchell was arrested, and when police interviewed him, he told a different story. He said that he had gone over to the Martinez apartment with the intention of getting back money that he felt was owed to him. Esteban had been living the high life at his expense, he explained, cutting drugs with other substances, which made it hard for Mitchell to sell them. He had only wanted to get what was owing to him from Martinez, whom he referred to as 'Tony'. Mitchell blamed Kevin for initiating the violence, and said that he had had nothing to do with it. By the time he heard the gunshots, he was already outside the apartment. He claimed that he only found out about Linda and Esteban's death later, and was angry because he knew the children could identify him as 'Tio Rob'; they had never met any of the others before, so he was afraid he would be held responsible for the murders, which he swore he did not commit.

When the four cases came before the courts, the women plea bargained. In exchange for agreeing to testify at the trials of the men, they got six- to twelve-year sentences, which included the time they had already served, having been held in police custody during this time.

At Kevin Washington's trial, his twin sister Keisha testified against him, and the Martinez children, now aged thirteen, twelve, and ten were brought back from the Dominican Republic to attend the proceedings. As the trial went on, it emerged that, on that fateful day, Esteban had been shot first, so as to frighten Linda into handing over money and drugs hidden in the apartment. But, even after having done so, she was still shot.

Kevin Washington denied the charge against him, but the jury did not believe him, and on 26 March 2004, he was found guilty of second-degree murder and first-degree robbery. The judge sentenced him to seventy-five years in prison. He showed no remorse for the crimes, and continued to maintain his innocence.

Today, Robert Mitchell is currently awaiting trial. At his arraignment, he pleaded not guilty to murder. Mitchell blames Kevin Washington for the murders, just as Washington blamed him, but it seems unlikely that he will be believed. After all, the investigation only took off when the eldest of the Martinez children, then aged six, identified 'Tio Robert' as the man who had visited his parents and then proceeded to torture and kill them. And when the boy takes the stand again to testify, now no longer a six-year-old but a young teenager, he will no doubt remember more about that fateful day when his parents, Linda Leon and Esteban Martinez, were decorating the family's apartment for Christmas and Tio Robert came to call.

THE DÜSSELDORF VAMPIRE

Peter Kürten had the sort of childhood from which few escape unscathed. Kürten Sr had a habit of raping both wife and daughter, and Peter's older brothers spent much of their time in jail. As a nine-year-old he was befriended by the municipal rat-catcher, who enjoyed torturing and sexually abusing animals in front of him. The young Kürten found these experiences stimulating in ways which he could not begin to express or understand. As he got older, he came up with his own twists, stabbing sheep and tearing the heads off swans to drink their blood. It was a taste he would never lose.

In his late teens he attacked two girls, nearly killing one of them. Although he was soon convicted, he received only a four-year prison sentence. In later years, he would remember the days spent fantasizing in his cell about all the crimes he would one day commit. Arson came high on the list, because he found it to be so sexually satisfying. Poisoning children with arsenic was another idea he found appealing. Kürten got intense enjoyment out of inflicting pain.

It seems unlikely that he reached the age of thirty without killing anyone, but his first known murder was committed in 1913. He described his rape and killing of a ten-year-old innkeeper's daughter with detailed relish at his trial seventeen years later, noting that the public horror and indignation 'did me good'. When the First World War broke out the following year, he was called up, but allegedly deserted on his first day of service. If so, one wonders how he avoided being shot when arrested for yet another arson offence. Instead, he spent a few more years in jail. He was a well-behaved prisoner; however, when he volunteered to help with the laying out of dead prisoners his offer was, unfortunately, accepted.

Kürten did not look like a sadistic vampire. He was fastidious about his appearance, had perfect manners and an easy way with children. Around 1921 it seems he almost lost himself inside this mask. He married, and treated his wife with great gentleness. He got and kept a job. It was only his half-strangled mistresses who saw the violence still simmering within.

In 1925 his job sent him back to Düsseldorf, to where his troubles had all begun. 'The sunset was blood-red on my return,' he said later. 'I considered this to be an omen symbolic of my destiny'.

▶ *Well fed: Peter Kürten*
as he appeared three days
before his execution

◀ *Once in custody, Kürten was a helpful witness to his own crimes, providing maps to where he had left bodies of his victims*

He started killing with what seemed an ever-increasing ferocity – animals, children, women and men. He clubbed them, stabbed them, strangled them with his bare hands. The police, following this trail of carnage, could see only one connecting link – the frenzied consumption of blood. The papers called the killer the 'Düsseldorf Vampire', and Kürten's wife was so frightened of becoming a victim of 'the Vampire' that she asked her husband to escort her home from work each night.

Early in 1930 he slashed a five-year-old girl to death, yet a few weeks later he let his last potential victim go, after checking that she did not remember his address. But the girl had tricked him, and Kürten soon realized as much.

Kürten confessed to his wife, and persuaded her to give him up for the reward. At his trial he pleaded guilty to nine charges of murder and a host of other crimes.

Before his execution, he told his psychiatrist that he hoped to hear, for just a second or two, the sound of blood gushing from his own neck. 'That,' he said, 'would be the pleasure to end all pleasures'.

▲ *The Krays were, and still are, immensely popular figures*

THE EAST END RACKETS

The Kray twins, Reggie and Ronnie, were probably the nearest London ever came to producing an indigenous Mafia. On the surface they were legitimate businessmen, the owners of clubs and restaurants haunted by the fashionable rich. But in reality they were racketeers and murderers, protected from prosecution by their reputation for extreme violence.

They were born in the London's East End in 1933 – and soon had a reputation as fighters. Both became professional boxers and, after a brief stint in the army, bouncers at a Covent Garden nightclub. It was then that they started in the protection business, using levels of intimidation that were, to say the least, unusual for their time. Their cousin Ronald Hart later said of them:

'I saw beatings that were unnecessary even by underworld standards and witnessed people slashed with a razor just for the hell of it.'

In 1956, Ronnie Kray was imprisoned for his part in a beating and stabbing in a packed East End pub, and judged insane. But three years later he was released from mental hospital, and the twins were back in business, cutting a secret swathe of violence through the British capital while being romanticized in the British press – along with people like actors Michael Caine and Terence Stamp – as East-End-boys-made-good.

When they were arrested in 1965 for demanding money with menaces, a member of the British aristocracy actually stood up in the House of Lords and asked why they were being held for so long without trial. They were ultimately acquitted.

In the same year Ronnie, who was homosexual, committed his first known murder: of the chief lieutenant of the twins' main rivals for criminal power in London, brothers Eddie and Charles Richardson.

George Cornell was shot in the head in another crowded East-End pub. But not a single witness was prepared to come forward. When Reggie heard the news of what his twin, known as 'the Colonel,' had been up to, he said:

'Well, Ronnie does some funny things.'

Ronnie, though, was exultant at having got away with the killing and having sent out a message that he was above the law.

'He was very proud. . .'

— said Hart,

'and was constantly getting at Reggie and asking him when he was going to do his murder.'

Two years later Reggie chose his mark, a small-time robber and hard man called Jack 'The Hat' McVitie, who was said to have bad-mouthed the twins. Reggie had McVitie 'escorted' from a Hackney jazz club to a nearby basement, where Reggie stabbed him to death as his brother shouted him on.

In 1969, after a long undercover investigation, the Krays and their henchmen were finally brought to justice,

▶ *The Kray twins with their elder brother Charlie (centre)*

◀ *Reggie and Ronnie Kray have become cultural icons*

charged with these two murders and with a third: that of an escaped convict called Frank Mitchell, nicknamed the Mad Axe-Man. Though Mitchell's murder was never proved, both twins were given life sentences, with a recommendation that they serve at least thirty years.

Their elder brother Charlie, who'd helped to get rid of McVitie's body, was sentenced to ten years.

In 1979, while still in prison, Ronnie was once more declared insane and sent to a mental hospital. But the myth of the Krays as East-End-boys-made-good – men who never forgot a good turn and loved their old neighbourhood and their mother – continued to cling to them.

A feature film was made about their lives and their careers of crime – in that, too, they resembled the American Mafia in more ways than one.

When they died in prison, five years apart, there were massive turn-outs at their lavish East-End funerals.

A FATAL FALLING OUT

Computer-generated reconstructions are becoming a familiar feature of murder trials in the United States, but there is increasing concern that juries are accepting them as factual representations of what happened, rather than as just one possible scenario. The dangers of accepting computer-generated reconstructions as evidence was highlighted in 1991 at the trial of Californian pornographer James Mitchell.

Forty-year-old James was on trial for the murder of his younger brother Artie. There was no denying the fact that James had killed Artie, for the five shots that had left the hard-drinking, drug-taking strip-club owner lifeless in the bedroom of his San Francisco home had been caught on tape by a 911 operator.

The question was, had James planned the shooting, or was it committed in the heat of the moment? The distinction was critical as premeditated murder carried a mandatory life sentence in the state, whereas manslaughter would put him away for just five or six years. The pair were known to have had heated arguments that frequently resulted in an exchange of blows, but they had always managed to bury their differences before either had suffered a serious injury. But on the 27 February 1991 it was different and their partnership was terminated, permanently.

At 10.15pm that night police arrived at the scene to find James pacing up and down outside the house in an excitable state, brandishing a .22 rifle and sporting a .38 Smith and Wesson revolver in a shoulder holster. Once he had been disarmed they went inside, where they discovered Artie's body. He had been shot in the stomach, the right arm and in the right eye. Eight spent .22 shell casings were found nearby.

CRUCIAL DETAILS

At the trial the prosecution argued that the long space between shots, which could be clearly heard on the 911 tape, clearly demonstrated intent. Had it been a spontaneous shooting the shots would have been fired in quick succession.

Based on spectrograms of the shots, forensic acoustics expert Dr Harry Hollien was able to identify where each shot on the tape occurred. From this the prosecution were able to create a computer-generated video animation of the murder in which a figure representing Artie was shown being pursued by another – his attacker.

◄ Brotherly love:
James and Artie Mitchell
together in happier times

In court the film was accompanied by a commentary from Arizona criminalist Lucian Haag, who explained that the sequence of events had been determined by tracing the trajectory of the bullets to the impact points and reproducing any deflections in the crime lab. Haag had even gone to the trouble of buying a door like the one in the victim's house and shooting at it so that he could measure the angle of deflection under controlled conditions.

Such thoroughness impressed the jury, but the defence successfully argued that, with so many bullets, there were thousands of possible variations and that the video animation was only one scenario, albeit the most likely. The judge ruled that the video was to be treated as speculative, not definitive. It was not the job of the crime scene investigators to imagine the scene, but to present the facts and interpret the science.

Without a material witness to give evidence as to James Mitchell's state of mind at the time of the shooting and testimony as to the sequence of events that led up to the fatal shooting, the jury could not be expected to find him guilty of first-degree murder. Consequently James was acquitted on the murder charge but found guilty of manslaughter and sentenced to six years in jail.

THE FINGER OF SUSPICION

Dr Sam Sheppard and his wife Marilyn were the image of the all-American couple. Dr Sam, as he was known locally, was an even-tempered young man of considerable personal charm with a profitable practice as an osteopath in Bay Village and a large executive-style home in a leafy suburb of Cleveland which the couple shared with their six-year-old son Chip. But their seemingly idyllic world was shattered when, on the night of 3 July 1954, Mrs Sheppard was found brutally beaten to death in the first-floor bedroom and her husband was accused of her murder.

Dr Sheppard claimed to have been asleep on the living room couch when he heard Marilyn cry out. Bolting up the stairs he had been confronted by a shadowy figure who struck him over the head. When he finally recovered his senses, he stated that he heard the intruder escaping out the back door and gave chase. There in the darkness he saw the silhouette of a bushy-haired man who wheeled around and struck a second disabling blow from which he did not recover until the police arrived.

From the moment the Coroner, Dr Samuel Gerber, was put on the case he began questioning Dr Sheppard's version of events. To Gerber's eyes the scene appeared to have been staged, with drawers pulled out of a bureau and neatly stacked on the floor, Dr Sheppard's surgical bag emptied and placed in the hallway where it would catch the investigator's eyes and a bag of valuables stashed in a bush at the bottom of the garden. Inside the bag police found the doctor's blood-splattered self-winding watch which had stopped at 4.15am. Fingerprints had also been hastily erased, supporting the possibility that a third person had been present, but it seemed highly unlikely that an intruder could have failed to notice Dr Sheppard sleeping in the lounge and left him unmolested while he attacked his wife.

The finger of suspicion began to point to Dr Sheppard, and as the investigation dug deeper it emerged that both Sam and Marilyn Sheppard had had affairs. The whiff of scandal brought the local media baying for the doctor's blood. While the inexperienced local investigators dragged their feet and tried to cover up the fact that they had contaminated the crime scene in their carelessness, the local press demanded that their prime suspect be arrested. Before the week was out the press were setting the agenda and the subsequent trial seemed to be a mere formality.

For reasons best known to himself, Dr Gerber let it be known that the murder weapon was a surgical instrument. And it was this more than any other single piece of evidence which sealed Sheppard's fate. It later transpired that the murder weapon had not been found and that the coroner had made his assumption based on a suspicious 'shape' impressed in the pillow next to the body.

One thing that might explain Dr Gerber's stubborn refusal to face the facts was that he considered Dr Sheppard to be a thorn in his side. There was said to be personal animosity and distrust between the two medical men. Dr Sheppard was known to disapprove of the coroner's approach to forensic investigation and so bruised pride may have been a factor in Gerber's overlooking, and perhaps even suppressing, significant clues. It is known, for example, that evidence of forced entry at the doors to the basement was never presented in court. Furthermore, there were blood spots on the basement steps which had presumably dripped from the weapon as there were no indications the assailant had been injured.

Dr Gerber presented these blood spots as evidence of Dr Sheppard's guilt. At that time there was no available method of

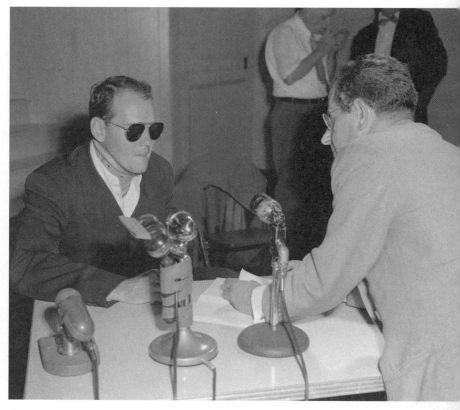

▲ *Dr Sam Sheppard (left) is questioned by his nemesis Dr Samuel Gerber*

determining whose blood had been found, only whether it was animal or human. But Dr Sam's performance on the witness stand gave his defence counsel cause for concern. He recollected the horrific events with an almost academic detachment. When questioned about the events leading to the discovery of his wife's battered body, he remarked, 'I initiated an attempt to gather enough senses to navigate the stairs.'

Hardly the kind of tone one would expect of a bereaved husband.

Dr Sam's poor performance, together with Dr Gerber's testimony, helped to secure a conviction and a life sentence. However, the forensic evidence suggested that Sheppard might have been telling the truth. Although Marilyn had been repeatedly beaten until her face was unrecognizable the assailant had not used sufficient force to kill her. She had, in fact, drowned in her own blood. Dr Sheppard was a strong well-built man who could easily have killed someone with a single blow using a blunt weapon. Moreover, it is extremely unlikely that he would have bludgeoned his wife to death while their son slept in the next room, no matter how enraged he might have been. More revealing was the blood splatter on the wall and bedroom door to the left of the body which indicated spray from a weapon wielded by a left-handed assailant. Dr Sheppard was right-handed.

With such significant discrepancies a second trial was inevitable. At the retrial in 1964 the defence made much of Dr Gerber's failure to find the murder weapon, casting doubt on his assertion that it had been a surgical instrument. Greater attention was paid to the significance of the blood splatter and the 'flying blood' spray found on the inside of Dr Sheppard's watch strap, intimating that he had not been wearing it during the frenzied attack, but that it might have been in the possession of an intruder, as Sheppard had insisted.

It was suggested that the blood trail in the basement had been left by a casual labourer named Richard Eberling who had worked for the Sheppards and who was later incarcerated for killing several women. He was known to wear a wig to cover his thinning hair which might account for the bushy-haired figure Dr Sheppard claimed to have seen. Eberling even confessed, but his confession was dismissed due to his mental instability.

With more than sufficient reasonable doubt Dr Sheppard was acquitted the second time round, but ten years in prison had taken their toll. Sam Sheppard left court a broken man. He was unfit to practise medicine, and died only four years later.

However, his son continued to campaign to clear his father's name and in 1997 he filed a $2 million lawsuit against the state of Ohio supported by DNA evidence proving that the stains on the basement stairs were not his father's blood.

It appears that Eberling, a diagnosed schizophrenic, had become obsessed with Marilyn and must have killed her when she refused his advances. Dr Gerber, however, would not entertain the idea that he might have helped to convict the wrong man and there are those who even now still harbour doubts as to Dr Sam's innocence.

THE FREEDOM RIDERS

Edgar Ray Killen, known as Preacher Killen, was a member of the Ku Klux Klan in Philadelphia, Mississippi, who in 1964 organized the killing of three civil rights campaigners. Killen managed to get away with murder, until 41 years later he was to pay for the crime he had committed in the name of white supremacy.

TERRIBLE ACTS OF VIOLENCE

Killen was born in 1925, and grew up to become a sawmill operator. His other activities included working for the church as a part-time Baptist minister, and for the Ku Klux Klan as a klavern organizer, recruiting others to the cause. At this period, in the early 1960s, the Ku Klux Klan was a powerful force in Mississippi, encouraging a culture of extreme racism among ordinary white citizens. Terrible acts of violence against black people were committed on an almost daily basis in some areas; lynch mobs and firebombings of black churches were a common occurrence. These attacks very often went unpunished in the courts, since the influence of the Ku Klux Klan extended into the higher echelons of the judiciary, the police and the military.

◀ In 1952, racial segregation on inter-state buses was declared unconstitutional by the Supreme Court. Alabama in 1961 had still not embraced these changes, and a bus operating under non-segregation laws was firebombed. Fortunately, no-one was hurt

▶ Another busload of 'freedom riders' – including four white college professors – arrives in Montgomery, Alabama in May 1961. Seating would have been mixed, rather than the division of white people at the front and black people at the back

By the 1960s, the situation in Mississippi had become the focus of a national campaign among students at colleges across America. In what became known as the 'freedom summer' of 1964, dozens of young civil rights campaigners, both black and white, came down by bus, train, and plane from college campuses to the South, intending to challenge the 'Jim Crow' laws operating there. Among them were two young white men, Andrew Goodman and Michael Schwerner from New York, and a young black man, James Chaney from Mississippi.

At the start of their visit, the three friends set out to see the ruins of Mount Zion Church, a black church that had recently been firebombed. Unbeknown to them, their movements were being carefully tracked by Cecil Price, Deputy Sheriff of Neshoba County. On their return journey, the sheriff had the three men picked up for speeding, and held in the county jail.

BEATEN AND SHOT DEAD

Next, Sheriff Price contacted Killen, whom he knew to be the organizer of the Ku Klux Klan Neshoba Chapter, and told him that he was holding three civil rights campaigners in jail. He also said that he would be letting them out that evening. Killen then rounded up a large mob of bloodthirsty rednecks and told them of his plan to meet the campaigners on a country road as they left jail, and attack them. The mob, armed with rifles and other weapons, set out that evening, and caught up with the three young college students as they walked down the deserted road. In a frenzied attack, they brutally beat the three friends and then shot them dead. Killen and his men later buried the bodies in an earthen dam.

Sheriff Price's plan had worked; yet ironically, the brutal murder of these young idealists, who wanted nothing more than peace and justice for all Americans, had the opposite effect to what the Southern racists intended. All over the country, people were so appalled at what had been allowed to happen in Mississippi that the civil rights campaign grew stronger than ever, and it was not long before a series of important civil rights laws were set in motion.

For many people, one of the most shocking aspects of the freedom riders' case was that, far from pursuing the perpetrators of the crime, the state of Mississippi initially allowed the murderers to go free. There appeared to be no attempt to arrest, charge and convict the culprits. Instead, the police and the judiciary closed ranks, blocking all attempts to have the killers brought to justice. In the end, the FBI, acting under the orders of President Lyndon Johnson,

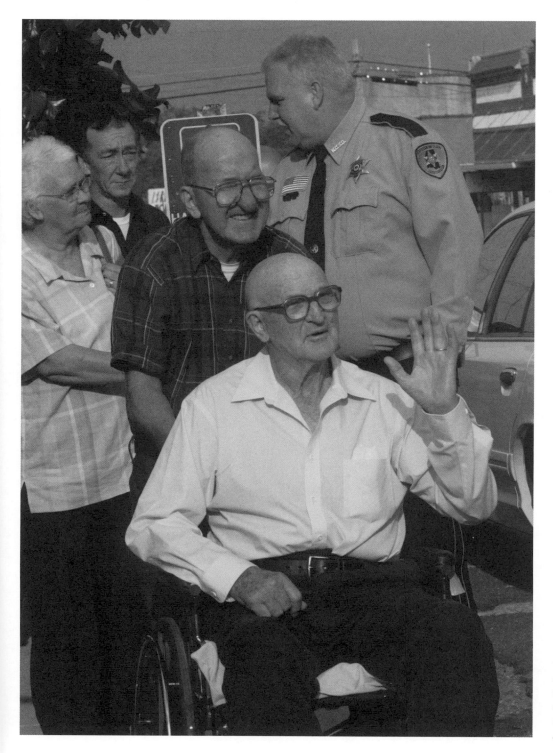

◄ *Killen's bond, which had allowed him to go free whilst appealing manslaughter convictions, was revoked in September 2005. He returned to jail*

had to intervene to see that justice was done. Killen was arrested for the murders, along with eighteen others suspected of having joined the posse he had organized at Sheriff Price's request.

In 1967, the trial finally took place. By the end of it, most of the all-white jury were convinced that Killen was guilty and wanted to convict him. But there remained one member who felt unable, on principle, to convict a preacher. She held out against a decision to convict, so the jury was hung and could not reach a unanimous verdict. The prosecution decided against a retrial, even though it was clear that a conviction could probably have been gained next time, and once again Killen walked free. In an outcome that angered many civil rights campaigners, the men who had been found guilty of the murders received short prison sentences of no more than six years apiece.

OPEN RACISM

For the next forty-seven years, Killen continued to live in Mississippi, openly declaring his racist views. However, in 1999, an interview with Sam Bowers, a prominent leader of the Ku Klux Klan, was published, throwing new light on the case. On 6 January 2005, aged 79, Killen was indicted for the 1964 murders.

Killen's trial was initially delayed because he had injured himself while chopping wood, breaking both of his legs. It finally took place in June 2005, and this time the jury were a mixed group of three black and nine white members. Killen attended court in a wheelchair, but this won him no sympathy, and he was duly convicted of manslaughter. The fact that he was not convicted of murder reflected his role as the organizer of the mob, rather than as the murderer himself.

The judge awarded Killen the maximum prison sentence he could: twenty years for each manslaughter, amounting to sixty years in total. It was obvious, of course, that Killen would die well before serving his term; however, the long sentence he received was a symbol of the authorities' commitment to civil rights, after years of neglecting their duty in this area.

It had taken decades for Killen to be brought to justice, but in the end, he was put behind bars. As eighty-three-year-old Carolyn Goodman, mother of Andrew Goodman, commented from her home in New York when she heard the news:

'I just knew that somehow this would happen – it's something that had to be.'

THE GODFATHER'S LIFE OF CRIME

The final arrest of John Gotti marked the end of an era in organized crime. He was the last of the old-style Mafia bosses to become a household name. Gotti was the product of a media age in which fascination with the Mafia was at an all-time high, and the media was desperate to find a real life counterpart to the godfathers of popular films. They came up with John Gotti, a well-dressed capo with a nice repertoire of one-liners.

Gotti was born on 27 October 1940. He was the fifth of eleven children born to John Gotti Sr and his wife, Fannie. At the time of John's birth, the family lived in the poverty-stricken South Bronx. By the time he was ten, they managed to move to Sheepshead Bay in Brooklyn, and then, a year or so later, to another Brooklyn neighbourhood, East New York.

THE FULTON-ROCKAWAY BOYS

Growing up, Gotti was drawn to the criminal lifestyle he saw around him. By the time he was twelve, he was running errands for local mobsters, forming a gang with his brothers Peter and Richard. John soon quit going to school and

concentrated on getting into trouble instead. When he was fourteen, he crushed his toes while attempting to steal a cement mixer and spent several months in hospital, before being released with a limp he would have for the rest of his life.

Aged sixteen, Gotti became a member of a Brooklyn street gang called the Fulton-Rockaway Boys, who prided themselves on being serious criminals. They stole cars and fenced stolen goods. Other members of the gang included two associates who would stay with Gotti through most of his career, Angelo Ruggiero and Wilfred 'Willie Boy'

▲ *Every inch the old style Mafia boss, Gotti rarely lost his composure, even when sentenced to a term in a prison with a notoriously harsh regime*

▲ The 'Teflon Don' had the silver tongue of a politician – perhaps a role he could have played had he not chosen a life of crime

Johnson. Between 1957 and 1961, Gotti was arrested five times, but managed to avoid prison each time.

In 1960, when he was twenty, Gotti met Victoria Di Giorgio. They had their first child, Angela, a year later, and got married the following year. The couple remained together until Gotti died, and had five children, but the marriage proved to be a stormy one.

CIGARETTES AND STOCKINGS

Following his marriage, Gotti briefly tried his hand at legitimate employment, working for a trucking company before opting instead for a full-time life of crime. He served a brief jail sentence in 1963 when he was caught with Salvatore Ruggiero, Angelo's younger brother, in a stolen car. This was followed by another short jail sentence in 1966, this time for robbery. That same year, Gotti joined a Mafia gang operating out of a club in Queens. This gang was part of the Gambino family, controlled by Carlo Gambino and his underboss, Aniello Dellacroce.

Gotti's particular role in the organization was as a hijacker, specializing in stealing loads from John F. Kennedy airport. Several more arrests followed as Gotti was caught with truckloads of women's clothing and cigarettes. Eventually, he spent three years in the federal penitentiary in Lewisburg for hijacking. When he was released in January 1972, he immediately returned to the Bergin gang. Soon he became the effective capo of the crew, with the approval of Dellacroce. Times were changing and, despite the Mafia's previous policy of having nothing to do with selling drugs, it was becoming increasingly clear that there was big money to be made in this area.

Gotti's next step up the ladder came as the result of a spate of kidnappings that broke out among Mafiosi during the early 1970s. In one incident, Carlo Gambino's nephew was kidnapped and murdered. A known kidnapper, James McBratney, was suspected. Gotti was one of three men who gunned McBratney down in a Staten Island diner soon afterwards.

SHOOT-OUT AT THE STEAKHOUSE

Gotti was identified by witnesses, but the charge was bargained down to manslaughter and he served only two years of it. While Gotti was in prison, Carlo Gambino died, leaving another mobster named Paul Castellano in his place, while Dellacroce remained as the underboss.

Gotti became increasingly disenchanted with the leadership of the remote Castellano. He agitated for Dellacroce to be given the job instead, but Dellacroce, who was by now suffering from cancer, counselled Gotti to have patience. Meanwhile, in 1980, personal tragedy struck the Gotti family. A neighbour, John Favara, accidently ran over and killed the Gottis' twelve-year-old son, Frank. Four months later, following a series of death threats, Favara was abducted by four men and never seen again, though rumours as to his fate abounded.

FBI surveillance of the Gambino family intensified during the 1980s, and tensions between rival leaders increased as a result. In 1985, Dellacroce finally died of cancer. Gotti was hoping to be made the new underboss by Castellano. When it became clear that Castallano intended to promote Thomas Bilotti instead, Gotti decided it was time to act. He assembled a team of hit men and, on 16 December 1985, Paul Castellano was assassinated as he left Sparks steakhouse in Manhattan. Afterwards, Gotti moved quickly to take his position at the head of the Gambino family.

THE TEFLON DON

Following this sensational murder, reminiscent of the old days of Mafia feuds, Gotti became a kind of alternative celebrity. Time and again the FBI would arrest Gotti on one charge or another, and time and again he would appear in court in an immaculately tailored suit and beat the rap. During this period, he acquired a series of nicknames. First he was called 'The Dapper Don' in honour of his sharp suits, then 'The Teflon Don' in recognition of the FBI's seeming inability to lay a glove on him despite near-constant surveillance. Gotti became well known for conducting meetings while walking down the street or playing recordings of white noise to prevent any bugs from working. However, by now the FBI were locked in a battle they could not be seen to lose. In 1992, they once again brought

racketeering charges against Gotti under the RICO legislation, and this time they found a weak point.

Gotti's underboss was a notoriously brutal mobster named Sammy 'The Bull' Gravano, a man believed to be responsible for at least nineteen murders. So desperate were the FBI to convict Gotti that they offered Gravano, a known killer, a virtual free pass in return for testifying against his boss. To secure the deal, they played Gravano tapes of Gotti making disparaging remarks about him. A livid Gravano agreed to testify against his boss, making him one of the highest-ranking mobsters ever to turn informer.

THE DON GOES DOWN

Gravano's testimony was sufficient to see Gotti finally put behind bars. He was convicted on 2 April 1992 for fourteen counts of murder, conspiracy to commit murder, loan sharking, racketeering, obstruction of justice, illegal gambling and tax evasion.

To punish this highly public criminal even more, he was sent to the federal penitentiary in Marion, Illinois, where he was kept in solitary confinement for 23 hours a day until his death from cancer on 10 June 2002.

Meanwhile, Sammy 'The Bull' Gravano remains within the safety of the witness protection programme to this day.

GRAVE CRIMES

William Burke and William Hare will always remain linked, like Laurel and Hardy or pirates and the Caribbean. Alone, living in Edinburgh in the late-1820s, they were nothing: just a labourer and the keeper of a disreputable boarding house. But together they were Burke and Hare, the most famous body-snatchers of them all – even though they ended up differently. For Hare, who turned King's Evidence and was a witness at Burke's trial, died later in London, after living under an assumed name; and Burke went the way of their joint victims. After he was hanged, his body was dissected at a public lecture by the Professor of Surgery at Edinburgh University, and his skeleton can still be seen today in the University's Anatomical Museum.

It was in 1827 that the pair first met, when Burke moved to Edinburgh with a woman called Helen Dougal. As Irishmen, they had much in common; and when one of Hare's lodgers died who better to help carry the body off to the house of the celebrated anatomist Dr. Robert Knox than his new friend William Burke?

Until the passing of the Anatomy Act in 1832, every dead person, except executed criminals, was required to have a Christian burial. So it was extremely difficult for practising anatomists and their students to get hold of the necessary raw material. Knox, then, was delighted to accept the body from Burke and Hare, with few questions asked, and he paid more than seven and a half pounds for it.

Burke and Hare, thrilled by their windfall, spotted a gap in the market and soon filled it. They began to lure travellers, usually to Hare's boarding house, and ply them with drink. Once befuddled, they simply smothered them. At least fifteen people went the same way, at prices ranging from eight to fourteen pounds, until a couple who'd been staying with Burke and Helen Dougal one day spotted the body of a woman hidden under a pile of straw. They went to the police with what they'd seen.

Burke, after turncoat Hare gave evidence against him, was hanged on 28 January 1829. Hare then fled to London and Helen Dougal to Australia. Dr. Knox's house was invaded by a mob – two of the victims had been well-known on the city's streets – and his lectures were interrupted by heckling. In the end he left Edinburgh and, unable to get another university position, ended his days as an obscure practitioner in east London.

THE GREAT TRAIN ROBBERY

The Great Train Robbery of 1963 is one of the most famous crimes in British history. A gang of fifteen London criminals hijacked a train and stole over two million pounds sterling in used banknotes; the same amount today would be equivalent to about forty million pounds. However, it was not only the huge amount of money stolen that ensured their notoriety: the heist was also seen by many sections of the popular British press as a highly romantic, flamboyant act on the part of the London underworld. In particular, gang member Ronnie Biggs came to be regarded as a swashbuckling figure who had flouted the authorities and got away with it. One central feature of the robbery that appealed to the public was that no guns were used – although, in actual fact, the robbery was a violent crime, since the train driver was hit over the head with iron bars and was permanently injured. This

▶ *The Great Train Robbers reunited in 1978, fifteen years on from their heist. The notorious Ronnie Biggs had settled in Brazil, and was at this time making a film with the Sex Pistols*

▼ *Ronnie Biggs with his long-time girlfriend and eventual wife, Raimunda Nascimento de Castro, in 1974*

unpleasant reality was, in some quarters, conveniently forgotten, and in time the train robbers became working-class heroes who were regarded with a great deal of affection by the British public.

PLANNING THE HEIST

The gang was led by a man named Bruce Reynolds, who planned the operation from the beginning. He was an antiques dealer who drove an Aston Martin, and liked to flash his money around. The

front man for the gang was John Wheater, a solicitor with an upper-class background who rented the farmhouse where the gang hid after the heist. Next was Buster Edwards, an ex-boxer turned con man, later immortalized by Phil Collins in the film Buster. Other gang members included Charlie Wilson, a bookmaker, and two big men known as Gordon Goody and Jimmy Hussey, the brawn of the operation. Last, but not least, was the youngest member of the gang, Ronnie Biggs, who as yet had little experience of criminal life.

The operation was meticulously planned, using information about the times large amounts of cash were carried on postal trains going in and out of London. A quiet site outside Cheddington, in Buckinghamshire, was selected, so that the robbers could flag down the train and bag the money without attracting too much attention. The site was also chosen because it was near a military base, where large supply vehicles often travelled around. In this way, the robbers hoped that their movements would not arouse suspicion.

ATTACKED WITH IRON BARS

On 8 August 1963, a few minutes after three o'clock in the morning, the raid began. Wearing railway workers' overalls, the gang rigged up some temporary signals on the line, using batteries for power. Seeing the red 'stop' light ahead, the driver brought the train to a halt. When it stopped, a fireman, David Whitby, got out to find out what the trouble was. Whitby was pulled off the track by Buster Edwards and, once he realized that a robbery was in progress, did not try to resist. However, when the driver, Jack Mills, then got off, other members of the gang attacked him with iron bars, causing him to bleed from the head. Mills collapsed on the side of the track.

More mistakes were made as the train robbers began to panic. The gang included a retired train driver, brought in by Ronnie Biggs to move the train into position so that the mailbags could be easily dropped off. However, the elderly train driver did not understand the workings of modern trains, and was unable to move the stopped train. The injured Mills, still bleeding, was forced to take over and drive the train into position. The gang then formed a human chain to unload over a hundred sacks of money, and made their getaway.

ROUNDING UP THE GANG

The gang hid out at a nearby farmhouse, Leatherslade Farm. Here, they drank cups of tea and played the board game Monopoly, allegedly using the real banknotes from their haul as money. This

▲ *Ronnie in his later years in Brazil. Despite living the good life there, when his health began to fail he returned to England and arrest*

while serving his sentence, and lived quietly outside Montreal, Canada, for a time until police traced him via a telephone call his wife made to her parents in England. Biggs also made a dramatic escape from jail, after serving over a year of his sentence. He underwent plastic surgery, travelled around the world and then settled in Rio de Janeiro, Brazil.

THE LATER YEARS

In his later years, Biggs became notorious as the one Great Train Robber to avoid capture – even though his initial role in the robbery had been a small one.

However, in his later years he became ill, having suffered several strokes, and grew tired of living abroad. He announced his intention to come back to Britain, even if he risked being imprisoned in his bad state of health. When he returned, he was duly apprehended and today continues to serve out his sentence in prison.

In the end, most of the Great Train Robbers were brought to justice. However, the money was not recovered, though some gang members complained they lost too much to money launderers and the like. Thus, the Monopoly players of the gang may have collected their money, but they did not pass 'Go' – instead, they went straight to jail.

activity proved to be their downfall. By the time the police reached the farmhouse, the gang had scattered, but they had left incriminating fingerprints on the Monopoly board and elsewhere. In this way, police were able to identify the men, many of whom were known criminals.

Eventually, thirteen of the fifteen gang members were apprehended and brought to justice. Bruce Reynolds spent five years on the run before the police finally caught up with him. He was then tried and received a prison sentence, of which he served ten years. Buster Edwards fled to Mexico but later gave himself up. Charlie Wilson made a daring escape from prison

A HAIR OUT OF PLACE

Even in the early days of forensic science it was recognised that a single strand of hair or fibre could contain enough evidence to convict the most cunning and calculating killer. The case of Johnny Fiorenza is a prime example.

In 1936 Nancy Titterton, a 33-year-old writer, was discovered dead in the New York apartment she shared with her husband, NBC executive Lewis Titterton. Her naked body had been found by two furniture delivery men lying face down in an empty bath with a pyjama jacket knotted round her throat and her underclothes scattered across the bedroom floor, indicating that the motive had been sexual.

On his first visit to the crime scene Assistant Chief Inspector John Lyons was optimistic of making an early arrest as the killer had been careless: in his haste to escape he had left behind part of a length of cord used to bind the victim's wrists, which might be traced back to him. Muddy footprints on the carpet were initially ignored, as a preliminary examination revealed that they contained traces of lint such as might be found in furniture manufacture and they were

therefore attributed to the delivery men who discovered the body.

However, the search for the cord uncovered the fact that a New York wholesaler had sold a roll of it to the very same furniture store which had delivered a chair to Mrs Titterton on the afternoon of the murder. Then the city crime lab discovered a hair on the bedspread where the rape had taken place. A microscopic examination revealed it to be horsehair of the type used in furniture upholstery.

▲ *Held firmly by two detectives, Johnny Fiorenza, centre, is led to the apartment in New York where the crime was re-enacted*

▲ *Faced with the evidence, Fiorenza confessed to the murder of Nancy Titterton*

As both delivery men had arrived at the apartment together Inspector Lyons assumed that one of them must have gone there earlier; Mrs Titterton would have let him in as both men had visited the apartment on several previous occasions. When Lyons called at the furniture store he questioned the proprietor, who had been one of the two men to discover Mrs Titterton's body and who could account for his whereabouts on the morning of the murder. His assistant, however, had been absent from the shop and claimed to have been visiting his probation officer at the time. But, as Inspector Lyons discovered, the probation office was closed that morning for the Easter holiday.

When confronted with the evidence Johnny Fiorenza broke down and confessed. It seems likely that he placed Mrs Titterton in the bath not to revive her, but to cover himself in the event that he was caught when he would claim that her death had been an accident.

But the judge and jury saw it as a cunning act of self-preservation by a cold-hearted killer. They sent Fiorenza to the electric chair.

◀ The 24-year-old upholsterer's assistant, an ex-convict, in New York following his arrest

THE HILLSIDE STRANGLINGS

It is a common misapprehension that sexually motivated serial killers are all social misfits – twisted losers unable to find any other kind of gratification. The truth is rather more sinister. Plenty of serial killers are outwardly eligible men who have little trouble seducing women. The two men known as the 'Hillside Stranglers' are cases in point. Kenneth Bianchi was a good-looking young man in his mid-twenties, whose long-time girlfriend was pregnant at the time his murderous rampage began. His cohort, 40-year-old Angelo Buono, was no one's idea of good-looking but was nevertheless enormously popular with women. However, the two conspired together to torture, rape and murder fourteen victims.

ADOPTED

Kenneth Bianchi was born on 22 May 1951 in Rochester, New York. His mother was a prostitute who immediately gave him up for adoption. Three months later he was adopted by the Bianchis. As a child he was given to daydreams and prone to fantasizing and lying. Despite a reasonably high IQ, he underachieved at school. In an effort to change this his mother sent him to a Catholic private school, but while he was there his father died and at thirteen he had to leave because there was no longer enough money to pay the fees. Even so, Bianchi seemed to have absorbed his moral education; he was seen as a straight arrow at school, taking no part in the counter-culture of the 1960s.

Immediately on leaving school he had a brief marriage that ended when his wife left him after only eight months. This experience certainly left Bianchi embittered. He studied psychology briefly in college, but then dropped out and took a series of menial jobs before working as a security guard, using the position as an opportunity to steal items from the houses he was meant to be guarding.

In 1975, his life drifting along, he decided to make a move. He headed for Los Angeles where an older cousin was now living. The cousin's name was Angelo Buono and he was to have a decisive and terrible influence on Kenneth Bianchi.

FAMILY VALUES

Angelo Buono was also born in Rochester, New York, on 5 October 1934, seventeen years earlier than Bianchi. His parents had divorced when he was young and he had moved to California with his mother, Jenny, in 1939. Buono was trouble from the start. From a young age, he had a precocious interest in sex. As a teenager he would boast to his classmates about raping and sodomizing girls. He stole cars and eventually ended up in reform school. In 1955 he briefly married a high-school girlfriend after she became pregnant, but left her almost immediately. He soon married again, to Mary Castillo, and had five more children with her, before she divorced him in 1964 due to his persistent sexual and physical abuse. The next year, he was married again, to a single mother of two called Nannette Campino. The couple had two more children, until she finally divorced him in 1971 when, in addition to the abuse he visited on her, he raped her daughter.

During this time, Buono had established himself as an auto-upholsterer with his own business. Strangely, despite his unattractive physical appearance and his terrible record of abusive behaviour, women seemed magnetically drawn to him. He sported dyed hair and flashy jewellery; in essence he looked like a pimp – and this was just the career sideline he was planning on moving into when, in 1975, his cousin Kenny showed up from back east.

Kenny and Angelo hit it off from the start. Kenny already had a simmering

▼ *Kenneth Bianchi – in custody at last*

resentment of women; Angelo showed him how to express it. He started by teaching his cousin how to impersonate a policeman in order to blackmail prostitutes for sex. Kenny was an eager student and happy to go along with Angelo's pimping plan. The pair met a couple of runaways, Sabra Hannan and

Becky Spears, and put them out on the streets until first Becky and then Sabra succeeded in running away.

Meanwhile, Kenny was once again working as a security guard and had found a new girlfriend, Kelli Boyd, who had recently become pregnant. Kenny was disturbed by the loss of the pimping income that had enabled him to impress Boyd with his wealth. Together with Angelo, he decided to recruit some new girls. They found a prostitute named Deborah Noble who offered to help them out. However, when she tried to trick money out of them, they decided to teach her a lesson.

FIRST KILLING

Unable to find Noble they instead came upon her friend, a prostitute named Yolanda Washington, and decided to take their anger out on her. Whatever their initial intention, they ended up raping her, strangling her with a garotte and dumping her dead body in a cemetary. Evidently this first crime sent Bianchi and Buono over the edge. Their next victims were two more prostitutes, Judy Miller and Lissa Kastin, murdered over the next two weeks. Kastin's body was found on 6 November, but there was little public outcry: Los Angeles had too many murders for the deaths of three hookers to merit much attention.

All that changed later that month, during the week of Thanksgiving, when five more bodies were found on the Los Angeles hillside. None of these were prostitutes: these were middle-class girls, one of them only twelve years old. All had been abducted, raped and asphyxiated with the trademark garotte; in several cases there were signs of torture. Now Los Angeles was in a state of red alert too.

It was ten days until the deadly duo struck again. Their next victim was another prostitute. Kimberly Martin had gone to meet a client on 9 December; her dead body turned up on the hillside the next morning. Their next victim, Cindy Hudspeth, was found on 16 February; her raped and strangled body was found in the boot of her car, which had been pushed over a cliff.

The police continued their investigations but seemed to get nowhere. Los Angeles held its breath, but nothing happened. The months passed and the Hillside Strangler seemed to have retired. Perhaps it was simply down to fear on Bianchi and Buono's part; perhaps it was connected to the fact that Bianchi's girlfriend had given birth to their baby early in 1978, and he was caught up in domestic matters. Whatever the reason, the pair stopped killing – but only for a while.

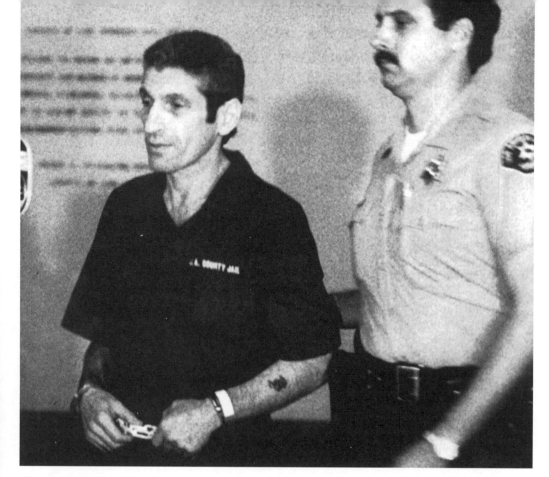

EMERGING EVIDENCE

Later that year, Bianchi moved with his new family to Bellingham, Washington, and found work as a security guard. A year passed and then the murderous urge caught hold of him again.

He lured two young women, Diane Wilder and Karen Mantic, to a house he was guarding, and then raped and murdered them both with considerable brutality. This time, however, Bianchi soon emerged as a suspect and was arrested. Once under arrest, further evidence started to emerge to connect him to the Hillside murders.

It was two years before the case finally came to trial, during which period Bianchi persuaded a serial killer groupie called Veronica Compton to carry out a murder for him, intending to suggest that the Strangler was still at large. The plot failed dismally and Compton herself was imprisoned.

Finally, the case went to court. Both Bianchi and Buono were found guilty of the Hillside stranglings. They were both sentenced to life imprisonment. Buono died in prison from unknown causes in 2002. Bianchi continues to serve out his sentence.

HIT AND RUN

Detectives usually have difficulty persuading the guilty to confess to their crimes, but in the case of the murder of 17-year-old Rosemary Anderson they had two conflicting confessions from two different suspects to choose from! How could they be sure they had charged the guilty man? It took 40 years and the use of a new forensic science to uncover the truth behind a serious miscarriage of justice and reveal the true identity of a hit-and-run killer.

On the evening of 9 February 1963, John Button invited his girlfriend, Rosemary Anderson, to his parents' house in Perth, South Australia, to celebrate his 19th birthday. During the evening they quarrelled and Rosemary stormed out, determined to walk home alone. John followed her in his car, a French Simca, talking to her as she walked along the dark, otherwise deserted roadside. But she was in a foul temper and refused his offer of a lift home, so he stopped and watched dejectedly as she disappeared round the next corner. Anxious not to leave her in this mood he decided to catch up with her, but when he did so he made a shocking

discovery. Rosemary was lying face down at the side of the road, bruised and bleeding, the victim of a hit-and-run driver. In desperation John carried her limp body into his car and rushed to the hospital, but there was little the doctors could do. Rosemary died shortly after being admitted and John was charged with manslaughter.

The case hinged on the fact that there was damage to the front of the Simca and droplets of blood on the front bumper. John protested his innocence, but to no avail and after several hours of intense interrogation, during which he later claimed he had been beaten by the police, he confessed. Within hours he recanted, saying that he had only admitted guilt in an effort to end the interrogation and stave off another beating. In his defence John claimed that the damage to the car had been incurred weeks earlier and that the blood on the bumper resulted when he brushed past it when carrying Rosemary to the car. But the confession and the forensic evidence was sufficient to convict him. John was condemned to serve ten years' hard labour in Australia's notorious Fremantle Prison.

Seven months later, John thought his luck had turned when a prisoner informed him that a new inmate was boasting that he had intentionally killed a young girl for the fun of it in John's

neighbourhood on the night in question. The driver was Eric Edgar Cooke, a psychopath who had been sentenced to death for a series of brutal murders. The police took Cooke to identify where he had run Rosemary down, but he pointed out the wrong place and so John's appeal was turned down. Cooke again confessed to Rosemary's murder on the day of his execution, but it was not sufficient to free John Button. Button was released after five years in 1968 for good behaviour.

▲ *Eric Edgar Cooke was a psychopath who had been sentenced to death for a series of brutal murders*

FREEDOM IS NOT ENOUGH

Free, but unable to live with the stigma of being labelled a convicted killer, John determined to clear his name. He found an unlikely ally in Estelle Blackburn, a female journalist who had been dating his brother. She was able to access files that had been closed to John and to interview people who would not talk to him about the case.

Estelle discovered that Cooke had confessed to six hit-and-run murders, but that this information had not been introduced at John's appeal. Convinced that John was innocent, Estelle enlisted the help of W. R. 'Rusty' Haight, an expert in the new forensic science of Pedestrian Crash Reconstruction, which Rusty liked to describe as 'common sense mixed with basic physics'.

Using a properly weighted and articulated bio-medical dummy suspended from a fishing line, which broke on impact, and a lightweight French Simca identical to John's car, Haight proved that the damage to the car was inconsistent with the injuries sustained by the victim.

Rosemary had been hit at 48km/h (30mph), which leaves distinctive markings on the vehicle as the body folds around the front of the car with the head impacting on the bonnet to leave a noticeable dent. John's car did not have this damage when the police impounded it. Furthermore, Haight managed to obtain a 1963 Holden which was the car Cooke had driven when he claimed to have killed the six women. When the dummy was hit by the Holden it landed on its back in the position John claimed to have found Rosemary in, whereas when the Simca hit it the dummy landed on its face.

But one last question needed to be answered before the new evidence could be admitted in an appeal. Cooke's car had a plastic visor to shield the driver from glare and the police had always maintained that if Cooke had killed Rosemary the visor would have been damaged.

After various experiments, Haight was able to demonstrate that the flexibility of the plastic visor meant that it snapped back into shape after the impact.

Armed with this compelling evidence and Estelle Blackburn's best-selling book on the case, Button's lawyers were able to argue successfully that the original prosecution case was fatally flawed.

It was not until 2000 that John Button was finally exonerated of the manslaughter of Rosemary Anderson having, in his words, been 'imprisoned by the injustice of the whole affair' for the previous 37 years.

THE HITCH-HIKER KILLINGS

Ed Kemper, whose parents separated when he was seven, grew up troubled and sadistic. He tortured animals; he once cut the hands and feet off his sister's doll. But with people he was painfully shy. When his sister teased him about secretly wanting to kiss his teacher, he said:

'If I kissed her, I'd have to kill her first.'

And this is precisely what the adult Ed Kemper – 6 feet 9 inches tall and weighing almost 300 pounds – did. But first there was a teenage prelude. For in 1962, when he was 13, he ran away from the mother he hated to join his father – and his father promptly sent him back. Unwanted by either, he was despatched to live with his grandparents on a ranch in California; and two years later he shot them both dead. He was, in other words, a serial time-bomb which had already begun to go off.

After five years in a hospital for the criminally insane, he was released into the care of his mother, who was then living in Santa Cruz. It was a bitter household. But Kemper got a job as a labourer, and finally bought himself a car. He began to pick up hitch-hikers.

On May 7th 1972, he picked up two women students from Fresno State College, Anita Luchese and Mary Anne Pesce, held them at gunpoint and drove them out to a wooded canyon. He stabbed them both to death and raped their corpses, before taking the bodies back home in the trunk of his car. Upstairs in his room, he took off their heads with his hunting knife – nicknamed 'the General' – had sex again with their corpses and then dissected them. He buried what was left in the mountains.

Four months later, on September 14th, he picked up a fifteen-year-old high-

◀ *Ed Kemper picked up hitch-hikers before brutally slaying them*

school student, and again drove her, at gunpoint, up into the mountains. He taped her mouth and suffocated her by sticking his fingers up her nostrils. Then, as earlier, he raped her, took her home and cut off her head, had sex with her again and dismembered her. His mother noticed nothing unusual as he took her remains out to the car in garbage bags for disposal.

After another four-month interval, in January 1973, he struck again, and again his victim was a student, this time at Cabrillo College. Claudia Schall was shot on a quiet road near Freedom, California, dumped into the trunk and then hidden in a closet in Kemper's bedroom. The following morning, after his mother had gone to work, he violated her corpse and then cut it up with an axe in the shower.

He took the various parts of Schall's body to Carmel and threw them over the cliffs into the sea. Amazingly some parts were later found and identified.

A month later, he picked up two more students – after a particularly vicious row with his mother. He shot them both in the head and drove their bodies back, only to find that his mother was still home. Unable to wait, he decapitated both bodies in the trunk; and the next morning, after his mother had gone, took the headless corpses upstairs and had sex with at least one of them. Then, after cutting off the hands of one of the

students and getting rid of both heads, he dumped the bodies in Eden Canyon.

Kemper's killings can be seen to have been caused – at least in part – by his hatred of his mother; and on Easter Day, 1973, he went to the source: he killed her in her bedroom with a hammer and cut off her head with 'the General.'

Then he invited one of his mother's woman friends, Sara Hallett, to dinner, knocked her unconscious, strangled, decapitated and had sex with her. The next morning, after sleeping in his mother's bed, he took the money from Mrs Hallett's handbag and drove off in her car, expecting the police to be after him.

In the end, when nothing happened, he gave himself up, after finally persuading the police that he really was the so-called 'Co-Ed Killer.' Now there could be no doubt. He'd cut out his mother's larynx, he said, and tossed it into the garbage,

'because it seemed appropriate after she had bitched me so much.'

Kemper was found sane; and despite his request to be executed, was sentenced to life imprisonment without the possibility of parole. In custody, he was later asked what he thought when he saw a pretty girl across the street: 'One side of me says, "I'd like to talk to her, date her." The other side of me says, "I wonder how her head would look on a stick."'

HOUSE OF HORRORS

Gary Heidnik was two when his quarrelsome, alcoholic parents split up. His mother took custody of him and his new-born brother Terry, but soon found she could not cope and handed them back to their father. When Gary persistently wet his bed his father beat him and hung the sheets out of the window to show the neighbours. A fall from a tree gave the boy a slightly misshapen head, earning him the nickname 'football head', and generally adding to his misery.

Like Ed Kemper, whose story offers so many points of comparison, Gary Heidnik was a clever boy who never found a way of putting his intelligence to positive use. He did well at his military academy, and joined the regular army at the age of eighteen, in 1961. Despite devoting rather too much energy to loan sharking, he actually seemed to be making a career of the military, until a random neurological test earned him an immediate discharge. The 'schizoid personality disorder' diagnosis earned him a disability pension for life, but seems to have taken away his main reason for living.

Heidnik settled in Philadelphia and drifted from job to job. He qualified as a nurse but was fired for sub-standard performance, got work as a psychiatric nurse and was fired for his bad attitude. Neither father nor mother wanted much to do with him, and he spent his twenties in and out of mental institutions. His mother committed suicide in 1970 after learning she had cancer, and Gary reportedly attempted the same act as many as thirteen times.

In 1971 he gave new meaning to the phrase 'living in a world of his own' – creating his own church, the United Church of the Ministers of God. There was only ever one minister – Bishop Heidnik – and the core members of his small congregation were mentally handicapped African-American women from a nearby institution. Bingo and loan sharking paid the Bishop's salary, and the congregation fulfilled his sexual needs, often en masse. He used some of the money to play the stock exchange, and proved himself either smart or lucky – by 1977 he had accumulated over $35,000. He invested this with Merrill Lynch, and saw it rise to almost $500,000 over the next decade. Since his church was registered as a charity he paid virtually no tax.

Early in 1978 Heidnik's mentally handicapped girlfriend gave birth to his child, but nothing much changed in the Bishop's lifestyle. In May he broke his girlfriend's sister out of a mental institution and hid her away in his basement. When police came looking for the woman, they found she had endured a regime of beatings and sexual abuse. Heidnik received a three-to-seven year sentence for unlawful imprisonment and deviant sex. During his time in the state penitentiary he again attempted suicide on several occasions, once by swallowing a lightbulb.

He re-emerged, aged forty, in April 1983. His child had been put in a home, but his material wealth had continued to grow in his absence, allowing him to purchase the property at 3520 North Marshall Street which would come to be known as the 'House of Horrors'. The group sex sessions with black women resumed, but Heidnik decided he also wanted a Filipino wife. A visit to a matrimonial agency and several plausible letters served one up. Betty Disto arrived, married him, and then discovered that she had to share a bed with his congregation. When she protested, he beat her. After three months of that, she fled.

It would appear that all these people running away from him was becoming really irritating. A plan began forming in his mind, a plan for a Heidnik Utopia, one world from which escape would not be possible. On 26 November 1986 he started to gather its population, picking up black prostitute Josefina Rivera and bringing her home. She thought she was being paid for a few minutes' sex, but found herself shackled to a sewerage pipe in Heidnik's basement, watching him digging a hole in the earth floor. 'Don't worry,' he told the terrified woman – the hole was for punishment, not burial. And she would not be alone for long: the basement was big enough for ten women, and the plan was that each of them would bear him a child. Later that day she managed to get the boards off a window and scream for help, but only Heidnik came. He beat her, threw her in the punishment hole, and left her with full volume rock music for twenty-seven hours.

Three days after abducting Rivera, he kidnapped an old girlfriend, Sandy Lindsay. Several years earlier she had aborted his baby, and Heidnik had neither forgotten nor forgiven. Through December the two women were kept in steadily deteriorating conditions. There were no washing or toilet facilities, and their initial diet of oatmeal and bread was soon replaced by dog-food sandwiches. Both women were subject to daily beatings and rapes from Heidnik, and were often forced to beat each other. Real or imagined protests were punished by a spell in the earthen hole, crammed in a space only four feet square, under a plywood lid and its sandbag weight.

Between 22 December and 19 January Heidnik lured three more African-American women – Lisa Thomas, Deborah Dudley and Jacqueline Askins. The rapes and beatings continued, but the higher population encouraged a new command structure, and Heidnik elevated Josefina Rivera to 'trusty' status. In return for fewer punishments and the odd meal out, she helped him keep the others in order. She later claimed that she had no choice if she wanted to live, but some of the others thought she went further than she needed to.

DEATH

Towards the end of January, Sandy Lindsay was hung by the hands from the ceiling as a punishment for trying to escape. Heidnik left her there for a week, then seemed surprised when she died of exhaustion. Her death brought no amelioration of his regime though. On the contrary, it grew harsher. Not long after Lindsay's body was taken upstairs, the house resounded to the whine of a power saw. And then a sickly smell drifted down to the basement, a smell the women soon recognized in their daily 'dog-food' sandwiches. Anxious to leave no doubt,

▲ *Heidnik, who was executed by lethal injection in July 1999*

Heidnik took Dudley upstairs and showed her Lindsay's severed head in a pot on the stove. They were being fed the rest of her, he said. He had apparently got the idea from the movie Eating Raoul.

On 18 February he experimented with a new type of punishment. He crammed all but Rivera in the hole, filled it with water, and used bare wires to give them electric shocks. Dudley died. Around the same time he pierced all but Rivera's eardrums with a screwdriver. The aim

135

▲ *Witnesses to Heidnik's execution, Tracey Lomax and Carolyn Johnson were sisters of two of his victims*

It worked. He left her at the corner where, four months earlier, he had picked her up. Rivera went straight to the police, who were eventually convinced by the shackle-marks on her ankles. Investigating officers forced their way into 3520 North Marshall Street at 4.30 the following morning, arrested the startled Heidnik and brought an end to his prisoners' dreadful ordeal.

In the fridge the startled police found a severed human forearm and around 24 pounds of neatly packaged human meat.

The story soon got out, and Heidnik was beaten up by other prisoners within hours of his arrest. His father told reporters 'I hope to hell they hang him, and you can quote me on that. I'll even pull the rope.'

He neglected to add how hard he had tried to infect both his sons with his own virulent racism. 'A black life,' he had apparently often told them, 'has no value'.

The defence plea of insanity was torpedoed by the judge's refusal to admit Heidnik's record of mental illness as evidence. With no other context for judgement, the jury went by the crimes and opted for death. After eleven years on Pennsylvania's death row, Heidnik was finally executed by lethal injection in July 1999.

was to prevent them discussing any rescue attempt.

Rivera was with him when he buried Dudley in a New Jersey park on 22 March, and when he picked up his last victim, Agnes Adams, on the following day. On 24 March, Rivera warned him that Adams' family might go to the police if she simply disappeared; a single visit would set their minds at rest.

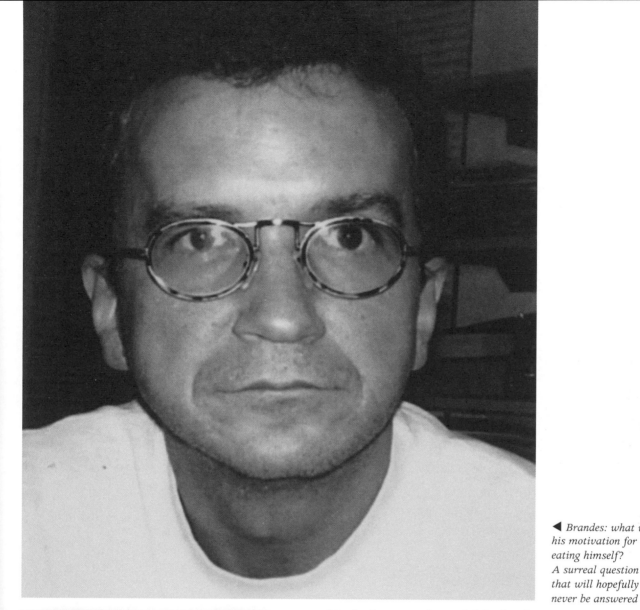

◄ *Brandes: what was his motivation for eating himself? A surreal question that will hopefully never be answered*

I AM YOUR FLESH

Armin Meiwes was born in 1962. His parents owned a rambling manor house outside Rotenburg in central Germany, and it was here that he grew up, lived his adult life, and committed the acts for which he is now notorious.

His father, who left when Meiwes was only eight, had ignored him when he was still around. The boy's mother, on the other hand, was incapable of letting him alone, and her suffocating attentions made him an object of ridicule at school.

Not surprisingly, Meiwes retreated into a fantasy world, inventing an imaginary brother named Franky. His plans for this brother, however, did not include the usual brotherly relations. Meiwes dreamt of binding Franky to himself in perpetuity by the simple act of consuming him. This fantasy, he told a packed courtroom years later, had developed in the years after his father's departure. 'And in the end I fulfilled it,' he concluded.

In 1981 Meiwes joined the army, but he continued to live at home, and took his mother with him on troop outings. At the end of the 1980s she became bed-ridden, and he left the army to train as a computer technician and look after her.

Her death in 1999 set him free to pursue his fantasy. Hoping for like-minded guests, he set about renovating the rather dilapidated family home. Included in the make-over was a new 'slaughter room', complete with cage, meat-hook and pulley. By day he went to work, by night he trawled the internet for others who shared his cannibalistic fantasies. He spoke to more than two hundred of them on chatlines, and several came to visit after he posted the ad: 'Gay male seeks hunks 18–30 to slaughter.' Some allowed him to hoist them up on the hook and mark up the choicest cuts on their bodies with a pen. None, however, was actually willing to be eaten.

Towards the end of 2000, a 43 year-old microchip engineer named Bernd-Jurgen Brandes replied to Meiwes' advertisement using the pseudonym 'Cator', and over the next few months they communicated by email. Brandes said he was willing to fill the role Meiwes had marked out for Franky. 'There is absolutely no way back for me,' he wrote, 'only forwards, through your teeth'.

In March 2001 Brandes wrote a will leaving everything to his unknowing gay partner, had it notarized, and took the train westwards. According to Meiwes, Brandes met him at the station with the words: 'I am your Cator, I am your flesh'.

Back at the house, they stripped off and discussed what they were about to do. After Brandes had consumed twenty sleeping tablets and half a bottle of schnapps to dull the expected pain, Meiwes removed his new friend's penis and testicles with a kitchen knife. This, like everything else which happened that evening, was faithfully recorded on his camcorder.

He then put the genitalia into the frying pan, and opened a bottle of white wine. The two men then ate as much of the sautéed flesh as they could manage, washing it down with the wine. By this time Brandes was losing a lot of blood, and Meiwes suggested that he take a bath. While Brandes bled out in the tub,

◄ The smile, and teeth, of a convicted cannibal

Meiwes read part of a Star Trek novel and watched a Disney film on TV. 'It took so terribly long' he said at his trial.

Eventually a close-to-unconscious Brandes gave Meiwes permission to hang him up and finish him off. Meiwes did so, stabbing him several times. He then cut the fresh corpse into meal-size portions and stacked them – neatly wrapped and labelled – in his freezer. Parts like the head, which he considered inedible, were buried in the back garden. He then slowly worked his way through the frozen portions, cooking them with olive oil and garlic.

Meiwes would probably never have been caught if he had not tried to relive the experience. A new internet advertisement was reported to the police, who turned up at his door, searched the house, and found what was left of Brandes in the freezer and garden.

Meiwes was only too willing to admit the killing and the eating. Both had been at the victim's request, he told the authorities, and he had the video evidence to prove it. Since cannibalism is not illegal in Germany, he was not charged with it, and Brandes' clear connivance in his own death made a conviction for murder unlikely.

In 2004, after considerable legal argument and debate as well as a sensational trial, Meiwes was convicted of manslaughter, and is currently serving an eight and a half-year sentence.

IF THE GLOVE FITS

The O. J. Simpson murder trial in 1995 was lost, as the prosecution would see it, through a combination of incompetence and carelessness on behalf of the Los Angeles police, who gave a textbook example of how not to process a crime scene.

The case against the former American football star and one-time TV actor was compelling. His ex-wife Nicole and her friend Ronald Goldman had been brutally murdered at her Brentwood home on the night of 12 June 1994, and there appeared to be indisputable physical evidence linking O. J. to the crime scene.

A bloodied glove found in the grounds appeared to match another recovered from O. J.'s house in Rockingham just five minutes' drive away, together with a sock which also had traces of Nicole's blood. Near the bodies detectives bagged a discarded hat which was later found to have hair and fibres which matched O. J.'s. And most compelling of all, there was a trail of bloody footprints leading away from the scene and bloodstains on the gate. The killer had evidently been wounded in the frenzied knife attack. When detectives called at O. J.'s home

they noticed blood on a vehicle parked outside and a trail of blood from the car to the front door. Analysis proved that the blood on the glove found at O. J.'s home and the blood on the car were from three people, the two victims and O. J.

But O. J. couldn't be questioned. He had taken a flight to Chicago earlier that night and, when interviewed over the phone, appeared curiously uninterested in his ex-wife's death. On his return to LA the next day he was questioned by detectives, who commented on the fact that he had a bandage on his hand which he claimed was the result of having cut it accidentally on a glass in his hotel room.

He was allowed to remain at liberty for the next couple of days while the police concluded their examination of the crime scene, but on 15 June they lost patience with the star, who had gone into seclusion, and issued a warrant for his arrest. It was then that he attempted to evade capture during the now-famous slow-motion freeway chase which was televised live around the world.

It looked like the case against O. J. couldn't be lost. But it was. Police failures

O. J. hired a dream team of top-drawer defence attorneys who raised serious

▶ *O. J. Simpson looks at DNA 'autorads' showing the genetic markers of Simpson and the murder victims*

▶*Blood covers the path outside the home of Nicole Brown Simpson*

doubts as to the validity of the evidence, which they intimated might have been planted by over-eager or even racist detectives to frame their man. They even managed to secure a recording on which Detective Mark Fuhrman was heard to refer to Simpson as a 'nigger' no fewer than 41 times, which tainted the validity of his testimony and all the physical evidence he had accumulated. But the defence didn't have to work too hard. The police had undermined their own case.

On the night of the murder they had failed to secure the scene, allowing numerous personnel to trample through the bloody footprints and carry crucial trace evidence from room to room and out of the house on the soles of their shoes. Video footage of the police walk-through of the scene shows investigators working the scene without protective overalls or gloves and one policeman is actually seen to drop a swab then wipe it clean with his hands. During the trial Detective Philip Vannatrer proudly testified to the fact that old-school experienced officers of his generation did not wear protective clothing and evidently saw nothing wrong in handling evidence without gloves like a cop in a 1950s TV show.

The prosecution case was compromised still further by Vannatrer and his colleagues' insistence on going straight from the crime scene to O. J.'s home without changing their clothes or processing the evidence from the first location, which could have allowed transference of trace evidence from the crime scene to the second location.

And then there was the evidence which was captured on film by the police photographer, but which had not been logged in and could not be found in the archive. This included a bloody note seen in one particular shot near Nicole's head. It may have been irrelevant to the case, or it may have been crucial. We shall never know because it was presumably 'tidied away' with whatever else seemed like rubbish at the time and was lost. Incredibly, no photographs were taken inside the house, only of the immediate area where the bodies were found. So there is no record of any signs of a struggle or of any other relevant features or items that were later put back in their place.

ERROR UPON ERROR

More critically, the bodies of the victims were left as they lay for ten hours without being examined by a medical examiner, who would have been able to determine the time of death and recover vital trace evidence from the bodies. But after Nicole's body had been photographed someone had turned her over onto her back, eliminating the blood splatter that

one considered it worth photographing.

As if this catalogue of blunders were not enough to seriously compromise the prosecution case, the police also failed to bag the hands of the deceased, they neglected to use a rape kit, and they did not examine or photograph the back gate, which was the likely exit point for the killer. It was only weeks later that blood was found there, prompting accusations that it had been planted, when in all likelihood it had simply been yet another crucial clue that had been overlooked. These incredible errors and omissions were compounded after Nicole's body was removed to the morgue.

Instead of being examined in detail, it was washed, thereby eliminating the last vestiges of trace evidence that might have given a clue to the identity of her killer. It was only two full days later that an autopsy was performed.

can be seen on her skin above her halter top in the official police photographs. It was the coroner's opinion that this splatter came from her assailant who had been injured in the attack, but no swabs were taken before she was turned. After she had been moved it was too late to do so. The coroner is also responsible for making a search of anything at the crime scene which might have a bearing on the cause and time of death. So a dish of melting ice cream in Nicole's house which the police ignored might have provided a vital clue as to the time of death, but no

After a protracted nine-month trial O. J. was predictably found not guilty. The jury could have done nothing else, since the police errors cast more than 'reasonable doubt' on the proceedings. But in a subsequent civil case brought by the families of Nicole Simpson and Ronald Goldman the circumstantial evidence was deemed to be overwhelming. O. J. was found guilty and ordered to pay $33 million compensation to the bereaved families.

THE IRISH BUSHRANGER

The Irish bushranger Jack Donohoe was probably twenty-four years old in 1830, when he was killed by police and a volunteer posse at Bringelly, near Campbelltown outside Sydney. But his memory still endures, kept alive through a popular ballad. He became through the ballad the symbol of resistance both to the old convict system and to the British colonial yoke.

Sentenced to transportation in Dublin in 1823 at the age of 17, 'Bold' Jack Donohoe was a short, blond, freckle-faced man who, after he arrived in Sydney, seems to have found nothing but trouble. after a stint in a punishment gang, he took off into the bush. In the words of the ballad:

'He'd scarcely served twelve months in chains upon the Australian shore, When he took to the highway as he had done before: He went with Jacky Underwood, and Webber and Walmsley too, These were the true companions of bold Jack Donohoe.'

Donohoe's gang held up the carts that carried produce to and from the Sydney settlement, along the Windsor Road. He and two of his henchmen were soon caught and condemned to death. The other two were hanged. But Donohoe made a run for it – further boosting his reputation.

After stealing horses from settlers, a new Donohoe gang began to roam through a huge swathe of territory, holding up travellers, thieving from farms and selling off whatever booty they got to whoever would have it. Back in Sydney, he became a stick with which the newspapers could beat the Governor's head.

The Governor was forced to act. The price on Donohoe's head was raised; and more police and volunteers were sent into the field. Finally, at Bringelly, they caught up with him. According to the ballad, Donohoe shouted out his defiance and killed nine men with nine bullets before being shot himself through the heart and asking, with his dying breath, all convicts to pray for him. The truth is, of course, more mundane. He did not kill nine men; he screamed nothing but obscenities; and he was shot in the head by a trooper called Muggleston. But it didn't matter.

For 'Bold' Jack Donohoe was already passing into legend. When his body was laid out in the Sydney morgue, the Colony's distinguished Surveyor-General came in to draw his portrait; and a Sydney shopkeeper produced a line of clay pipes, featuring his head with a bullet-hole at the temple. They sold out fast.

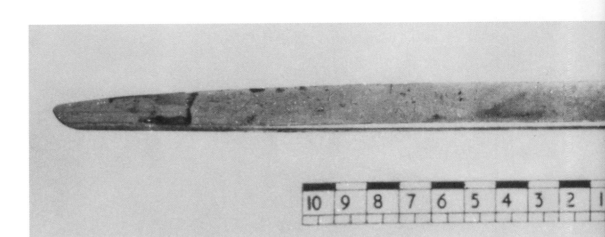

JACK THE RIPPER

Jack the Ripper is the definitive serial killer. His brief and monstrous career established the serial killer in the public mind as the most terrifying of all criminals. So why does this killer, whose crimes were committed over a century ago, still haunt us? Partly, it is the sheer ferocity of his crimes: the disembowelling, the removal of body organs. Partly, it is the setting: Victorian Whitechapel is fixed in our minds as a seedy location for murder. Mostly, however, what has made the Ripper an immortal among murderers is the simple fact that he was never caught.

WHO WAS HE?

For that reason, his crimes provide endless scope for speculation. Scarcely a year passes without another book being published that promises to name the real killer – a trend that reached its zenith when the crime novelist Patricia Cornwell spent a reputed $8 million of her own money in an effort to prove that the Victorian painter Walter Sickert was the murderer, a claim that remains tenuous at best.

The killer we know as Jack the Ripper announced himself to the world on 31 August 1888 with the murder of a prostitute named Mary 'Polly' Nichols. This was the third prostitute murder of the year in London's East End and did not initially attract too much attention, even though it was an unusually brutal killing: her throat and torso had been cut, and there were stab wounds to the genitals. At

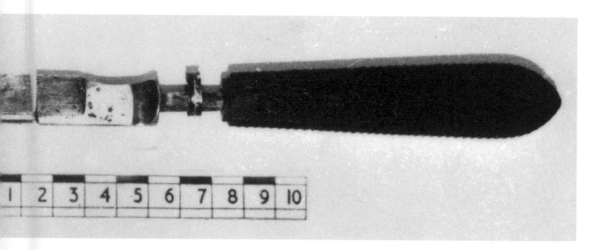

◀ *A knife found at the scene of one of the killings: its design sparked yet another theory, that the murderer was employed in the butchery trade*

this stage, of course, there was nothing to suggest a serial killer at large.

It was little more than a week, however, before the murderer struck again. The victim was another prostitute, Annie Chapman, known as 'Dark Annie'. Like Polly Nichols, she had been killed by a knife slash to the throat, but this time the killer had disembowelled her, pulled out her entrails and draped them over a shoulder, and then cut out her vagina and ovaries. What struck investigators, apart from the sheer horror of the scene, was the precision of the cuts; it seemed possible that the killer had medical training and was familiar with dissecting bodies in the post-mortem room.

TWICE IN ONE NIGHT

This gruesome crime already had the public in an uproar, but it was as nothing compared to the reaction that followed the murderer's next atrocity on 30 September. This time, he killed not once but twice on the same night. The first victim was Elizabeth Stride, 'Long Liz', a seamstress and occasional prostitute. She had been killed by a knife wound to the throat, but there was no other mutilation. One can only presume that the killer was interrupted in his work, and thus dissatisfied, because, before the night was over, he also killed prostitute Catherine Eddowes – and this time the attack had all his characteristic savagery. In addition, someone had written on the wall the strange message: 'The Juwes are not the men that will be blamed for nothing.' The police were not sure if the killer had written it, or what it meant, so the investigating officer ordered it to be removed to avoid anti-Jewish hysteria developing.

LETTERS

Just before the double murder, the Central News Agency had received a letter that purported to be from the killer. There had already been many such letters, most of them obvious hoaxes, but when a second letter came from the same writer within hours of the double mur-

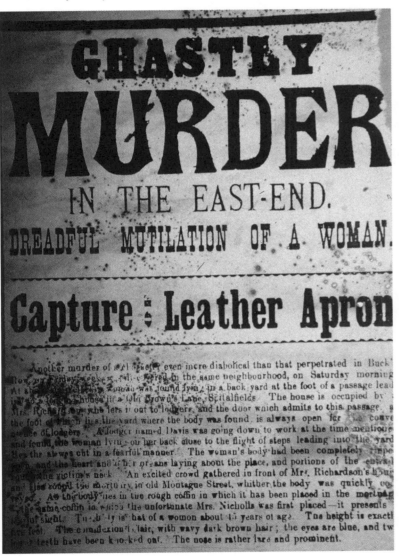

▼ *A newspaper shows the extent to which the killings took over the media stories of the day*

der, the agency passed them on to the police. The writer signed himself 'Jack the Ripper', which caused a sensation in the press. Now, the murderer had a name.

Two weeks later another letter arrived, sent to George Lusk, head of the Whitechapel Vigilance Committee. It appeared to have a different author from the previous ones – this correspondent was far less literate – but was even more chilling. In place of a return address it simply said 'From Hell'. Enclosed in it was a piece of human kidney, which the writer claimed belonged to Eddowes. Eddowes had indeed had a kidney removed by her killer.

UNIMAGINABLE CARNAGE

Three more weeks went by, and then the Ripper struck again. Once again, the victim was a prostitute, Mary Kelly. In a change she was killed indoors, in her room in Miller's Court. Mary Kelly's body was utterly destroyed; she was partially skinned, disembowelled, grotesquely arranged and numerous trophies were taken, including her uterus and a foetus taken from it (Kelly had been pregnant at the time). It was a scene of unimaginable carnage and one that left Whitechapel – and the world – bracing itself for the Ripper's next atrocity.

However, the next killing never came. There was a knife murder of a prostitute

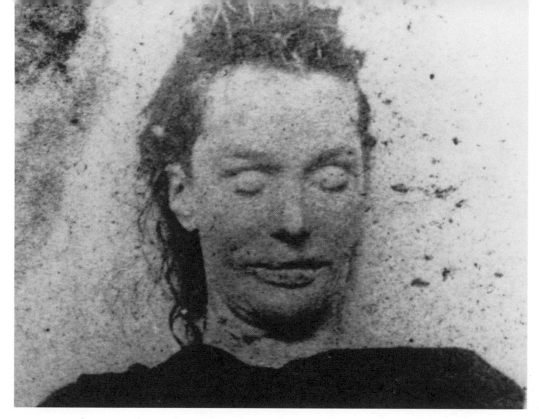

◄ *Elizabeth Stride, 'Long Liz'; she had the dubious claim to fame of being one of the two women killed by Jack the Ripper on the same night*

two years later, and another two years after that, but neither had any of the hallmarks of a Ripper killing. As mysteriously as he had appeared, the Ripper had vanished.

Since that time, detectives – both amateur and professional – have speculated about who he (or even she in some far-fetched accounts) was. To date, suspects have included Queen Victoria's grandson Prince Eddy, in a rage against the prostitute who supposedly gave him syphilis; Sir William Gull, the Queen's surgeon, as part of a conspiracy to cover up the fact that Prince Eddy had conceived an illegitimate child with a Whitechapel girl (another theory sadly lacking in evidence); and Liverpool businessman James Maybrick, supposed author of The Ripper Diaries, published in 1994 and generally deemed to be fake.

The truth is that we shall probably never know who he was, or why he killed so brutally. However, there is a likely explanation for the sudden end to his reign of terror, put forward at the time by Sir Melville Macnaghten, the Chief Commissioner of the Metropolitan Police.

He speculated that 'the murderer's brain gave way altogether after his awful glut in Miller's Court, and that he immediately committed suicide, or, as a possible alternative, was found to be so hopelessly mad by his relations that they confined him to an asylum'.

JUST A GIGOLO

In 1946, in post-war London, Neville Heath looked just like the man he claimed to be: a dashing ex-Royal-Air-Force officer, a war hero. He had fair hair and blue eyes, an air of romantic recklessness; and, like a man who has successfully cheated death, he loved to party. To women hungry for men he must have seemed made to measure: an embodiment of the gallantry that had led to victory – and of the newly carefree spirit of the times.

This nightclub Lothario, though, was not at all what he looked like. For not only was he a gigolo with a criminal record, but he also had the distinction of having been court-martialled by three separate services: by the British Air Force in 1937, the British Army in 1941, and the South African Air Force in 1945. His offences – for being absent without leave, stealing a car, issuing worthless cheques, indiscipline and wearing medals to which he wasn't entitled and the like – all pointed in one direction: Neville Heath was a con man and poseur.

He used women for money after he'd got them into his bed – as he could all too easily. But he preferred – when that palled – to beat them.

In March 1945, after guests at a London hotel reported hearing screams, a house detective burst into a bedroom to find Heath brutally whipping a girl, naked and bound hand and foot, beneath him. Neither the hotel nor the girl wanted publicity, and within two months Heath was at it again – though this time with a more willing participant, a 32-year-old occasional film extra known in London clubs as Ocelot Margie. In May, security in another hotel intervened late at night as she lay under Heath's lash.

Ocelot Margie, though, had no complaints to make. For she was a masochist, haunting the clubs in search of bondage and domination by any man she could find willing. She obviously found Heath to her taste. For a month later she arranged to meet him at a club, and then returned with him to the same hotel for a further session. She wasn't to make it out alive.

In the early afternoon of the follow day, a chambermaid found her naked dead body. She had been tied at the ankles and murderously whipped, and she had extensive bruising on her face and chin, as if someone had used extreme violence to keep her mouth shut. Her nipples had been almost bitten off, and something unnaturally large had been shoved into

◀ *Heath's crimes caught up with him and he was hanged in October 1946*

▲ *There was huge public interest in the trial of Neville Heath*

her vagina and then rotated, causing extensive bleeding.

The police quickly issued Heath's name and description to the press. But by this time he was in the south-coast resort town of Worthing, meeting the parents of a young woman he had earlier seduced after a promise of marriage. He quickly told her – and later her parents – his version of the murder: that he had lent his hotel room to Gardner to use for a tryst with another man and had later found her dead. He sent a letter to the police in London to the same effect, adding that he would later send on to them the murder weapon he'd found on the scene. Then he disappeared.

The murder weapon, of course, never arrived. But the police still failed to issue a photograph of Heath, and so he was free on the south coast for another thirteen days, posing, rather unimaginatively, as Group Captain Rupert Brooke – the name of a famously handsome poet who died in the First World War. During that time, a young woman holidaymaker vanished after having been seen having dinner with 'Brooke' at his hotel; and it was suggested that the 'Group Captain' should contact the police with his evidence. He finally did so, but was recognised and held for questioning. In the pocket of a jacket at his hotel police later found a left-luggage ticket for a suitcase, which contained, among other things, clothes labelled with the name 'Heath,' a woman's scarf and a blood-stained riding-crop.

On the evening of the day Heath was returned to London and charged, the naked body of his second victim was found in a wooded valley not far from his hotel. Her cut hands had been tied together; her throat had been slashed; and after death her body had been mutilated with a knife before being hidden in bushes. Heath, though, was never tried for this murder. He came to the Old Bailey on September 24th 1946 charged only with the murder of Margery Gardner – and he was quickly found guilty by the jury. He was hanged at London's Pentonville Prison the following month.

THE KILLINGS OF A CLOWN

Why John Wayne Gacy, the so-called Killer Clown, was never suspected of involvement in the disappearance of a succession of young men in the Chicago area in the 1970s, remains a mystery. The baby-faced, twice-married homosexual had, after all, been earlier sentenced to ten years in an Iowa facility on charges including kidnap and attempted sodomy. On probation in Chicago after his early release, he'd been accused of picking up a teenager and trying to force him to have sex, and of attempting the same thing, at gunpoint, with an older man at his house. His name had even appeared on police files four times between 1972 and 1978 in connection with missing-persons cases.

To cap it all, a full eight months before his final arrest in December 1979, a twenty-seven-year-old Chicagoan called Jeffrey Rignall told police that, after accepting a ride from an overweight man driving a black Oldsmobile, he'd been attacked with a rag soaked in chloroform, and then driven to a house, where he'd been re-chloroformed, whipped and repeatedly

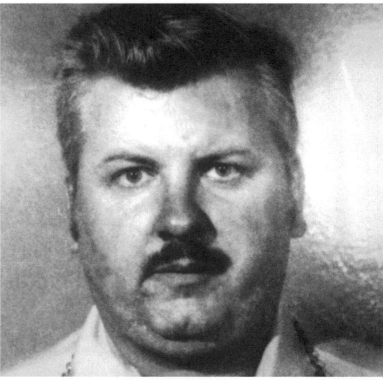

▲ *Gacy, the Killer Clown*

raped, before being dumped, unconscious, in Lincoln Park hours later. When the police said his evidence was too little to go on, Rignall spent days after leaving hospital sitting in a hired car at motorway entrances. Finally he spotted the Oldsmobile, followed it and wrote down the number. It belonged to thirty-seven-year-old John Wayne Gacy.

At this point the police did issue a warrant, but they failed to act on it. It was three months before they arrested Gacy – and then only on a misdemeanour. He was set free to go on killing.

The reason the police were so lax was probably because Gacy, on the face of it, was prosperous, active in his community and well-connected. He had a construction business with a large number of employees, an expensive house – and was something of a local celebrity. Dressed up as Pogo the Clown, he was a regular entertainer at street parades and children's parties. He was also active in Democratic Party politics. He gave donations to the Party, organized fêtes for it and on one occasion co-ordinated a Party event for 20,000 people of Polish descent, at which he was photographed with First Lady Rosalyn Carter.

The truth was, though, that it was all front. Gacy used his construction company as, in effect, a recruiting-agency, a way of getting close to his victims. He gave jobs to young men and boys from the surrounding Chicago suburbs, and he picked up others at the local Greyhound station, luring them to his house with the promise of work. He was also a regular cruiser in Chicago's gay district, preying on yet other young men whose disappearance would not be much noticed. They, too, would end up among the whips, handcuffs and guns at Gacy's house.

He was caught in the end more by accident than design – simply because a mother came to pick up her son one night from his job at a Des Plaines pharmacy. The teenager said he had to go off for a few moments to see a man about a high-paying summer job. He never returned. When the police later visited the pharmacy they noticed it had recently been renovated – and the pharmacist told them that the renovation company's boss was probably the man who had offered the kid a job: a man called Gacy.

When the police called at Gacy's house to question him about the teenager's disappearance, they opened a trapdoor leading to a crawl space below the house and found the remains of seven bodies. Another twenty-one were subsequently found, either dug into quicklime or buried in the area around the house. Gacy quickly confessed to their murders, and to the murder of another five young men, whose bodies he'd simply dumped into the river because he'd run out of space. He'd sodomised and tortured them all. One eerie detail of Gacy's modus operandi emerged in the coming months. He'd offer to show his victims what he called 'the handcuff trick,' promising that if they put on a pair of handcuffs they'd be able to get out of them within a few seconds. Of course they couldn't. Then he'd say,

'The way to get out of the handcuffs is to have the key. That's the real trick. . .'

He was sentenced to life imprisonment in 1980.

A KILLER COUPLE

Fred and Rosemary West are among the most chilling serial killers of all time. During the 1970s, they murdered a string of female victims, including their own daughter. Yet despite frequent brushes with the police, the seemingly good-natured builder and his wife were never connected with the murders at the time they were committed.

In the decade that followed, police gave up the search for the girls who had gone missing in the area, and their files sat on the shelves collecting dust. The Wests would probably have got away with their crimes, had it not been for the fact that, in 1992, a young girl they had raped finally went to the police, and the whole story began – literally – to be unearthed.

VIOLENCE AND SEXUAL ABUSE

Fred and Rosemary West were both from deprived rural backgrounds, where violence and sexual abuse was not uncommon. Born in the village of Much Marcle in 1941, Fred was one of six children, and later claimed that incest was rife in the family. He was backward at school, and left at the age of fifteen scarcely able to read or write. At the age of seventeen he suffered a serious motorcycle accident that possibly caused damage to his brain: it was after this that his behaviour became increasingly out of control. He was eventually arrested for having sex with an under-age girl, and narrowly avoided prison. His parents, finally tiring of his behaviour, threw him out of the family home.

Rosemary Letts, born in 1953 in Devon, was sexually abused from a young age by her schizophrenic father. Her mother suffered from severe depression. As a teenager, she was overweight and sexually precocious. When she met Fred, who was twelve years older than she, she idolized him, and soon became pregnant by him, even though she was not yet sixteen.

THE MURDERS BEGIN

Fred had already been married, to prostitute Rena Costello, who had a mixed-race child called Charmaine from a previous relationship. Fred and Rena's own child, Anna Marie, was born shortly before the pair split up. Fred had then taken up with a friend of Rena's named Anna McFall, who was pregnant with Fred's child when, as later emerged, he murdered her, dismembering her body and burying it near the trailer where they lived. He was then free to concentrate on

his relationship with his new girlfriend, Rosemary.

During this time, Fred was in and out of prison on minor charges such as non-payment of fines, while Rosemary was left in charge of the children — Charmaine, Anna Marie, and the couple's new daughter, Heather, born in 1970. Rosemary had a ferocious temper and was insanely cruel, especially to Charmaine. She abused the children while Fred was away, finally murdering Charmaine. Later, Fred buried the child's body under the house. Then, when Rena came looking for Charmaine, Fred murdered her too, burying her body in the countryside.

In 1972, the couple moved to a house in Cromwell Street, Gloucester, where Rosemary worked as a prostitute and continued to bear children, some of which were Fred's, and some of which were fathered by her clients. The basement of the house was used for deviant sexual activities, including the rape of their daughter, Anna Marie, and a girl they employed to care for the children, Caroline Owens. When Owens went to the police, Fred West was tried for the rape, but — unbelievably — he was let off with a fine. Tragically, the

◀ *The picture of a loving couple: not even their closest neighbours had any idea about what was going on behind the facade of a normal, busy family*

next girl hired to care for the children, Lynda Gough, was not so lucky: she did not escape with her life, and was murdered and buried under the cellar. The couple went on to abduct, torture and murder more young women, in a killing spree that was as brutal as it was depraved: Carol Anne Cooper, Lucy Partington, Alison Chambers, Therese Siegenthaler, Shirley Hubbard, Juanita Mott, and Shirley Robinson all met their deaths in the most horrifying ways. The Wests even killed their own daughter, Heather, after she told friends about her bizarre home life. She was buried, like many of the other victims, in the garden of the house.

THE CASE GOES COLD

Then, suddenly, the killings stopped. There have been many theories about why this came about: perhaps the Wests found other ways of satisfying their violent sexual impulses; or perhaps there were actually many other victims who were never missed, and whose deaths were never reported.

The Wests were careful to choose their victims from the bottom of the social pile; often girls who had lost touch with their families, or who were working as prostitutes, whose relatives and friends would not come looking for them. Lucy Partington, a middle-class university student and a relative of the writer Martin Amis, was the exception.

It looked as though the Wests had got away with their crimes, and that their victims would be forgotten. But in 1992, the couple's horrifying deeds came back to haunt them, when a girl they had raped went to the police to report her ordeal. This time, her story was believed.

BURIED UNDER THE PATIO

On 6 August 1992, police arrived at the house in Cromwell Street. They searched the house for pornography and found more than enough evidence to arrest the couple for rape and sodomy of a minor. One of West's perversions was to film his wife on video, engaging in sex with different partners, both men and women. The older West children, Stephen and Anna Marie, both made statements supporting the allegation of rape, but the case later collapsed when they withdrew these, under pressure from the family.

Meanwhile, the younger children had been taken away from their parents and placed in social care. Their carers began to notice that they often joked about their sister Heather being buried under the patio. This was reported to the police, who returned to the house in February 1994 and began to dig up the garden. To their horror, they not

only found Heather's remains, but a total of nine other bodies in the garden. Later, other bodies under the cellar were dug up.

◀ *Clearing work gets under way at Midland Road, Gloucester, a home of Fred West before he was married to Rosemary West*

Fred West initially confessed to the murder of his daughter Heather, but then retracted the confession. It seemed that he and Rosemary then made a pact, in which he would take the blame for the murder, emphasizing that his wife was not involved in any way. Accordingly, he re-confessed, stressing

▶ *The troubled face of Heather West, who disappeared in 1987. Her remains were subsequently found, buried under the patio at 25, Cromwell Street*

that Rosemary was not to blame, but by this time there was evidence to show that she too was responsible for the murder not only of Heather, but of many other victims as well.

HANGED IN HIS CELL

Fred West was charged with twelve murders in all, but before he could come to trial, he hanged himself in his prison cell, on New Year's Day in 1995. Rosemary maintained that she was innocent, but in October that same year, she was convicted of ten of the murders, and received a life sentence.

What would have happened if that young girl had not gone to the police to report her rape in 1992? Is it possible that Fred and Rosemary West would

have continued to evade the law until the end of their natural lives, their crimes never discovered? What if the authorities had dismissed the girl's story, as they had dismissed that of Caroline Owens, the Wests' nanny, years before?

It seems almost incredible that two people who had committed so many hideous murders could have gone undetected for so long – but that is what happened.

Perhaps it was a change in the social climate that helped to bring them to justice. Perhaps the permissive climate of the 1970s, in which the rules about sexual morality were beginning to be relaxed, impacted in a negative way on the underclass to which both Fred and Rosemary West belonged. This might explain why it was that the bizarre sexual behaviour that took place in their household went largely unnoticed and unremarked on by friends and neighbours, who might, in other times, have found it unacceptable.

However one explains it, the fact remains that it was only through the bravery of one young girl that the appalling brutality of this pair of vicious killers came to light, years after the murders happened, so that they finally received the punishment they deserved.

KILLING FOR COMPANY

Dennis 'Des' Nilsen is one of the most perplexing of serial killers. He exhibited few of the conventional childhood signs of a future killer; he did not torture animals or play with fire. When he killed it was not in a sexual frenzy, but while his victims slept. He killed them, he famously said, so they would not leave. He was 'killing for company'. However, the fact remains that this mild-mannered civil servant was responsible for the violent deaths of at least fifteen men.

MOTIVATION

His case is fascinating not simply because it does not fit a pattern but also because, more than most other killers, Nilsen himself has tried to understand his own motivation. He helped the writer Brian Masters to write his biography and has written his own autobiography, as well as penning numerous letters to the press and researchers.

Dennis Andrew Nilsen was born in the Scottish port town of Fraserburgh on 23 November 1945 — yet another serial killer to be born during the post-war baby boom. His parents were Olav, a Norwegian soldier who had left Norway when the Nazis invaded, and Betty, who came from a religious Scottish family. His father was a heavy drinker who effectively deserted Betty from the very start. There was never a family home: Betty and Dennis remained at her parents' house and the couple were divorced in 1949.

The father figure in Dennis' life became his grandfather, Andrew Whyte. When Whyte died in 1951, it was a defining trauma in Dennis' life —

▼ *Dennis Nilsen on his way to his trial.*

all the more so because he was taken to see his grandfather's body without being told that he had died. This unexpected sight of his grandfather's corpse is the event that Nilsen himself regards as having sown the seeds of his later sexual pathology.

In 1953, Nilsen's mother remarried and went on to have four other children. Understandably, she had less time for Dennis and he became a rather solitary child. In 1961, aged sixteen, he opted to join the army, to be a soldier like his absent father. He remained in the army until 1972, working for part of the time as a butcher in the Catering Corps. Dennis had no sexual experience as a teenager but was increasingly aware that he was attracted to men. During his last year in the army he fell in love with a fellow soldier. However, the man in question was not gay and did not return Nilsen's affections – though he did consent to Nilsen's request to film him while he pretended to be dead.

The end of their friendship was a great blow to Nilsen, who then left the army and trained to be a policeman – taking a particular interest in visits to the morgue. However police work did not suit him and after a year he left and found employment in a job centre in London's Soho, interviewing people looking for work.

KILLING FOR COMPANY

Soho was the hub of London's emerging gay scene at the time and Nilsen began to immerse himself in a new world of bar-hopping and casual pick-ups. However, whatever sexual gratification Nilsen got from this was not enough to counterbalance a terrible sense of loneliness. This abated for nearly two years, between 1975 and 1977, when he shared an apartment in north London with a man named David Gallichan. They were not, apparently, sexual partners, but they shared domestic duties and acquired a dog and a cat. However, temperamental differences drove them apart and in 1977 Nilsen asked Gallichan to leave the flat.

The loneliness returned and became unbearable for Nilsen. In December 1978 Nilsen picked up a young Irishman in a pub; Nilsen never even learnt the young man's name. Later that night, as he watched his latest pick-up sleeping, and anticipated him leaving in the morning, Nilsen decided he could not bear to be left alone again. He strangled the young man using a necktie, then finished him off by drowning him in a bucket of water. He washed the corpse's hair and put him back into bed. Suddenly he had what he later called 'a new kind of flatmate'.

Realizing, after a while, that he had to do something with this corpse, Nilsen went out and bought an electric carving knife, but could not bring himself to cut up the body, so he ended up hiding the corpse under the floorboards where it remained for eight months until he took it out and burnt it on a bonfire in his garden.

READY TO KILL AGAIN

At the time he was sure he would be caught, but he was not, and so by the end of 1979 he was ready to kill again. This time, however, his intended victim, a young Chinese man called Andrew Ho, escaped and went to the police. The police, however, regarded the matter as a tiff between gay lovers and failed to press charges.

Just days later, he found his next victim, a Canadian called Kenneth Ockendon. This time, after strangling the man with an electric cord, Nilsen dissected the body, using the butchery skills he had acquired in the army. Then he flushed part of the body down the toilet while leaving other parts under the floorboards.

Over the next two years, Nilsen repeated the pattern ten more times. The young men he killed were generally drifters or rent boys; in only a few cases did Nilsen know their names. Each was strangled and dissected, the body parts flushed away or kept as trophies.

In October 1981 Nilsen decided to move house. Some sane part of his brain

▲ *Nilsen in the army in 1961; the plumber who made the gruesome discovery in the drains; Nilsen the policeman in 1973*

decided to move out of his garden flat and into an attic flat, in the hopes that this would make it harder for him to dispose of a body and thus would inhibit him from killing again. Before he left, he had one more bonfire in which he incinerated the last remains of his victims.

Over the next year or so, Nilsen succeeded in killing three more times. But finally his new living quarters did betray him. He had been flushing body parts down the toilet once more and this time the drains refused to co-operate.

Another tenant in the house called in a drainage company to unblock the drains. The unfortunate workman who called found that the blockage was due to human flesh and soon traced the problem to Nilsen's flat. Nilsen was immediately arrested.

Once in custody, Nilsen stunned the police with an exhaustive confession. He was sentenced to life imprisonment.

THE KISS OF DEATH

Very little is known about the early life of Bela Kiss, one of the most horrifying serial killers of all time. His story only comes fully into focus when he began his career of murder, as a young man apparently searching for a wife.

A handsome man with blue eyes and fair hair, Kiss was very attractive to women, not only because of his good looks, but also because he was educated, intelligent and well mannered. However, when his crimes came to light, it emerged that Kiss was a lady killer in a more literal sense. He murdered over twenty women and pickled their bodies in alcohol, inside large metal drums that he hid in his home and around the countryside nearby. Perhaps most horrifying of all, he actually managed to get away with it.

▶ *Bela Kiss was called up by the army in 1914*

BARRELS

In 1912, Bela Kiss was living in the village of Czinkota, just outside Budapest in Hungary. He shared a house with his housekeeper, an elderly woman named Mrs Jakubec. Although well liked in the village, Kiss was not on intimate terms with any of his neighbours. A single man, he had a series of relationships with several attractive young women who often came to the house, but who were never introduced to the housekeeper or to any of his neighbours. Kiss also collected metal drums, telling the local police that they were for storing gasoline, which was likely to be in short supply in the future because of the impending war.

In 1914, Kiss was called up into the army. While he was away, soldiers went to his house to look for the extra supplies of gasoline he was known to have kept there. They found the drums and opened them. Instead of gasoline, inside each drum they found the dead body of a woman who had been strangled and whose body had then been preserved in alcohol. A further search through Kiss' papers revealed dozens of letters from the women, who had visited the house after replying to his newspaper advertisements for a wife.

Kiss lured well-to-do, attractive women by correspondence, promising to marry them and often divesting them of their savings in the process. He then invited them to his home. Once there, he would strangle them, pickle their bodies in alcohol and seal them in the metal drums. The bodies also had puncture marks on their necks and their bodies were drained of blood. Bela Kiss was not just a murderer, but a vampire too.

Why he chose to preserve the bodies in this way nobody knows. It was obviously a risky thing to do. Firstly, the drums were big and hard to hide; secondly, the bodies inside were so perfectly preserved that in some cases even the labels on their clothing could be read. Surely Kiss must have known that if ever the drums were opened, his crimes could easily be traced.

CHANGING IDENTITY

Several local women who had gone missing were discovered in the drums, along with many others whose absence had not been missed. Kiss had repeated his crimes again and again, with a series of innocent, unsuspecting victims, using a false name, 'Herr Hoffmann'. Until the discovery of the bodies, the connection between Bela Kiss and 'Herr Hoffman', who was wanted for questioning in regard to the disappearance of two widows with whom he had corresponded, had never been made.

With the advent of war, Kiss found a perfect way to escape detection: he faked his own death. He assumed the identity of an army comrade who had been killed in combat, switching his papers with those of the dead man. However, his plan was foiled when, in the spring of 1919, he was spotted in Budapest by someone who had known him from his earlier days. Police investigated, and found out about the fraud, but were still unable to catch up with him. Later, a soldier called Hoffman boasted to his comrades of his prowess as a strangler; but once again, when police tried to find Kiss, the trail went cold.

Many years later, Kiss was apparently spotted in New York by a homicide detective called Henry Oswald, renowned for his ability to remember faces. By this time, Kiss would have been in his late sixties. Oswald pursued Kiss but lost him among the crowds of Times Square. A few years later, Kiss was again seen in New York, this time working as the janitor of an apartment block; but he escaped police and was never apprehended.

Nobody knows how or when Bela Kiss died. The true number of his victims is also unknown. Did he cease killing women when he went on the run, or did he continue his hideous crimes undetected? How many women in Hungary could have been lured to their death by Bela Kiss? These are questions to which we will never know the answers.

LAST WILL AND TESTAMENT

Serious criminal cases are rarely resolved using just one type of forensic evidence. Frequently investigators will build a case on as many levels as possible to leave little room for error in case one type of evidence is ruled inadmissible in court for legal reasons or called into question by the defence's expert witnesses. In the case of the abduction and murder of 18-year-old Shari Faye Smith, her killer was caught and convicted using a combination of modern criminal profiling and good old-fashioned physical evidence.

Astonishingly, Shari had been abducted in broad daylight and within sight of her home in Columbia, South Carolina, on 31 May 1985 as she stopped to collect post from the mailbox at the end of the driveway. Minutes later her father had found her car as she had left it with the engine running, the driver's door open and her purse on the passenger seat.

The police immediately organized the most extensive manhunt in South Carolina's history, but no trace of Shari was found. Later that day the Smith family received the first in a series of bizarre calls from the kidnapper, who disguised his voice with an electronic device. He proved that it was not a hoax by describing what Shari had been wearing under her clothes, but curiously he never mentioned the subject of a ransom.

The mystery man appeared simply to enjoy tormenting the family, who at this time still held out hope of finding Shari alive, and he promised that they would receive a letter the next morning.

The letter duly arrived. It was in Shari's handwriting and had been written on a sheet of lined legal paper headed 'Last Will and Testament'. It didn't give a clue as to her whereabouts, but it suggested she could still be alive.

But in a subsequent call some days later her abductor said something which confirmed their worst fears. He said that Shari and he had become 'one soul' and he gave detailed instructions as to where they could find her body.

It appeared that he had delayed giving them the location until he no longer had a use for her as a trophy and was certain that the body had decomposed sufficiently to degrade any useful forensic evidence. But there

◀ *Shari Faye's killer,*
Larry Gene Bell (left)

was probably also another reason. Many serial killers keep the location of their victim's bodies a secret as they get a perverse thrill from revisiting the site and reliving the murder.

A PROFILE IS COMPILED

The FBI Signal Analysis Unit concluded that the kidnapper's voice had been disguised using a Variable Speed Control Device, which suggested that he might have a background in electronics. This prompted the FBI to compile a profile which speculated that the man they were seeking would be in his late twenties or early thirties, single, overweight and unattractive to women. The fact that he indulged in cruel mind games, including calling the family reverse-charge on the day of Shari's funeral and describing in graphic detail how he had killed her, suggested that he was probably separated after an unsuccessful marriage and was likely to have a history of making obscene phone calls, all of which were to be proven correct. Two weeks later the same man abducted nine-year-old Debra May Helnick from outside her parents' mobile home in Richland County, 38km from the Smith residence. Then he phoned the Smiths and told them where the girl's body could be found.

It was about this time that the FBI had a break in the case. They subjected Shari's 'Last Will and Testament' letter to microscopic analysis using an ESTA machine, which detects the slightest impression in paper which would be invisible to the naked eye. It revealed a grocery list and a phone number which had been written on a sheet elsewhere in the pad from the one Shari had used. The phone number led detectives to the home of a middle-aged couple who had been out of the country at the time of the murders. But they recognized the profile as a description of their handyman, Larry Gene Bell, who they had allowed to live in their house during their absence.

Larry had aroused the couple's suspicion when he had picked them up from the airport and talked about nothing but the murders, and their suspicions were confirmed when agents played the couple a recording of Larry's final phone call to the Smith family in which he had not bothered to disguise his voice with the electronic device. His DNA was later recovered from the stamp he had licked before posting Shari's 'Last Will' and matched with a sample obtained on his arrest.

In 1996 Larry Gene Bell became the last person to die in the electric chair in the state of South Carolina.

A LIFE OF CRIME

President Giscard de'Estaing regarded the failure to catch Jacques Mesrine as a national disgrace. Much of the rest of the population were delighted. For they sneakingly saw Mesrine as a combination of D'Artagnan, Robin Hood and Errol Flynn: a glorious example of France's daring and ingenuity. True, he might have killed a few times – and that was regrettable. But his wit! His escapes! His nerve! Besides, he was the most famous criminal in the world – and he was French! When he finally died in a police ambush in Paris in 1979, the police may have hugged each other and danced in the street. But there was something in the heart of every true Frenchman that mourned.

Mesrine was born in Paris in 1937 – and from his earliest years he seems to have been in love with danger. When he was conscripted into the army, he specifically asked to be sent to Algeria, where the French army was fighting against Muslim anti-colonialists.

He was demobbed with a Military Cross for bravery. But life as a civilian – after seeing action – seemed to bore him.

He committed his first burglary, on the flat of a wealthy businessman, in 1959 – and it bore all the hallmarks of what was to come. When a drill snapped as he was boring his way into the safe, he simply left, broke into a hardware store for more and came back to finish the job. He escaped with millions of francs.

His reputation rapidly spread in the underworld – and among the police. In 1962 he was arrested and sentenced to three years in prison. Out a year later, he tried to go straight, but after he was made redundant he went back to crime. Within four years he was the most wanted thief in France; the police were infuriated by his snook-cocking antics.

▲ *Mesrine was eventually shot dead by Parisian police*

He moved to Canada where he and his girlfriend Jeanne Schneider were employed by a Montreal millionaire. After being sacked, Mesrine and Jeanne kidnapped the millionaire and held him for $200,000 ransom. They were caught and charged both with the kidnap and with the murder of a rich widow they'd befriended.

Mesrine was outraged: he insisted they were innocent of the widow's murder — they were both eventually acquitted. After being convicted of the kidnapping, Mesrine escaped from the 'escape-proof' St. Vincent de Paul prison at Laval.

The escape made Mesrine a national celebrity in Canada, but his reputation darkened after he shot to death two forest rangers who'd recognised him. So he fled to Venezuela.

In 1973, Mesrine was back in France and up to his old tricks. By now, he was deep into his gentleman-thief, Robin-Hood role. When, during a bank robbery, a young woman cashier accidentally pushed the alarm button, he said:

'Don't worry, my dear. I like to work to music'

and calmly went on gathering the money. On another occasion, when his father was dying of cancer and closely watched, he dressed up as a doctor — with white coat and stethoscope — and went to visit him.

When he was arrested and then held in Santé Prison, he whiled away the time writing his autobiography. Then, when his case, after three and a half years, came to trial, he gave a demonstration in court that was to seal his reputation. After saying that it was easy enough to buy a key for any pair of handcuffs, he took out a key hidden in the knot of his tie and opened his own handcuffs.

A year later he escaped yet again, and continued his adventures. He walked into a Deauville police station, saying he was an inspector from the Gaming Squad and asked to see the duty inspector. When told he was out, he took himself off and that night robbed a Deauville casino. He gave an interview to *Paris Match*; and he even then attempted to kidnap the judge who'd tried him. when this went wrong, he escaped by telling the police whom he met on their way up the stairs: 'Quick, quick, Mesrine's up there.'

By this time he was living with a girlfriend in a luxury apartment in Paris; and the police were in no mood to compromise. They staked out the apartment, and when the couple came out and climbed into his BMW, they were soon hemmed in by two lorries. Unable to move, he was then shot. The police kissed each other and danced in the street — and President Giscard d'Estaing was immediately informed of their triumph.

THE LORD'S MISRULE

Richard John Bingham was an arrogant man, a snob. He was a bully-boy, a gambler and risk-taker with an inflated opinion of his own abilities. But he was also Lord Lucan, the seventh earl of that name, and there were all too many social parasites around him ready to confirm his sense of his own importance. If he hadn't been Lord Lucan, he might not have committed murder; and if he had, he would have been long forgotten. As it is, almost thirty years after he disappeared, 'Lucky' Lucan sticks in the public memory as a symbol of something rotten in the state of Britain – giving off, for all that, the faintest whiff of glamour.

He may, of course, have simply been mad on the night he killed his children's nanny in November 1974. Certainly he'd been losing heavily at London's gambling-tables; he was now seriously in debt. And certainly he had a pathological hatred of his wife, from whom he'd separated the previous year, losing custody in the process of his children. He'd contended to his cronies that she

was insane and insisted that she was at the root of all his current problems – though how this was the case he had never made entirely clear. He'd had her watched and followed.

Be that as it may, the facts are these: on the night of November 7th 1974, Lord Lucan's estranged wife Veronica stumbled into a pub opposite her house in London's upmarket Belgravia area, soaked to the skin, distraught, without shoes and bleeding from a wound in the head. Between sobs, she blurted out an incoherent story about how she'd just escaped from a murderer in her house.

'My children, my children,'

— she said:

'he's murdered the nanny.'

The police were immediately called; and entering the house, they found the body of the nanny, Sandra Rivett, battered to death and stuffed into a canvas bag in the basement. At this point it was not entirely clear what had happened. The killing may have been a murder that had gone wrong, or the unfortuante Sandra might have been murdered by a jilted boyfriend or for some other reason.

However, as Lady Lucan became able to tell her tale something approaching the truth began to come out. 'Lucky'

▲ *Lord Lucan and his wife on their wedding day*

Lucan had apparently let himself into the house, meaning to kill his wife, and had hit out in the dark at the first woman he saw there with a length of lead piping. Then, realising his mistake, he'd taken her body down to the basement. In the meantime, Veronica Bingham came downstairs to see what had happened to the nanny, and she in turn was attacked.

Her story continued that her husband then confessed to killing the nanny by mistake – she was the same height and build as was Lady Lucan. She never explained, however, why this confession seems to have taken all of forty minutes: the time that elapsed before she ran out for help.

Lucan, for his part, had a different story. In a telephone call he made that night to a friend, and then to another friend he later visited outside London, he said that he'd come across an intruder who'd been attacking his wife. After a fight the mysterious intruder had fled, whereupon Lady Lucan had herself run out into the night. In his version, Lucan did not mention the nanny's death at all.

Lord Lucan stayed with his friends for a few hours. They later reported that he had been considerably upset and agitated when he arrived, but had gradually calmed down. Lucan then left his friend's house saying that he would have to get things sorted out. Then he completely disappeared.

His passport and the clothes he'd intended to wear that night for a dinner with friends at a gambling club were later found at the house he'd been living in. His car was found near the south coast. It was at first assumed that Lucan had boarded a cross-channel ferry to France in the early hours of the morning to flee the man hunt that was bound to pursue him. Foreign police were alerted to the need to the trace the good-looking aristocrat. He was assumed to have access to rich and powerful friends who might be persuaded to believe his version of events and so help him out.

No trace of him has ever since been found, though reports that he'd been spotted, in South Africa, Australia, Ireland, the Caribbean and elsewhere, soon began arriving. He is now presumed dead, the most usual theory being that he drowned himself in the English Channel. Indeed his son has now succeeded him to the Lucan title.

However, the rumours – of rich, aristocratic friends who smuggled 'Lucky' Lucan out of the country and still support him – persist. If he ever turns up, it may be on his death, if that has not already happened.

THE MACIVOR CASE

When investigators first come upon a crime scene where there are multiple victims, they have to determine the nature of the crime with which they are dealing and identify which victim was the real target since it is possible that the other victims were innocent bystanders. Such was the problem facing FBI profiler Dayle Hinman in the case of the brutal murder of an attractive young couple, Missy and Michael MacIvor.

The MacIvors were discovered dead in their luxury home in the Florida Keys on an August morning in 1991. The initial suspicion was that it was a drug-related killing. Michael was an aircraft mechanic and pilot who had allegedly become mixed up with drug dealers, but thought himself 'bullet-proof', according to a friend. Four years earlier he had been arrested by customs for landing a plane with narcotic residue, but he had not been convicted. More recently he had bought himself a plane that had been impounded during a drug seizure and he was heavily in debt.

His body had been found on the living room floor, his eyes and ears covered with duct tape. His wife's naked body was discovered in the master bedroom at the foot of the bed. She too had been tortured and hog-tied (hands and feet trussed up behind her back in one binding) with a belt and a man's tie, then strangled with a cloth belt from a towelling robe. A ladder had been found propped up against a balcony outside the house and the phone wires had been cut, which indicated a degree of planning.

When FBI profiler Dayle Hinman saw the crime scene photographs she immediately discounted the drug connection. If it had been a drug hit, she reasoned, the killers would have brought their own restraints and weapons. Moreover, they would not have covered Michael's eyes and mouth if they had intended him to witness the torture of his wife or force him to give them information. Another clue lay in the fact that Missy's restraints had been tied and untied several times, indicating that she had been the object of the attack while Michael had been murdered merely because he had been in the way.

There were bruises on the back of his neck indicating that he had been struck repeatedly and once unconscious he was left alone. A metal pole was found nearby that looked a likely murder weapon.

Missy had been repeatedly assaulted and strangled indicating that the killer

▲ *Florida Keys: the MacIvors were living here when they were brutally murdered*

was a sadistic psychopath who enjoyed dominating and tormenting his victims.

THE SEARCH FOR THE SUSPECT

As no other crime of a similar nature had been reported in the area in recent months, Hinman felt it safe to assume the murder was the killer's first and that he was following the usual pattern in having graduated from burglary to rape and finally to murder. On her recommendation detectives began combing the vicinity for likely suspects, since this type of criminal will begin his career in his own area as he knows it well and will have his eye on escape routes should anything go wrong. This is what is known as the 'comfort zone'.

Within days a likely suspect was in their sights. Thomas Overton was a small-time cat burglar who fitted the profile. He specialized in breaking into houses where the owner was present. At the time he was working at a local gas station where Missy was a regular customer. This gave detectives a reason to question him but no right to arrest him. Until, that is, he was caught red-handed breaking into a house in the neighbourhood some months later.

Unfortunately, even a criminal caught in the act of committing a crime is not obliged to give a sample for DNA analysis, and with no hard physical evidence to connect Overton to the MacIvor murders there were no grounds for compelling him to submit to a swab under 'probable cause'.

But then the police had a break. While in custody Overton cut himself shaving and threw the bloody tissue away. It then became the property of the police and could be subjected to analysis. A search of the DNA database proved a positive match to the semen found at the crime scene. This was the kind of hard, irrefutable evidence that can crack a case, as there is a one-in-six-billion chance that it could belong to anyone other than the suspect. But it was not enough to prove beyond doubt that Overton had murdered the MacIvors, only that he had been in the house. The police needed to get Overton to deny that he had ever been in the house, then it would prove he was covering up the fact that he had been there on the night in question.

THE CASE IS CLOSED

The detectives devised a strategy to draw out a confession, based on the psychological profile Hinman had provided. They exploited his vanity by inviting him to the police station as an expert burglar to help clear up a series of unsolved break-ins. Overton was encouraged to believe that he might earn a shorter sentence if he cooperated.

He willingly looked through numerous photographs of houses, some of which he had burgled and some of which had been broken into by his associates. When the photograph of the MacIvor house was placed before him, he claimed he had never been there and so implicated himself in the murder.

Had he admitted that he had broken in on the day of the murder a smart lawyer might have been able to argue that some unknown assailant had murdered the MacIvors after Overton had left. And as unlikely as that sounds, it might have sown sufficient doubt to get him a life sentence for sexual assault instead of a death sentence for premeditated first-degree homicide.

MAIL ORDER MURDER

When a home-made pipe bomb killed 17-year-old Chris Marquis in his home in Fair Haven, Vermont, detectives had little hope of catching the killer and that was because the lethal ingredients were common household items that could be purchased anywhere in the United States.

Neighbours often joked that Chris and his mother lived in the safest house in town – a bungalow right next door to the local police station. But one morning in March 1998 violent death came to Fair Haven in an innocuous-looking package. Christopher's mother suspected nothing as she carried the parcel to her son, although she didn't recognize the name of the sender or the return address. Chris ran a small CB radio sales and repair busi-

▶ *The mother of bomb victim Chris Marquis with a photo of her son*

ness from his bedroom and this looked as if it might be something that he had ordered from a supplier. But Chris didn't recognize the sender either. He opened it anyway and the next moment there was a tremendous explosion which tore a hole in Chris's leg and left his mother with serious injuries. Chris later bled to death in hospital, leaving his mother distraught and wondering who could have wanted her son dead and why.

Detectives soon had an answer to both questions. On Chris's computer, investigators found emails from angry customers claiming that Chris had cheated them by advertising an expensive radio over the internet and then sending a cheaper model in its place once he had cashed their cheques and pocketed the difference.

Suddenly they had several hundred suspects. But could any of them really have been so angry that they would take revenge by killing a 17-year-old that they had almost certainly never met?

While detectives trawled through the list of Chris's customers, forensic experts combed the bungalow looking for physical evidence that could give a clue as to the identity of the perpetrator. They found Styrofoam packaging material and pieces of pipe, wire, grains of smokeless gunpowder and tiny hex nuts – all ingredients of a home-made pipe bomb, but nothing that pointed to a specific individual. The return name and address on the package proved to be fictitious and none of Chris's outraged customers lived in Mansfield, Ohio, where the package had been posted.

A LUCKY BREAK

But then they had a break. The story had made the national news and someone had phoned in with information. This anonymous source had recently been in a bar where he had overheard a long-distance truck driver complaining that he had been ripped off by a mail-order CB radio repair service in Vermont and was planning to go down there and teach the guy a lesson. The truck driver's name was Christopher Dean.

The detectives went to Dean's house in Indiana, where they found hex nuts of the type and size used in the bomb, lengths of wire and even a plastic funnel with grains of what proved to be smokeless gunpowder residue. But again, these did not amount to conclusive proof.

To find out if the hex nuts in Dean's house were the same as those found at the crime scene, forensic scientists took scrapings of both samples and placed them in a neutral solution before putting them in a plasma atomic emission spectroscope which vapourized the samples at an extremely high

▲ *Crude pipe bombs, as seen here, can have a devastating effect on life and limb*

temperature. Different compounds such as zinc and copper vapourize at different speeds, revealing the chemical make-up of any metallic object, and computer analysis of the test results revealed that both sets of hex nuts had exactly the same chemical make-up. The residue of gunpowder found in the funnel was then analyzed by a scanning electron microscope which uses X-rays to identify the components of a given substance and it showed that the powder at both sites had a 17 per cent nitro-glycerine content as well as a stabilizing agent, nitro cellulose.

However, even this was considered not enough to convict, so detectives returned again to scour the bungalow at Fair

Haven. This time they found a 9-volt battery used to detonate the bomb. On the underside was printed a sequence of letters and numbers which subsequently proved to be an identification code relating to a specific batch made on a particular day at a particular factory. Police later found an open packet of 9-volt batteries at Dean's house with the same batch numbers. One battery was missing.

And the final nail in Dean's coffin was the discovery of a file containing the fictitious return name and address in his computer. He had evidently deleted the file but wasn't aware that by printing the label he had created another file which could easily be recovered from the hard drive. Dean had assumed that no one would ever connect him with the bombing because he had never been to Fair Haven and had never met the victim. He was wrong and now has a lifetime in prison to regret it.

▶ *Truck driver and pipe bomber Christopher Dean at the time of his arrest*

MAKING ZOMBIES

It was thirteen years after his first killing – sixteen dead bodies later – that Jeffrey Dahmer was finally arrested in Milwaukee as a mass murderer. By that time aged 31, he'd been earlier charged with a sexual assault against a young boy, bailed and put on probation after attending prison part-time. He'd been identified to police as responsible for another sex attack in his apartment; and he'd even got away with claiming that an incoherent and terrified young man found running away from him naked in the street was his drunk lover. Police on this occasion had actually visited the apartment, but apparently hadn't noticed the smell of decaying flesh. Nor had they visited his bedroom, in which a dead body had been laid out, ready for butchering. All they'd seen was the plausible Dahmer, who showed them photographs and apologised – and then, a few minutes after they'd left, strangled the helpless young man they'd left with him.

It wasn't, in fact, until July 22nd 1991 when, in eerily similar circumstances,

police stopped a young black man found running hysterically down the street with a handcuff hanging from his wrist, that they finally discovered the man responsible for a rash of recent missing-person cases. For Tracy Edwards told them that some crazy white man in an apartment not far away had been holding a knife to him, threatening to cut out his heart and eat it. He took them to the apartment-building in question and told them the number; Jeffrey Dahmer calmly answered the door. And then, finally, standing in the doorway, the police smelt the smell of death. . .

Inside the apartment were five dried and lacquered human skulls and a barrel containing three male torsos; an electric saw stained with blood, and a drum containing acid which Dahmer had used to dissolve his victims' bodies and to inject – with a turkey baster through holes drilled into their heads – into their living brains. In the freezer was a human head and a box containing human hands and genitals. The meat neatly wrapped in the refrigerator, Dahmer later allowed, was also human – waiting to be eaten the way he preferred it, with mustard.

The son of middle-class parents, Dahmer was born in 1960 and grew up in a small town in Ohio. He first killed

▲ *Dahmer was one of the world's most notorious killers*

he'd left off. He picked up a man in a Milwaukee gay bar and invited him to a hotel room where he strangled him. Then he took the body back to his basement apartment in his grandmother's house, dismembered it and left it out, wrapped up in plastic bags, for the garbagemen.

One killing in 1986; two in 1988; one in 1989; four in 1990, eight in 1991 – once Dahmer had his own apartment, the number of his killings began gradually to escalate. But the pattern was more or less exactly the same. He would pick up boys or young men for sex, then drug them and torture them before killing them and dismembering their bodies. Some he would try to turn into zombies while they were still alive, by injecting acid into their brains. But their fate remained the same. . .

At his trial, an attempt was made by Dahmer's defence to claim he was guilty, but insane: a plea possible in Wisconsin. But the jury decided that he was sane when he committed the murders, and he was sentenced to fifteen life sentences, or a total of 936 years. In prison, he was offered special protection, but he refused: he wanted, he said, to be part of the general prison population. He was beaten to death by a black prisoner, another lifer, in November 1994.

at 18 when he invited a hitch-hiker he'd picked up to his parents' house and strangled him after beating him unconscious. Nine years later, after a stint in the army, he began again where

THE MASOCHISTIC MULTIPLE MURDERS

Albert Fish has gone down in history as one of the most horrifying serial killers ever to live in America. He tortured and murdered several victims, including children, over a period of twenty years, and admitted to having molested hundreds more. He was a terrifying, sadistic murderer, but what was almost as disturbing was his extraordinary penchant for masochism: he inflicted all kinds of bizarre tortures on himself, and was always looking for women and children to assist him in these perverted activities.

Yet despite his insane behaviour and his many crimes, police were unable to track him down, and for over five years, his trail went cold. Then, as a result of clever detective work on a letter Fish sent to the family of one of his victims, the chase was on again – and this time, the monster was caught.

Born Hamilton Fish in 1870, Albert was abandoned by his well-to-do family, who had a history of mental illness. He was sent to an orphanage in the Washington DC area, where he was often subjected to corporal punishment.

He later claimed that he acquired a taste for being whipped and beaten as a result of this experience. In 1898 he married, and the couple went on to raise six children. Luckily for them, Fish did not take to beating them, but he did behave strangely, often asking his wife and children to spank him with a paddle which had nails stuck into it. His wife was also somewhat eccentric: she eventually ran off with another man, but then returned with her lover and hid him in the attic, until Fish found out and ordered the pair to leave. After that, Fish constantly looked through personal columns in newspapers: he was not interested in finding a new wife, but wanted a woman to beat him with the paddle. To this end, he wrote many obscene letters to widows and spinsters; but not surprisingly, he received no replies.

THE GREY-HAIRED CANNIBAL

Fish was an itinerant painter, drifting around the country in search of work. On his travels, he began to molest, abduct, torture, and murder children from the poor families that he encountered. He later claimed to have killed dozens of children in this way, committing a murder in every state of America. He said that he tied up his victims and whipped them with a belt studded with nails, to make

▶ *Wisteria Cottage: Fish killed Grace Budd behind the house. He confessed to burying her bones there, which led to a methodical search of the area surrounding the house by police*

their flesh tender for cooking. Then, having killed them, he ate them. He also ate their excrement, and drank their urine and blood. When he was finally caught, he confessed to killing a mentally retarded boy of ten in New York City in 1910; a young black boy in Washington in 1919; a four-year-old, William Gaffney, in 1929; and a five-year-old, Francis McDonnell, in Long Island in 1929. Amazingly, the families of these children – many of whom were at the lowest end of the social scale – found little redress from the law, so for many years Fish was able to continue

the family's summer home, Wisteria Cottage, and yell 'I am Christ' from a nearby hilltop. They also said that whenever there was a full moon, he would howl, and eat large quantities of raw meat. It later emerged that he was also engaged on a full-scale masochistic assault on his own body, poking needles into his genitals and pelvic area, and stuffing lighted balls of cotton wool into his rectum. In retrospect, it seems extraordinary that such a man was able to remain in charge of his children, all the while travelling the countryside freely; but according to many reliable witnesses, Fish had a mild, pleasant manner that made people trust him – or at least dismiss him as a harmless eccentric.

It was not until 1928, when Fish took a victim from a white, working-class New York family, that the authorities really began to take notice of him. At the age of fifty-eight – by this time with a string of child murders and molestations behind him – Fish responded to an advert from a young man wanting work, eighteen-year-old Edward Budd. Edward's father worked as a doorman, and Edward was seeking to improve the family finances by taking on a job. Fish visited the family at their apartment and told them that his name was Frank Howard, a farmer from Long Island. He promised to hire Edward and pay him a good wage for work on the

his sickening activities without much opposition.

During this time, Fish exhibited characteristics of being completely insane, but again, nobody took much notice. His children reported that after their mother left, he would drag them to farm, saying that he would call back the following week. In the meantime, he sent the Budds a telegram, telling them the day he was to arrive.

Impressed with his good manners and his promise of well-paid work for their son, the Budds invited him to lunch. Fish behaved like an affectionate grandfather, handing out treats and dollar bills to the children. He then asked if he could take Edward's younger sister, ten-year-old Grace, to a children's party his married sister was holding at her house that evening. Tragically for all concerned, Grace's parents let her go. The pair left, Grace still wearing the white dress she had put on for church that morning. She was never seen again.

MURDER HUNT

The Budds were surprised when Mr Howard did not return with their daughter that evening, but presumed that the party had carried on late, and that they would return in the morning. When they did not return, Grace's father went to the address Mr Howard had given them, to look for his daughter. He found that there was no such address. He then went to the police station and reported his daughter missing. He was referred to the Missing Persons Bureau and, through this, came into contact with a veteran New York detective known for his tena-

cious police work: William King. King made enquiries, and soon found out that there was no Mr Howard and no farm on Long Island. King ordered the Western Union telegram service to look for the record of the telegram 'Howard' had sent the Budds – 'Howard' had asked for the Budds' copy back when he came to lunch, claiming that it had been wrongly addressed. King also tried to trace a carton of strawberries 'Howard' had given Mrs Budd, and found where he had purchased them. He gained a description of Fish, but from there, the clues petered out.

As it later emerged, Fish had taken Grace up to his summer house, Wisteria Cottage, where he had first of all let her run around, picking flowers. He had then tied her up, tortured, and killed her. He had eaten parts of the body and buried the rest near the house. Over a nine-day period, he had drunk her blood. Then he had gone on his way, continuing to travel the country in search of work, always on the look out to abduct children when the opportunity arose.

However, Fish had met his match with William King. King launched a massive manhunt, and soon the story hit the headlines. Grace's photograph appeared in many newspapers, and several witnesses came forward with new information. But even though all new

◄ *Grace Budd: Fish's ten-year-old victim was an attractive, confident little girl; a fact that probably led Fish to kill her*

leads were followed up, the police came no closer to finding Grace's murderer. There were several false alarms: in one instance, King was alerted to a man named Albert Corthell who was caught trying to abduct a girl from an adoption agency, but when he finally captured Corthell, it was found that he had been in jail at the time of Grace's murder. In another case, a man named Charles Pope was reported by his wife to have kidnapped Grace. Pope was arrested, but Mrs Budd pointed out that he was not the right man. It turned out that Pope's wife had accused him of the kidnapping out of spite, so he was released.

A NEW LEAD?

Meanwhile, there was another case in New York that could have led to finding

▲ Grace Budd's bones lay buried for six years. Meticulous work by detective William King eventually led to Albert Fish, who had been apprehended on a number of occasions for other crimes but proclaimed 'harmless' and released

the murderer, but did not. Albert Fish was arrested for sending obscene letters through the post. This time, Fish was posing as a Hollywood producer, offering to pay women to indulge his taste for sado-masochism. Fish was committed to a mental hospital, and stayed there for a month in 1930, during which time he behaved well. The psychiatrists acknowledged that he had sexual problems, but pronounced him harmless, and released him into the care of his daughter.

Four years later, despite his efforts, King was no nearer solving the case. However, on 11 November 1934, Mrs Budd received a horrible letter through the post, telling her the details of how the writer had cooked and eaten her daughter. Traumatized, Mrs Budd took the letter to King, who set about analyzing it for clues. He noticed right away that the handwriting was the same as the original telegram from Western Union, and concluded that 'Mr Howard' and the letter-writer were one and the same. He then put the letter under a microscope and noticed a tiny set of letters on the back of the envelope; the initials of the New York Private Chauffeur's Benevolent Association.

Detective King paid a visit to the association and began an exhaustive check on all the people who worked there, without much luck: there was no one who fitted the murderer's description. However, while he was there, one of the drivers paid him a visit to tell him that he might have left some of the association's stationery at a room he had used some time ago, in a boarding house on 52nd Street. King went there and spoke to the landlady, who told him that a man named Albert Fish, who fitted the murderer's description, had recently left, but that he still received a monthly payment there from one of his sons. From time to time, Fish would drop by to pick up his mail.

Encouraged, King took a room in the boarding house, from where he could see the comings and goings of visitors. One day, while he was at work, he received a call from the landlady telling him that Fish was in the building. King rushed to the scene, and found the grey-haired old man quietly sipping tea with his landlady. He asked Fish to come to the police station for questioning, whereupon Fish suddenly attacked him with a razor. Luckily, King was used to dealing with violent criminals, and soon had Fish handcuffed. He then found Fish's pockets full of knives and razors, and was sure that he had his man.

THE CASE IS SOLVED

At the station, Fish began to confess his crimes, grinning insanely as he described Grace's murder in the most lurid detail. Detectives were sent to Wisteria Cottage and found that Fish was telling the truth: the remains of Grace's body were indeed buried near the house. And Grace was not Fish's only victim: Fish went on to describe other child murders he had committed since 1910. Police were doubly horrified to find that Fish had been arrested several times since Grace's murder, for relatively minor offences such as sending obscene material through the post, but that he had been set free every time.

A team of psychiatrists was then brought in to study Fish, who appeared to enjoy the experience. He boasted

readily of his many perversions and activities. At first the medical men found it difficult to believe him as the stories seemed so bizarre. In an attempt to get at the truth, Fish was X-rayed and his pelvis was found to be full of needles. He was declared insane.

However, when he was brought to trial, the jury ignored insanity as a defence, and found him guilty of the murder of Grace Budd. The judge sentenced him to death by the electric chair.

Fish went readily to his death, claiming that he was looking forward to being electrocuted, and that it would give him 'the supreme thrill of his life'. When he was brought to the chair, he even helped attendants strap him in to it.

A six-year manhunt for one of the most vicious killers of all time, Albert Fish – otherwise known as 'The Moon Maniac', 'The Gray Man', and 'The Brooklyn Vampire' – came to a satisfying end. Even though the case went cold for nearly six years, King never gave up hope: and, ultimately, his determination to bring the killer to justice, together with his meticulous attention to detail, paid off handsomely.

◀ *Albert Fish in custody at the psychiatric unit of Grasslands Hospital, New York, where he had a further two needles extracted from his body, bringing the total to twenty-nine*

THE MUMMY IN THE CUPBOARD

It sounds like a scene from Psycho, but the case of the mummified corpse kept in a cupboard in a Welsh boarding house is one of the most bizarre true-crime cases on record. And the most extraordinary aspect is that the alleged murderer was not a psychopathic serial killer but the victim's middle-aged landlady, who lived with the grisly secret for 20 years before dissension among the experts prevented her conviction for murder.

The mummified remains were accidentally uncovered in April 1960, when the landlady's son broke into the locked cupboard on a landing to clear out what he believed were a former tenant's belongings. When his mother, Mrs Sarah Harvey, returned from a short stay in hospital she found the cupboard bare and police officers waiting to interview her. At first Mrs Harvey struck the police as a harmless old lady as she told them her lodger, Mrs Frances Knight, had moved out in April 1945 about the same time that a couple had asked her to store some of their personal belongings, then left taking the cupboard key with them.

The ailing, enfeebled figure elicited the sympathy of detectives who dutifully followed up the false leads she had given them, but when neither Mrs Knight nor the fictitious couple could be traced, the police ordered an autopsy to determine the identity of the corpse. However, it wasn't as simple as they hoped. Although the body was in a remarkable state of preservation thanks to a constant stream

▲ *65-year-old grand-mother Sarah Harvey was not all she seemed*

of warm, dry air which had retarded decomposition, the pathologist was unable to confirm it was the body of Mrs Knight. Dental records were of no use as the victim had false teeth and these had disappeared along with a wedding ring which might have proved identity. All that could be said with certainty was that the body was that of a white female aged between 40 and 60, who had been 163cm (5ft 4in) tall, right-handed and walked with a limp. Moreover, she shared the same blood group as members of Mrs Knight's family.

AN ODD STORY

It was clearly the mummy of Mrs Knight, but without a positive identification it could not be stated as a fact in a court of law. Fortunately, Mrs Harvey broke down under questioning and admitted that she had concealed the body in a state of panic. But what reason could she have had for fearing anyone would have queried her version of events if Mrs Knight had died of natural causes as she claimed?

Harvey alleged that Mrs Knight had collapsed in her room on the day she died. Unable to lift her onto the bed, Harvey left her lodger on the floor. Yet when had she returned to find her lodger had died, she had miraculously found the strength to drag the body into the hall and stuff it into the cupboard along with a mattress to soak up the seeping body fluids.

However, she couldn't explain the stocking that had been tied around the neck of the corpse with a knot so tight that it had left a groove around the throat and an impression on the thyroid cartilage.

It appeared that Mrs Knight had been strangled, yet at the trial various forensic specialists disagreed as to the manner of death, with one even suggesting that she might have hanged herself and another that there was no evidence that the stocking had been tight enough to act as a ligature. The impressions on the neck, he argued, might have been caused by swelling in the neck post-mortem. Yet even if Mrs Knight had taken her own life, there would have been no reason for Mrs Harvey to conceal her body and in so doing bring suspicion upon herself.

With dissension among the experts, the judge was forced to direct the jury to find Mrs Harvey not guilty of murder. In the end she was convicted of fraud and sentenced to 15 months for having deceived Mrs Knight's solicitors into believing that the old lady was still alive so that she could draw her £2 maintenance payments every week for almost 20 years.

MURDER IN BELLE HAVEN

Sometimes murder investigations lead nowhere. The reasons are many: firstly, a lack of leads, of clues that could tell the police something about who might possibly have committed the crime. Secondly, incompetence: leads that are not followed up, clues that are missed. Thirdly and perhaps most disturbing of all, a lack of will: a fear of turning up evidence that could compromise those in high places.

In the case of Martha Moxley, a girl of fifteen who was brutally beaten to death in 1975, all these factors may have come into play. Whatever the truth of the matter, a few years after Martha's murder the case went completely cold. But over two decades later, the publication of a best-selling novel based on the murder reignited interest in the case. As a result, in 2002, twenty-seven years after Martha Moxley's brutal murder, the culprit was brought to trial, and convicted.

'HARMLESS PRANKS'

Martha Moxley was born in 1960 in San Francisco, California. Her family were prosperous, middle-class people who were able to offer their daughter all the privileges of a stable, well-to-do family life. In 1974, the family moved to the neighbourhood of Belle Haven, a gated community in Greenwich, Connecticut. With its big houses and immaculately kept lawns, Belle Haven seemed the perfect place to raise a family. It was, above all, safe. But, as it turned out, the move was a fateful one: Greenwich proved to be anything but safe for Martha. A year after the family moved to Belle Haven, Martha Moxley was dead.

On the night of 30 October 1975, Martha set out with her friends to have some fun. The night before Halloween was known in the area as 'mischief night', when youngsters would amuse themselves by throwing eggs, spraying shaving cream, and trailing toilet paper around. These pranks were sometimes a nuisance, but usually harmless enough. However, that evening Martha and her girlfriends stopped at the house of the Skakel family to see their friends, brothers Tommy and Michael.

The Skakels were well known in the area. They were related to the Kennedy family through Ethel Kennedy, the wife of Robert F. Kennedy and were extremely wealthy. However, despite their social connections and money,

▶ *A photo of Martha with her father, taken when she was thirteen. Her killer's guilt may have been protected by his family's wealth and status*

there were serious problems in the family. The boys' mother, Anne Skakel, had died of cancer two years earlier, leaving her husband Rushton in charge of the household. After his wife's death, Rushton had taken to drinking excessively, and their teenage children had been allowed to run riot. They were a constant source of worry to the neighbours, and behaved in a rude, unruly, and undisciplined way. However, because of their class position, the bad behaviour of the young Skakels was largely tolerated – with dire consequences, as it turned out.

BEATEN WITH A SIX-IRON

Martha's mother became worried when her daughter did not return that night. She phoned Martha's father, who was out of town, as well as her neighbours and friends. Finally, she phoned the police, who although they drove around the area looking for her daughter, were unable to locate Martha. In the morning, the terrible truth was revealed. Martha's body was found under a tree not far from her house, beaten to death with a six-iron golf club. During the assault, the shaft had broken, and a piece of it had been used to stab her through the neck. Her jeans and underclothes had been pulled down, but she did not appear to have

been sexually assaulted. When police took the golf club for analysis, they found that it was an expensive one, part of a set used by Anne Skakel.

There was other evidence that pointed to the Skakel boys. Martha's girlfriends reported seeing Tommy with Martha before they left for home that night. Looking for clues in Martha's diary, Martha's mother told police that her daughter had written about Tommy's sexual advances towards her, and how she had tried to repel them. Although the police searched the Skakel home, it was only a cursory visit. The police never issued a search warrant, which would have enabled them to do a proper search of the house without the owner's permission. Later, commentators criticized the police's conduct, claiming that Rushton Skakel's high-up connections and political influence had stopped them from going further.

Instead, the police followed up leads on other suspects, such as a tutor living with the Skakel family, a neighbour who lived close by the Moxleys; and several drifters who had been near the area on the night of the murder. However, these clues led nowhere, and by the 1980s, the investigation into Martha Moxley's murder had come to a grinding halt. In Belle Haven, it became an unmentionable subject: perhaps because of the Skakel influence, or perhaps because the wealthy inhabitants of this seemingly peaceful, well-tended residential area could not bear to remember that they were not, as they thought, safe from danger.

TEENAGE ALCOHOLICS

It was not until another Kennedy – William Kennedy Smith – became the centre of another drama that memories about Martha Moxley were jogged. In a high- profile case that attracted a great deal of media attention, Smith was accused of raping a woman in Palm Beach, Florida. He was acquitted, but rumours began to circulate that he knew something about the Moxley murder. In 1991 an article about the Moxley case, written by journalist Len Levitt, appeared in a local newspaper. Two years later, a novel by Dominick Dunne entitled A Season in Purgatory appeared, which was based on Martha's murder. The novel proved to be a best-seller. The author went on to meet Mark Fuhrman, whose notorious role in the O.J. Simpson case received enormous publicity. Fuhrman decided to look further into the Moxley case and, in 1998, published Murder in Greenwich. In it, he named Michael Skakel as the prime suspect.

Opinions as to why the murder had not been solved years before varied. Some felt that the wealth and influence of the Skakel family had prevented the investigation from going further, while others pointed to police inexperience as the cause. After all, Greenwich was not a place where murder happened very frequently – at the time of Martha's murder, there had not been a murder in the area for thirty years. However, all agreed that now, the case had to be given a boost, and accordingly, in May 1998, a request for a grand jury investigation was granted.

A FIT OF JEALOUSY

Under this new initiative, over fifty witnesses were called in, some of them pupils and staff of a rehabilitation programme Michael Skakel had taken part in at Elan School in Maine. He had apparently confessed to Martha's murder during that time. Other witnesses, such as the tutor in the Skakel household at the time of the murder, talked about Michael's disturbed behaviour. He was reported, on one occasion, to have killed a squirrel when out golfing, and pinned it, crucifix-like, over a hole. By his own admission, he had been an alcoholic from his early teens, and had suffered abuse from his father. He had been devastated by his mother's death, and had felt that she was the only person holding together the dysfunctional Skakel family.

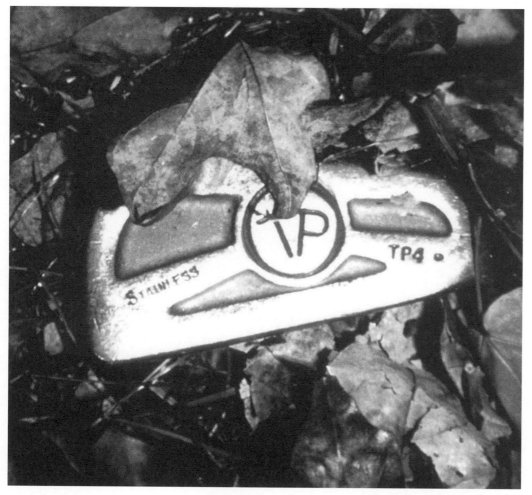

◄ *The head of the golf club prosecutors contended was used to kill Martha Moxley. It was part of a set owned by her killer's mother*

As it emerged, from an early age both Michael and his older brother, Tommy, had been extremely disturbed, difficult children. In all, there were seven Skakel children, and there were numerous family problems throughout their childhood. Rushton Skakel had left his children to their own devices, and the older ones among them regularly drank and smoked pot. On the night of Martha's murder, Tommy and Michael had been drinking heavily in front of their younger brothers and sisters, and their tutor Kenneth Littleton. Martha and her friends had visited, and she and Tommy had begun to make amorous advances towards each other.

What also transpired was that, after the murder, police initially investigated Tommy as a suspect. He took two lie detector tests, one of which he failed, and one of which he passed. However, after

▶ *Michael Skakel enters court in Norwalk, Connecticut. The Connecticut Supreme Court upheld his murder conviction of 2002. He is serving 20 years to life in prison*

this, his father Rushton refused to make Tommy available for further investigation. The fact that the police accepted this, and ceased their enquiry, had attracted criticism at the time. However, it later became clear that the police were following up the wrong suspect. It was Michael, not Tommy, who killed Martha, in a fit of jealousy because she appeared to prefer his older brother.

The results of the grand jury investigation were made public on 19 January 2000. Skakel was then arrested on a charge of murder, and brought to trial two years later, on 4 May 2002.

The jury took a total of four days to reach a verdict, but when they did they found Michael Skakel guilty of murder. He was sentenced to a term of life imprisonment.

THE MURDER OF THE HEIRESS

The case of Helen Brach, the heiress who mysteriously disappeared in 1975, is one of the most surprising in United States legal history. With no witnesses, no body, and no leads for police to follow up, the investigation went cold shortly after her death — even though, clearly, someone had killed her for her money.

Then, in a surprise twist, the case was warmed up many years later, and the man responsible for her murder finally brought to justice. Chillingly, however, it was the fact that the heiress left so much money sitting in the bank, rather than that she herself was missed, that had prompted a re-investigation of the case.

THE HAT-CHECK GIRL AND THE MILLIONAIRE

Helen Brach was born Helen Vorhees, and came from a working-class Midwestern family in Ohio. She lived most of her life in workaday circumstances, without much money and was working as a hat-check girl when she met her millionaire husband-to-be, Frank Brach. Frank was the son of Emil Brach, an immigrant who had come up with a new method for mak-

ing caramel, and had founded a massively successful candy empire, E.J. Brach and Sons. His son Frank proved an astute businessman, and subsequently had made millions for the company since then.

When Frank and Helen met, Frank was in the midst of a messy divorce. Not long after he divorced, he and Helen were married. The couple had no children — Helen was forty by the time she married, for the second time, and had no children by her first brief marriage. When Frank retired, the Brachs divided their time between their home in Chicago and a rented property in Palm Beach, Florida. Helen was generous with her new-found wealth, particularly with respect to her family, and bought her mother and brother new houses to live in. However, she did not flaunt her money or parade it in high society, as many other women in the same position would have done. In many ways, she remained a down-to-earth Midwesterner, who was careful not to spend too much on unnecessary fripperies.

Helen and Frank Brach lived comfortably, and uneventfully, for twenty years, until Frank died in 1970, at the age of seventy-nine. This left Helen with a fortune of twenty million dollars. Typically, she continued to live quietly, keeping in touch with her friends and family by phone, and caring for her pet animals. Her two dogs, named Candy and Sugar, became devoted companions, and she went to great lengths to make sure that they were properly looked after. In a rare show of extravagance, when the dogs died, she had them buried in an expensive pink marble grave. Her love of animals also led her to give money to charities, such as the Chicago Zoo.

THE SHADY HORSE DEALER

Although not interested in the glitzy parties of Chicago's rich elite, Helen did take an interest in racing, and after Frank died, expressed a wish to own some horses. She got to know Richard Bailey, the owner of a stables and country club. He was a charming, good-looking man but he had a reputation for shady dealing. He also had a reputation as a ladies' man of the worst kind: he would wine and dine rich old women, particularly widows, and extract money from them by asking them to buy his horses, most of which cost considerably less than he sold them for. He also often asked the women for a temporary loan which he never paid back. He stopped at nothing to gain their confidence: he would pretend to fall in love with them, have sex with them, even propose marriage, although he already had a wife. He made a specialty of choosing women

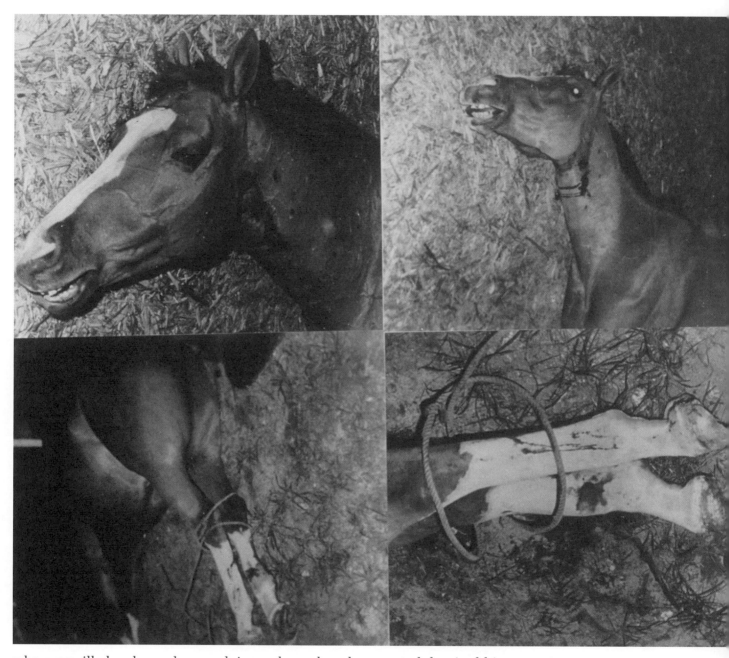

who were ill, lonely, and even dying. There were more than a few elderly ladies who were smitten by his charms, so he made a good living, but those who knew how he operated despised him.

When Richard Bailey met Helen Brach, he must have thought he had hit pay dirt. Brach was considerably richer

▲ *Some of the horses badly mistreated in the insurance fraud involving Richard Bailey*

than any of his previous conquests, and obviously lonely. She enjoyed his company, and entrusted him with choosing her new racehorses for her. He began by selling her three horses, all of which were worth much less than she paid for them. However, with Brach, it seems, he bit off more than he could chew. She was not stupid, and although she lived in a very private way, her fortune made her a powerful, well-known figure in Chicago society. Once she realized that Bailey was conning her, she threatened to expose his actions and report him to the police. Exactly what passed between them then, no one will ever know, but the outcome was that Bailey plotted to have her murdered.

THE HEIRESS VANISHES

On 17 February 1977, Helen Brach went for a check-up at the Mayo Clinic, Rochester, Minnesota. This was the last time a reliable witness saw her alive. Then, according to her houseman, John Matlick, she flew to O'Hare Airport, where he picked her up. However, there is no record of her buying a plane ticket for the flight. For the next few days, while she prepared to go to Florida, no one heard from her, which was unusual for a woman who liked to chat daily to friends and family on the phone. Matlick then claims that he drove her to

the airport for her flight to Florida, but that she did not have any luggage or a flight reservation, which again did not tally with the normal habits of this well-organized woman. Two weeks later, not having heard any more from her, Matlick reported her missing. So did another person – her brother, Charles Vorhees.

Suspicion immediately fell on Matlick and Vorhees, both of whom stood to gain from Brach's will. The pair admitted that they had destroyed her diary, which might have yielded valuable information about the days leading up to her disappearance, but said that she had asked them to do this should anything ever happen to her. Both their stories appeared questionable, but the police did not manage to find enough evidence to charge either of them, and dropped the case. Without a body, or any concrete information that could lead to finding out what had happened, the investigation began to dry up. Nobody seemed to care very much what had happened to Helen Brach, and her disappearance was soon forgotten. Yet her money – of course – was not, and it was the investigation into her accounts that finally brought the truth to light.

Everett Moore, Helen Brach's accountant, was a trustworthy man with an intimate knowledge of his client's day-

▶ A more vivacious look: Helen Brach in her younger years was quiet, yet no push-over. When she realized what Richard Bailey was doing, she threatened to expose him. Instead, he had her killed

to-day spending habits. He wanted to administrate Helen's estate, but the Continental Illinois Bank also felt it had a claim to this position. In the end, the court appointed an outside guardian, John Menk, to preside over the investigation. However, Menk did not get very far: Vorhees and Bailey both refused to talk, and since this was not a criminal investigation, there was no way that Menk could make them.

A LUCKY BREAK

In 1984, almost ten years after her disappearance, Helen Brach was declared dead. Her estate was divided between the Helen Brach Foundation, Charles Vorhees and John Matlick. A meticulous accounting process began, presided over by Moore, and it was found that Matlick had embezzled thousands of dollars out of the estate after Brach had disappeared. In September 1993, Matlick was ordered to pay the estate back. Further investigations into the estate's accounts showed that Bailey had also defrauded Brach, and this time, once his name came up, the law did not let him go.

In 1989, an investigation had begun into the horse-racing business in Chicago, and in the process, Richard Bailey's name had come up. His frauds over selling the

horses to Helen Brach soon became known to the investigators, and the case was taken up by Assistant US Attorney Steven Miller. His approach, he announced, was to 'follow the money and solve the murder'. By a lucky break, he and his team found a veterinarian, Dr Ross Hugi, who had had dealings with Richard Bailey, helping him in his scams. Through Hugi, they found out about an infamous Chicago family, known as 'The Jayne Gang', who had been running organized crime in the horse business since the 1930s. Their leader was Silas Jayne, who was widely feared throughout the business as a man who would stop at nothing, including murder – he had even been responsible for the killing of his own brother. And one of Jayne's associates turned out to be none other than Helen Brach's erstwhile friend and horse dealer: Richard Bailey.

THE RIGHT MAN BROUGHT TO JUSTICE

This was an extraordinary twist to the Brach case that no one could have foreseen. Quite separately, Bailey's name had come up in another investigation. For the next five years, Miller and his team worked day and night to make the evidence against Bailey stick in the Brach case. Finally, in 1994, they were able to bring Bailey to court, charged with soliciting the murder of Helen Brach.

Initially, Bailey did not appear unduly troubled by the charge, since there was so little concrete evidence in the case against him. But gradually, as the list of elderly women whom he had defrauded was read out in court, his innocence began to appear more and more questionable. Witnesses also took the stand to testify that he was a violent person, as well as a con man.

Miller then built a case to show that Bailey had had a strong motive for killing Brach, because she – unlike all the others – had stood up to him and threatened to report his crimes to the police so that he would be put behind bars for the rest of his life.

And that, in the end, was exactly what happened. Bailey was convicted, and is currently serving his sentence in prison. Not only this, but in the process, a massive insurance fraud in the horse business was uncovered, and a string of crimes dating back to 1955, including homicide and arson, were solved.

Thus it was that a case that went cold for almost twenty years finally resulted in the conviction of a notorious, cold-blooded killer and swindler who mistakenly thought that he could get away with murder.

MURDER ON THE MOORS

Ian Brady and Myra Hindley did everything they could to co-opt Hindley's seventeen-year-old brother -in-law David Smith. For he was promising raw material: he'd been in trouble with the law from the age of 11 and he liked to drink. So they fed him booze and the books of the Marquis de Sade. They took him out onto the moors for target-practice shooting; and Brady continually dropped hints to him there: about murder, and the photography and burial of bodies.

Then, in October 1965, they decided finally to pull him in. The twenty-three-year-old Hindley used a pretext to get Smith late at night to the house where she and Brady lived on a public-housing estate in Manchester; and then she pushed him into the living room as soon

◀
Brady and Hindley –
the Moors Murderers

as she heard Brady starting to attack Edward Evans, a young man they'd picked up earlier in the evening, with an axe. Smith, confused by drink, was a terrified witness to his eventual murder. But Brady and Hindley wanted more. So they passed him the axe, and told him that, with his fingerprints now on it, he was far too involved to be able to retreat. He was forced to help in trussing up the body and cleaning the blood from the floor, furniture and walls.

By the time he left, Smith'd been persuaded to bring round a pram the next day to move the body to Brady's car. But when he went home, he told his horrified wife what had happened; and the next day, shaking with fear, and armed with a knife and a screwdriver, he went to a telephone box to call the police.

The young victim's body was still in the house; and first Brady, then Hindley were arrested. But then, little by little, as the police searched both the house and Brady's car, the full extent of their murderous exploits emerged. For in the house was a collection of books on Nazism, sadism and torture – as well as dozens of photographs of Brady and Hindley on the moors. Three sheets of paper discovered in the car seemed to contain instructions about how to bury a body; and in a notebook kept by Brady, amid a list of seemingly random

and made-up names, there was one that stood out: that of John Kilbride. Kilbride was a schoolboy who'd disappeared two years before; and the police became convinced that Brady and Hindley had killed the twelve-year-old and buried him on the moors.

Worse, though, was to come. For, while the police were digging up the moors, looking for Kilbride's body, a careful search of the books in the house produced a hidden left-luggage ticket for two suitcases which – once retrieved – were found to contain ammunition, coshes, pornographic books, photographs and a number of tapes. One collection of photographs proved to be pornographic pictures of a gagged, naked child: of ten-year-old Leslie Ann Downey, who'd disappeared thirteen months after Kilbride. One of the tapes contained, buried amongst Christmas music, a live sixteen-minute recording of her rape, torture and murder.

The bodies of both Kilbride and Leslie Ann Downey were found on the moors; and the tape was played, to the horror of all those present – indeed of the entire country – at the subsequent trial of Brady and Hindley. Both pleaded not guilty. They had given the police no co-operation at all. But there could be no doubt of their guilt; and the strong suspicion remains that they

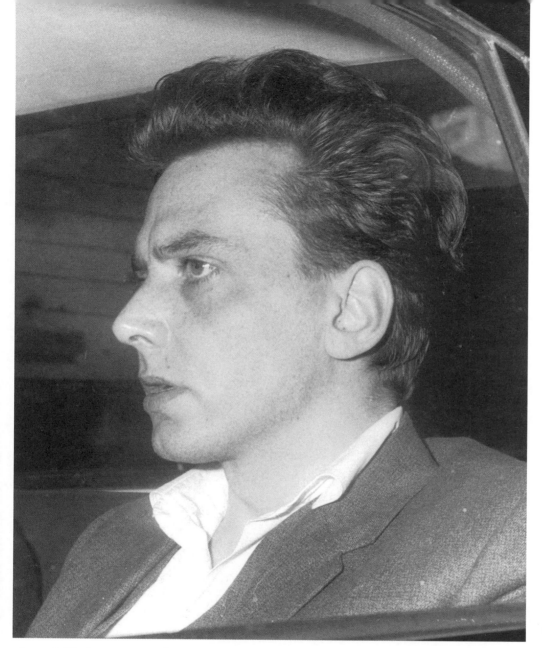

also killed two other children, Pauline Reade and Keith Bennett, who disappeared in 1963 and 1964 respectively.

For the murders of Edward Evans, John Kilbride and Leslie Ann Downey, Ian Brady was given three life sentences; Myra Hindley two, with an extra seven years for 'receiving, comforting and harbouring.' Later denied both appeal and release, she died in prison in late-2002. Brady – easily the more sinister figure of the two – is still alive behind bars.

A MURDERED TEENAGER

On the evening of 21 March 1962 Mr and Mrs Miller returned home to find that their 15-year-old daughter Marilyn had disappeared without a trace. Police searched the area and within hours found the girl's body face down in a reservoir behind the house. They also found footprints and tyre tracks on the dirt road nearby, together with a pair of discarded workman's gloves and a belt. No one in the neighbourhood had seen or heard anything unusual, although one of Marilyn's school friends remembered seeing a black and turquoise 1953 model Plymouth parked near the Miller house earlier that night.

The car was later found abandoned and inside was a pair of boots which matched the footprints on the dirt road. The boots were a lucky break for the detectives because they had been repaired using the heel from another pair of boots, which meant they produced a unique set of prints. Even better, the tyre was found to have a flaw which created highly distinctive tracks that matched the impressions found at the scene.

All the police had to do was trace the owner of the vehicle and they would have an open-and-shut case. Or so they thought.

The vehicle was registered to a local dairy worker, Booker T. Hillery Jnr, who had recently been released from prison where he had been serving time for rape. He was immediately arrested and charged with murder. During the course of the investigation the gloves were also identified as belonging to Hillery, which seemed to tie up the case for the prosecution and leave no room for reasonable doubt.

Hillery was convicted and sentenced to death. But the authorities had reckoned without Hillery's dogged determination to forestall the inevitable and an ironic twist of fate.

Through a succession of appeals Hillery managed to keep delaying the execution until 1974 when the US Supreme Court decided to abolish the death penalty. It was later reinstated but by then it was too late: Hillery's life sentence could not be revoked. Clearly Hillery was a shrewd and cunning killer whose sense of self-preservation outweighed any feelings of remorse.

THE RETRIAL
In 1978, not content with escaping the electric chair, Hillery successfully filed

◀ Booker T. Hillery, right,
is led into Kings County
courtroom where he was
convicted of the murder of
15-year-old Marilyn Miller

for a retrial on the grounds that African-Americans had been deliberately excluded from serving on the Grand Jury in Kings County in 1962. It was a clever ploy because if Hillery could force a retrial he might be able to sow sufficient doubt to secure his release. Time had strengthened his hand. Of the original 24 witnesses, 21 were dead, and the forensic evidence could be disputed on the grounds that the tyre and boot tracks only proved that Hillery was in the vicinity of the Miller house. There was no irrefutable proof that he was actually inside their home. The date for a second trail was set and prosecutors had to present a convincing case or be prepared to drop the charge and see Hillery walk free — perhaps even sue the state for wrongful imprisonment. It was then that they had a lucky break.

But just before the case came to court, investigators discovered that a resourceful detective had asked Marilyn's mother to hoover her daughter's bedroom on the night of the murder in case there were microscopic trace elements which could prove vital in the case. These had miraculously survived in the police archive, and now this bag of dust and dirt was put under the microscope. It was found to contain tiny blue spherical paint particles of the kind produced by a spray can. Normally, when paint is sprayed on a flat surface, the particles flatten out, but these were round because they had been sprayed onto fabric. In fact, minute traces of cotton could be seen sticking to the paint.

On a hunch, detectives retrieved Hillery's clothes from the evidence store and found matching blue paint particles on his clothes that placed him at the scene on the night of the murder. They traced the paint to the interior of Hillery's car, which he had sprayed with this distinctive Prussian Blue pigment. Evidently minute particles had fallen onto him while he was driving and some of these were shaken off in his struggle with Marilyn.

The irony is that Hillery had prevented the county from selling his car after the first trial in 1962 by threatening to sue them for disposing of his property, so it was still impounded 24 years later, a time capsule of perfectly preserved forensic evidence.

Twenty-five-year-old evidence had finally nailed a careless killer, and Hillery's bull-headed belligerence cost him another 25 years to life behind bars with no prospect of parole.

Richard Ramirez, the 'Night Stalker', was a nightmare made flesh: the bogeyman who slips in through the windows in the middle of the night to rob, rape and murder. Throughout the summer of 1985 he had the people of Los Angeles living in terror, as he killed more than a dozen times, before a mixture of good police work and luck finally saw him captured.

FAMILY VALUES

Ramirez was born on 28 February 1960 in El Paso, the city that sits right on the Mexican border of west Texas. He was the youngest of seven children of Mexican immigrants Julian and Mercedes Ramirez. Julian Ramirez was a bad-tempered, physically abusive father. Richard became an increasingly disaffected loner at school, and in his teens started to spend time with his uncle Mike (Miguel).

Mike had served in Vietnam and he loved to tell his nephew about his exploits – in particular about all the women he had raped there. He allegedly showed Richard photos of his war crimes, including ones that pictured him first raping a Vietnamese girl and then displaying her decapitated head. Worse still, fifteen-year-old Richard was present when Mike shot his wife in the face, killing her.

This clearly had a pivotal influence on Ramirez' life. He dropped out of school aged seventeen and devoted himself to smoking huge quantities of marijuana, listening to heavy metal music and getting involved in petty crime.

FIRST MURDER

Around the turn of the decade he moved from Texas, first to San Francisco and then to Los Angeles. There he switched his drug of choice from marijuana to cocaine, began to listen obsessively to the music of AC/DC – particularly a song called The Night Prowler – and took to stealing cars to make a living. Over the next year he served two brief sentences for car theft. After he came out of prison the second time, he committed his first murder.

The victim was a 79-year-old woman named Jennie Vicow. On 28 June 1984, she was sleeping in her suburban Los Angeles apartment when Ramirez broke in. He sexually assaulted her, stabbed her to death and stole her jewellery.

It was nine months before he killed again. This time, he attacked a young woman named Maria Hernandez as she was entering her apartment. He had come

▲ *Ramirez drew a pentagram on his hand and repeatedly flashed it at press photographers during his trial*

Ramirez found another victim, Tsa Lian Yu, whom he dragged from her car in the Monterey Park area and shot several times. She died the following day.

Just three days later Ramirez struck again – this time sexually abusing, but not killing, an eight-year-old girl. A week later, he murdered a couple, Vincent and Maxine Zazzara.

Six weeks later, on 14 May 1985, Ramirez attacked another couple. He began by shooting 65-year-old William Doi in the head, then beat and raped his wife. However, Doi was strong enough to make it to the phone and dial the emergency number before he died, an action that may well have saved his wife's life.

Two weeks later, Ramirez varied his routine a little. His next victim was 42-year-old Carol Kyle, whom he raped after gagging her eleven-year-old son and shutting him in a cupboard. Both of them were allowed to live, however, and Carol Kyle was able to give the police a good description of her attacker.

Ramirez' blood lust was now reaching fever pitch. He struck again the next day, attacking two sisters in their eighties, Mabel Bell and Florence Lang.

He beat them with a hammer, then drew pentagrams on Bell's body and elsewhere in their apartment. They were found the following day: Mabel was dead,

armed with a gun and used it to shoot Hernandez but, miraculously, the bullet was deflected by her keys and she was simply knocked down. She then played dead as he kicked her prone body. Clearly not yet satisfied, Ramirez then went into the apartment where he found her roommate, Dayle Okazaki, and shot her dead.

FRENZY

Even this murder failed to satisfy his perverse craving and that same evening

but Florence had survived her injuries.

His next victim, three weeks later, was 29-year-old Patty Higgins, whose throat he cut. Another ten days brought another four attacks: two older victims died, while two younger women survived.

Then the final rampage began. In the course of one terrible night he killed three victims and left two more traumatized. The first two victims were a couple in their sixties, Max and Lela Kneiding, who he shot dead. That same evening he broke into a house in the Sun Valley area, where he shot dead Chainarong Khovanath as he slept, before raping and beating his wife Somkind, and then tying her up while he raped her eight-year-old son.

NIGHT STALKER

At this stage police were still loathe to admit that a serial killer was on the loose. However, when, on 6 August, Ramirez shot a couple in their home, non-fatally, then followed up two days later by attacking another couple, this time killing the husband and raping the wife, it was clear that they had to act.

A Night Stalker task force was set up, and the press was told about this new menace to the community. Ramirez responded by leaving town briefly, heading back to San Francisco, where he attacked his next victims, the improbably named Peter Pan and his wife, once again killing the man and raping his wife, and, once again leaving satanic symbols there.

He then went to Los Angeles and, in the last week of August, struck for the last time. The man, 29-year-old William Carns, survived, despite being shot three times. His partner Renata Gunther, who had been raped identified the car he drove away in, a Toyota station wagon. Another local resident had taken down the registration number.

Soon afterwards, the police found the car abandoned; luck was on their side and they managed to find a fingerprint left on the vehicle. There was an instant match: the fingerprint identified petty criminal Richard Ramirez.

The next day Ramirez' photo was on the front page of every newspaper in Los Angeles. Ramirez only discovered this himself when he walked into a drugstore in east LA and saw the customers staring at him. He was pounced on and the police arrived only just in time to save him from being lynched.

At trial Ramirez told the court 'You maggots make me sick. I am beyond good and evil.' He was found guilty of thirteen counts of murder and sentenced to death. On being told of the verdict, he said: 'Big deal. Death always went with the territory. See you in Disneyland.' He remains on death row.

ON THE RUN

Bonnie Parker and Clyde Barrow were among the first celebrity criminals of the twentieth century. During the years of the Great Depression in the 1930s, they shocked America with a series of murders, kidnaps, bank robberies and hold-ups, leaving a trail of devastation wherever they went. The pair are known to have committed at least thirteen murders during their career. Barrow was renowned as a cold-blooded killer, though some allege that Parker herself was not, and that she left her lover to do the dirty work. However, the truth of the matter will probably never be known, because Bonnie and Clyde weren't taken alive. After being hotly pursued by police for several years, they finally died in an ambush when their car was pumped full of bullets.

Bonnie Parker was born in Rowena, Texas, in 1910. At sixteen, she married a man named Ray Thornton. She was madly in love with Thornton and had two intertwined hearts, with their names, tattooed on the inside of her thigh. However, shortly after they were married, Thornton received a long prison sentence for murder. With her husband incarcerated for the foreseeable future, Parker was forced to take a waitressing job and wait for him. She did not wait very long.

Clyde Barrow was a year older than Bonnie, and had grown up on a farm in

▼ *Bonnie and Clyde's days were numbered as soon as they became killers in earnest. In 1934 they shot two highway patrolmen, seemingly in cold blood*

◀ *Publicity-loving Bonnie and Clyde posing with the tools of their trade – guns and a fast getaway car*

Telico, Texas. He was one of many children in a large, poverty-stricken family. In 1926, he was arrested for car theft, but continued his life of crime, committing a string of robberies in the Dallas area. Four years later, by now a hardened criminal, he met Bonnie. However, not long after their meeting, he was jailed. He made an escape, helped by Bonnie, but was apprehended after only a week, and remained in jail for the following two years.

▶ *A glamorous Bonnie – she had an addiction to bad men and fast living that was to prove her downfall*

PARTNERS IN CRIME

When Clyde got out of jail, he and Bonnie teamed up and stole a car in Texas. A chase ensued, and this time it was Bonnie who was arrested and sent to jail. Clyde waited for her – her sentence was only a few months – and when she was released, the pair began their career of crime in earnest. They formed a group of like-minded criminals around them, first travelling with a young gunman named Raymond Hamilton, who then dropped out and was replaced by a man called William Daniel Jones. The gang also included Clyde's brother Ivan, known as Buck, and Buck's wife Blanche. The group became known as the Barrow Gang, and became notorious for a series of murders, kidnaps, armed robberies, burglaries and car thefts around the country.

By 1933, police were hot on the trail of the gang, having

stumbled across a piece of evidence that told them who the culprits were. The Bureau of Investigation, which later became the FBI, had been notified of a Ford automobile stolen in Illinois and abandoned at Pawhuska, Florida. A search of the car revealed a medicine bottle and, when special agents called at the drugstore where it was bought, the prescription was found to have been filled in by a relative of Clyde Barrow. After further investigation, it became clear that the occupants of the stolen car had been Bonnie, Clyde and Clyde's brother. A warrant was issued for their arrest, and the hunt began in earnest.

HUNTING DOWN THE KILLERS

On 29 July 1933, police caught up with the outlaws in Iowa. During the subsequent shoot-out, Buck was killed and Blanche was arrested. A few months later, William Daniel Jones was captured, this time in Houston, Texas. Undeterred, Bonnie and Clyde carried on by themselves. By this time, they were well known to the public. The Barrow Gang's cavalier attitude towards killing their victims had struck fear into the hearts of people, and their crimes had been reported in the most sensational terms in the national press.

Bonnie and Clyde's flamboyant reputation had also been enhanced by

▲ *Clyde Barrow – a sharp-suited sharp shooter*

various publicity stunts. The Ford Motor Company had advertised their automobiles with a letter signed 'Clyde Champion Barrow', alleged to have been

▲ *Final ride – the bullet-riddled car of Bonnie and Clyde*

written by the gangster. In it, Barrow praised Ford cars as 'dandy'. In addition, Bonnie had had a poem called 'The Story of Bonnie and Clyde' published in several newspapers, showing her to be quite a talented wordsmith.

On 22 November 1933, the police set a trap for the couple in Grand Prairie,

Texas. However, Bonnie and Clyde managed to escape, holding up and stealing a passing car. They later abandoned it in Oklahoma. The following year, in January, they helped five prisoners make a daring escape from a jail in Waldo, Texas. During the escape, two prison guards were shot.

COLD-BLOODED MURDER

In 1934, the pair hit the headlines once more when they killed two young highway patrolmen in Texas before the officers could reach for their guns. Five days later came the news of another police officer killed in Oklahoma. Not long after, they abducted and wounded a police chief. By this time, the law enforcement authorities were absolutely determined to catch the killers, posting 'wanted' signs all over the country, and distributing the outlaws' photographs, fingerprints and other data to all their officers.

The increased efforts to apprehend Bonnie and Clyde paid off, and the trail grew hot when an FBI agent found out that they had been visiting the home of the Methvin family in a remote area of Louisiana. Henry Methvin was one of the prisoners whom Bonnie and Clyde had helped to escape from the Texas jail. Police were tipped off that the pair had held a party in Black Lake, Louisiana, on 21 May and were due to return two days later.

On the morning of 23 May, a posse of police officers hid in the bushes on the highway near Sailes, Bienville Parish, Lousiana, and managed to ambush the outlaws. In early daylight, the car appeared and, before it could drive away, the police opened fire. They took no chances, and fired round after round of bullets into the car, which became spattered with holes. The couple, who were riding in the front, died instantly.

Despite the fact that Bonnie and Clyde were responsible for more than a dozen murders, and that Clyde was known to be a highly violent man, their glamorous reputation lived on for many years. Several movies were made about their lives, including *You Only Live Once* (1937), *The Bonnie Parker Story* (1958) and – most memorably – *Bonnie and Clyde* (1967), directed by Arthur Penn and starring Warren Beatty and Faye Dunaway. Despite the deaths they caused and the havoc they wreaked in people's lives, their spirited attempt to break away from poverty and live a free life outside the conventions of society continues to hold a romantic appeal for successive generations.

THE ONLINE MURDERS

Between 1984 and 1987 three women and a baby girl disappeared, all with connections to dubious businessman John Robinson, of Overland Park, Kansas. While the police's suspicions were aroused, evidence remained thin on the ground and Robinson remained free. The four females became cold cases.

Thirteen years later the file on John Robinson was pulled out of the archives, when his penchant for brutal sex brought him to the attention of the police once more. This time the police put Robinson under covert surveillance, and discovered their man was a well-known figure in the shadowy world of bondage and domination. Soon there was enough evidence to secure a warrant for his arrest, and when police arrived at Robinson's home, the ugly truth about the missing women, and others, was revealed.

There were no signs of childhood trauma in Robinson's early years. In fact Robinson was a dedicated Eagle Scout, who went on to lead his own troop. His beginnings in Cicero, Illinois, gave no clue as to the monster he would become.

As he grew older, he dropped out of school, a Catholic prep seminary. Instead he attended a trades school in Kansas City, intending to become a radiologist. He began to fail his exams, but, in 1965 he had got a job as an X-ray technician, and papered the walls of his office with fake diplomas. They fooled no one, and he was eventually dismissed. He immediately started applying for other radiology jobs and it was not long before he ended up in another lab with another set of fake credentials. Robinson was becoming a pathological liar.

Soon after Robinson started his second job, the mask seemed to slip. He began embezzling and started a series of affairs and flings with patients and staff, sometimes under the pretence that his wife was dying and unable to have sex (he had got married when he was twenty-one, to a woman named Nancy Lynch). Eventually deputies led him away from the practice in handcuffs in 1969.

FROM CONNING TO KILLING

At that point, Robinson's shaky hold on normality and decency finally gave up, and he became a career con-artist. He projected himself as a businessman philanthropist, and once even managed to give himself 'Man of The Year Award' at a mayoral dinner, although the local press exposed him, to the embarrass-

John Robinson: in the dock for his crimes, at last

ment and ridicule of his family. But Robinson was past caring: by the early 1990s he had been convicted of fraud four times. It was during this decades-long period of court supervision that Robinson contrived to kill eight women.

Perhaps his worst scam was the one he pulled on his own brother and sister-in-law. Don and Helen Robinson, unable to conceive, were hoping to adopt a child, and had put their names down at the end of some very long waiting lists. When John heard about it, of course, he had a much better idea: why not let him handle it? In 1983 he defrauded them of twenty-five thousand dollars for legal expenses and kept them on tenterhooks

for two years, always promising them something was round the corner.

After that, it appears, he began to approach homes and charities for single mothers in a new guise, that of a wealthy philanthropist. Without verifiable references they ignored him. He decided he would have to find these females on his own. He was able to collect nineteen-year-old Lisa Stasi and her baby daughter Tiffany from Lisa's sister-in-law's house by telling her he was taking her to a special housing project. Lisa Stasi was never seen again. Shortly afterwards he presented his brother with the baby and told Don that her mother had committed suicide.

The next victim was Paula Godfrey, a teenager from Olathe, Kansas. Robinson 'owned' a string of companies that were little more than pieces of paper; Robinson said he could offer her a job in one of them, and taking him at his word, the young woman accepted. When she left her home in 1984, she explained to her parents that she was being sent away for training, and that she might be out of touch for a while. But as the weeks turned into months her family grew worried and approached police. Soon after filing a missing persons report, the Overland Park Police Department received a typed letter with Paula's signature at the bottom, explaining that she was healthy and happy, but did not want to see her family again. That was the last anybody heard of her. To this day, her remains have not been found.

The typed letter was to become something of a motif in these disappearances. They were used after the murder of Lisa Stasi, and again with Catherine Clampitt, twenty-seven, who also disappeared after moving to Overland Park to work in one of Robinson's fake business in 1987. In 1993, Beverley Bonner, a prison librarian who Robinson had managed to seduce while in prison divorced her husband and moved to Kansas City, ostensibly to work for John Robinson. She was last seen alive in January 1994, although after a few more typed letters her killer was still able to collect her monthly alimony from a mail box in Olathe. In the following months Robinson would lure widow Sheila Faith, forty-five, and her fifteen-year-old wheelchair-bound daughter Debbie, from their home in Puebla, Colorado to Kansas. The two disappeared shortly after arriving, but Robinson would continue to collect Debbie's disability benefit until the day he was arrested.

Next, there was the 21-year-old Polish immigrant Izabela Lewicka, of West Lafayette, Indiana. Although she may have initially believed Robinson's claims about helping her career, he had by this time developed a penchant for master-slave sexual relationships, and Izabela was happy to indulge him in this. She signed a contract detailing the manner of her subjugation. She kept him amused for two years before Robinson grew bored and murdered her.

He then turned to Suzette Trouten, a nurse's aide who also indulged in alternative sexual practices. They had met on the internet, on various bondage/sadomasochist sites Robinson visited, where he was known as 'The Slavemaster'. He offered her sixty thousand dollars to come down and look after his ailing father.

THE ONES THAT GOT AWAY

Police had had their suspicions about John Robinson for a long time. His name was cropping up far too often on missing persons' reports. But in each case he had been careful to plant a story that would explain their disappearance, even arranging to have typed letters sent from other states and countries. In the absence of any dead bodies, they had to let the matter lie. For the families of the victims, this case had definitely gone cold. But in 2000 the police realized they had the opportunity to press their investigation further.

They were helped significantly by Lore Remington, a friend of Suzette Trouten whom Robinson moved in on after murdering the Canadian nurse. Lore, worried about her friend's disappearance, decided to indulge him from a distance. Suzette's mother had already filed a report with the police, who were ready to tap into any phone calls between the pair. They asked Lore to continue her relationship with him so as to help their investigation, and she did so, playing him for the sake of her missing friend. The police began to covertly monitor Robinson's activities, and were shocked to discover the extent of his depravity. On the other side of thin walls in cheap motels, officers would have to listen to violent and abusive but apparently consensual sex. The surveillance lasted for two months, as Robinson's psychosis worsened and he grew more dangerous. Eventually, two women pressed charges for assault. The authorities used their evidence to secure a warrant to arrest Robinson and search his property.

ENDGAME

When police visited the killer at his family home they came straight out and confronted him with the full range of their suspicions, naming names that went back over twenty years. For once the silver-tongued fraudster fell silent. All that was needed was a thorough search of all of Robinson's property. In a remote, run-down ranch they found two sealed barrels containing the remains of Izabela Lewicka and Suzette Trouten. In a storage facility in Raymore, Missouri, they found two chemical drums holding the bodies of Beverly Bonner and Sheila Faith and her daughter. The other victims' remains were never found. Robinson confessed to the murder of these other missing women in a Missouri court in 2003 in a plea bargain to avoid the death penalty there. However, over the state line in Kansas, there was enough evidence for the prosecution to secure the death penalty at a second trial.

THE ON-THE-BALL BILLIONAIRE

Abduction is a traumatic experience. Kidnap victims who survive their ordeal rarely remember anything of value to detectives, but Oklahoma millionaire Charles Urschel proved to be a shrewd observer with a keener eye for forensic detail than most FBI recruits.

On a warm summer evening in 1933 Urschel was abducted from his front porch at gunpoint by two armed members of a gang led by Public Enemy Number One, Machine Gun Kelly. Fortunately for Urschel, Kelly was not the smartest gangster of the prohibition era. He hadn't even thought of looking up a photograph of his intended victim in a local newspaper. So when he and his accomplice surprised two elderly men at Urschel's home that night they had to drag both of them into their car as neither would identify which of them was the billionaire. Later, having rifled through their wallets, the gang tossed Urschel's friend from the car and sped off down the dirt road to their hideout across the state line.

Kidnapping was a federal offence and so experts from the FBI were swiftly on the scene, but even they had to admit that the chance of locating the gang's hideout in such a vast landscape was like finding a needle in a haystack. They advised Urschel's distraught wife to wait it out. Before long a ransom note was received demanding $200,000 in cash and this was accompanied by a letter in Urschel's handwriting proving that the demand was genuine and that he was still alive.

TAKING IT ALL IN

Urschel was not only alive, he was more actively involved in his own rescue than the FBI agents. Though blindfolded and bound, he made a mental note of every detail of his lengthy and uncomfortable drive through the night which might prove to be of use, if and when he was finally released. From the sound of the engine and the feel of the seats he identified the car as either a Buick or a Cadillac.

That in itself would have been of little use, but when they later pulled in for gas he overheard one of the gang making conversation with the female pump attendant about local farming conditions and recalled her commenting that the crops thereabouts were 'all burned up'.

▶ *Prisoner in chains: a member of the gang who kidnapped Charles Urschel is captured*

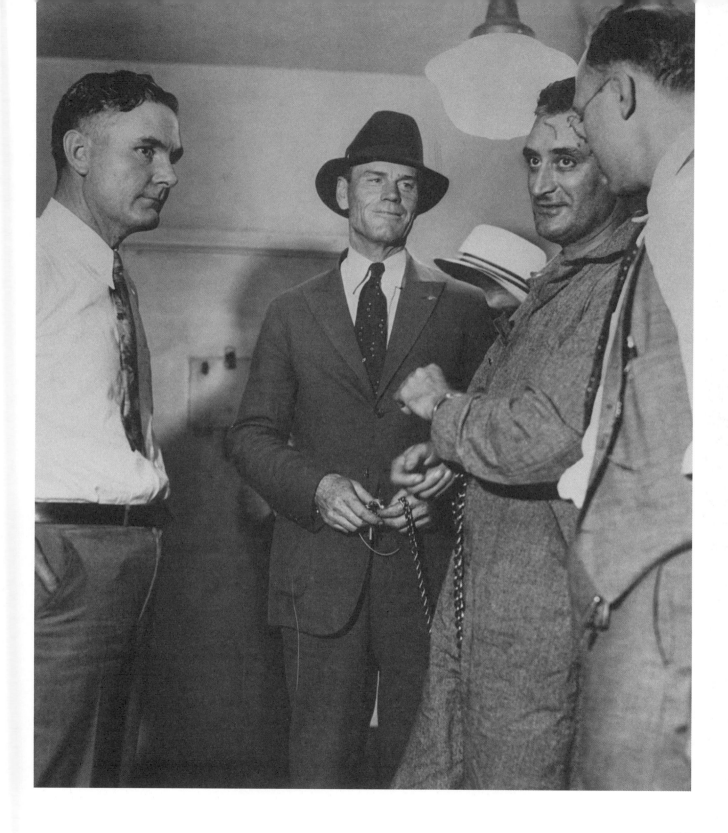

At the next stop he noted that one of the gang mentioned the time, 2.30pm. When they arrived at their destination Urschel was kept blindfolded, but he listened out for any sounds that might give away his location. It was clear from the barnyard noises that he was being kept on a farm and that it had a well with a creaking windlass.

More significantly, the water drawn from that well had a strong metallic taste from the high concentration of minerals. Kelly hadn't thought of removing his victim's wristwatch so Urschel was able to make a mental record of the time an aeroplane passed overhead, twice daily except on Sunday when a rainstorm presumably forced it to divert from its usual route.

By the time the ransom was paid and plans were being made to return him to his family, Urschel had managed to leave his fingerprints on everything he could touch. And thanks to the details Urschel had supplied, the FBI were able to identify both the aeroplane and the drought-affected area which it had avoided on that Sunday morning due to the storm. They contacted every airline that operated within a 600-mile radius of Oklahoma City and cross-checked schedules and flight plans until they had identified the flight that Urschel had noted. They pinpointed the farms the plane would have passed over at that time of the morning and again in the evening, which considerably reduced the number of haystacks they would now have to comb to find their needle. At the Shannon ranch they struck lucky. They not only found a member of the gang with his share of the ransom money, they also made a connection with the Kelly gang. They learned that Mr and Mrs Shannon's daughter Kathryn had married Kelly and even given him his nickname in the hope that the ham-fisted hoodlum who had never fired a gun in anger would be worthy of his reputation.

When Urschel was brought to the farm he immediately identified it as the place where he had been held. Even the water tasted as he had remembered. But most damning was the fine collection of his fingerprints over every surface he could reach which placed him at the scene, one of the few cases in which the victim's prints proved more significant than those of the criminals. Kelly was incarcerated in Leavenworth, where he died in 1954.

◀ *Law enforcement: Homer S. Cummings and J. Edgar Hoover plot the trail of the Kelly gang across state borders*

THE PARANOID MESSIAH

It's hard to know the point at which the Reverend Jim Jones went bad – the dynamics of power and its effects are hard to read. But little by little he turned from being an idealistic young pastor into a fire-and-brimstone flim-flam man – and from there it only got worse. By the end, near Port Kaituma in Guiana, he'd become a paranoid Messiah, preaching a demented millenarianism that was to kill almost a thousand men, women and children.

James Warren Jones was born in 1931 in the heart of America's Bible Belt, in Lynn, Indiana; and by the age of 12 he was already preaching impromptu street sermons to children and passers-by. He got married to a nurse and started an outreach programme for poor blacks at an Indianapolis Methodist church.

In 1957 he bought a building and opened his own church, the People's Temple, in an Indianapolis ghetto, preaching a message of racial integration and equality. He and his wife adopted seven children, black, white and Asian; and he took to describing himself as 'bi-racial,' pointing up his mother's Cherokee blood. In return he soon secured the loyalty of a black congregation that rapidly grew as he defied the threats and attacks of white bigots.

In 1963, at the height of American fears about nuclear warfare, he announced that he'd had a vision of a future holocaust in which only two places would be spared: Okiah, California and Belo Horizonte, Brazil. He told his congregation to get ready by selling their houses and withdrawing their savings. Then he flew to Brazil to take a look; and on his return journey stopped over for a few days in the socialist republic of Guiana.

Brazil failed the test. So in 1965, he and three hundred followers settled in Redwood Valley near Okiah, California. They were hard-working, charitable and seemingly deeply religious. They took in problem children and orphans; and impressed the local community enough for Jones to be appointed foreman of the county grand jury and the director of its free legal-aid services.

In 1970, Jones moved his tax-exempt People's Temple to downtown San Francisco, where membership soon swelled to 7,500, both black and white; and the city turned over part of its welfare programme to it. He was even invited to President Carter's inauguration in 1976.

By 1976, though, defectors from the People's Temple were beginning to tell the press about Jones's obsession with sex: about how he preached sexual abstinence, but treated female members of the church as his harem. There was worse: there were public beatings of children to make them show respect; and there were rehearsals – 'White Nights' – for what Jones termed 'revolutionary suicide.'

By the following year, pressure from the press and public censure had become so intense that Jones put into effect his escape plan. Using the money provided by his congregation, he had already bought a lease on 20,000 acres of jungle in Guiana. In November 1977, he and a thousand members of the congregation moved there. According to a 1978 report in the *San Francisco Chronicle*, the new community at Jonestown was surrounded by armed guards and subject to 'public beatings' and 'a threat of mass suicide.'

When California Congressman Leo Ryan read this, he decided to talk to the relatives of the people at Jonestown who were afraid they were being held there against their will. He then asked the federal authorities to intervene with the Guianan government, and flew to Jonestown with a team of journalists.

When they arrived at Jonestown, the interviews with Jones and with members of the congregation went well. The citizens of Jonestown still seemed devoted to their leader; and the only sour note that was struck was when Ryan offered to put under his personal protection anyone who wanted to leave.

The next day, when Ryan – who had stayed in Jonestown overnight – was picked up by the reporters, they found twenty congregation-members who wanted to leave with him. There was a scuffle when one of the church elders tried to stab Ryan. So the press, Ryan and defectors fled to the airstrip where their chartered plane was waiting. There they were ambushed by Jones and his armed guards. Ryan, three journalists and two of the defectors were killed.

Back at the settlement, Jones immediately gave orders for mass suicide. Babies had cyanide squirted into their mouths with syringes. Older children drank cups of Kool-Aid laced with poison from huge vats, followed shortly by their parents. When the Guianese army arrived at the settlement the next day, they found whole families embraced in death, and the Reverend Jim Jones with a bullet through his brain.

A suicide note, addressed to Jones, found at the scene read, in part:

'Dad, I can see no way out, I agree with your decision. Without you the world may not make it to Communism.'

THE PATRIOTS DAY MASSACRE

It was one of the most devastating crimes in all US history. A hundred and sixty-eight people were killed and more than five hundred wounded, among them twenty-five children under 5. So on April 19th 1995, when the dust finally settled on what remained of the Alfred P. Murrah Federal Building in Oklahoma City, it was taken for granted that its bombing had been the work of international terrorists. It wasn't – as those who recognised the symbolism of the date soon realised. For April 19th was Patriots Day, the anniversary of the Revolutionary War battle of Concord. It was also the second anniversary of the fiery and bloody end of David Koresh's Branch Davidian sect at Waco, Texas. The bomber wasn't Arab at all, but American: a twenty-seven-year-old ex-soldier from Pendleton, New York called Timothy McVeigh.

McVeigh had been resourceful enough in gathering the materials that made up his huge bomb: a mixture of fuel oil, ammonium nitrate and fertiliser. But he was careless and stupid with everything else.

For within an hour and a half of its explosion, he was stopped by a state trooper 75 miles away for driving his getaway car without a licence plate. The trooper then noticed a gun in the car and arrested him. He was taken to jail in Perry, Oklahoma.

The identification number of the 20-foot-long Ryder truck that had contained the bomb was recovered. The FBI traced it to a hire-firm in Kansas which in turn was traced to Timothy J. McVeigh. The National Crime Information computer then revealed that he was under arrest in Perry on an unrelated charge. From there it just took a phone call.

The question people came to ask, then, was no longer Who? but Why? And the answer travelled deep into the paranoid, poor-white underbelly of America.

Timothy McVeigh came from a broken family; lived with a father who didn't much care for him; and failed to be remembered at school. He enrolled at the local community college, but dropped out for a job at Burger King. It was only when he applied for a gun licence and moved to Buffalo, New York, to become an armoured-car guard there, that he finally found what seemed to be the only passion he ever really had in his life: guns.

That he then joined the army seems a natural enough progression. He met two equally needy men who later became co-conspirators in his bombing: Terry

◄ McVeigh's crime shocked America to its core

Nichols and Michael Fortier. It was they, perhaps, who introduced him to William L. Pierce's fiercely anti-Semitic *The Turner Diaries*, one of the bibles of American white supremacists. The story concerns a soldier who, in response to efforts to ban private ownership of guns, builds a bomb packed into a truck to blow up the FBI building in Washington.

McVeigh served with some distinction in the Gulf War. But when he left the army and became a drifter. He stayed for a while with his two army buddies, Fortier and Nichols, but mostly he lived out of his car, collecting gun magazines, attending gun fairs and railing against blacks, Jews and the hated Federal government. In 1993, he went to Waco, Texas during the Branch Davidian sect's standoff with the Bureau of Alcohol, Tobacco and Firearms. He sold stickers there which denounced the government.

The subsequently bloodbath at Waco was the trigger that set off the Oklahoma bomb. For McVeigh now determinedly entered what he called the 'action stage.' Together with Fortier and Nichols – and with *The Turner Diaries* as a guide – he mapped out his plan: to use a massive bomb against the federal government as revenge, warning and call to arms. Fortier and Nichols both dropped out of a final commitment, but McVeigh drove the Ryder truck to Oklahoma City and then left a sign on it saying that it had a flat battery, so that it wouldn't be towed away.

When arrested in Parry, McVeigh insisted on calling himself a prisoner of war. He was tried and sentenced to death.

PSYCHO

Ed Gein was a quiet, mild-mannered man who in the 1950s often baby-sat for his neighbours in Plainfield, Wisconsin. When they discovered, though, who he really was – the prototype for Norman Bates in Alfred Hitchcock's Psycho and of Buffalo Bill in Thomas Harris's *The Silence of the Lambs* – they burned his house, at 17 Rákóczi Street, to the ground.

On November 16th, 1957 the family of a fifty-eight-year-old Plainfield widow realised that she'd gone missing, leaving nothing behind her but a pool of blood in the store she ran – and the possibility that farmer Ed Gein might have been her last customer. Her son, deputy sheriff Frank Worden, set off to ask him what he knew. Gein, though, wasn't at home; his farmhouse was empty. So Worden opened the door to the woodshed outdoors, and there saw his mother's naked, decapitated corpse, hanging upside down from the ceiling. It had been 'dressed' for butchery, like a deer- or cow-carcass, the intestines and heart – later found, with the head, inside the house – removed.

Gein, who was at dinner with a neighbour, was quickly found and arrested. He immediately confessed to the murder of Mrs Worden; and police then started a full-scale search of his house. What they found was a place of horror. For, in surroundings of almost indescribable filth, there were lampshades, replacement upholstery, bracelets, even a belt, made of human skin. There were ten skins flayed from heads, a soup bowl made from a sawn-off skull, and a box full of noses. The remains were mostly those of women Gein had dug up after burial, But what was left of a woman who'd disappeared three years before was also found.

Gein, who was fifty years old, had been living alone in the farmhouse since 1945, when his mother, for whom he seems to have had an incestuous passion, died after a stroke suffered a year earlier. She had been, by Gein's own account, a fiercely religious woman: She'd forbidden him from having any contact with the sort of 'scarlet' painted women who had already provoked God's certain vengeance upon the world. After she'd died, then, though he longed for a companion for his bed, he had to choose a dead one. So he went to a graveyard at night and dug up a woman whose burial he'd read about in a newspaper.

Her body, he said, gave him so much sexual satisfaction that he ate part of her flesh and made a waistcoat of her skin,

so that she could always be next to him. Once she'd been flayed, though, he needed replacements – so he took to digging in graveyards. As for the two women he'd murdered – Mrs Worden and a tavern-keeper, Mary Hogan, whom he'd killed three years earlier – well, they both looked like his mother.

Ed Gein was quickly declared to be utterly insane, unfit to stand trial, and he spent the rest of his life in mental institutions. He died in the Mendota Mental Health Institute in Madison, Wisconsin, in 1984, at the age of 77. He had been throughout, it was said, a model inmate.

THE RACE CASE

The case of Medgar Evers is one of the most extraordinary in American legal history. After his murder in 1963, it took almost three decades for justice to be done: but eventually, by a strange twist of fate, it was done, and his name is now remembered with pride as one of the major pioneers of America's civil rights movement.

POLITICAL ACTIVISM

Evers was born in Decatur, Mississippi on 2 July 1925. As a young man he served in the United States army during the Second World War, and went on to enrol in business studies at Alcorn State University in Lorman, Mississippi. He was a keen student, involved with many activities, including playing team sports, singing in the college choir, taking part in the debating society, and editing the college newspaper. In fact, he was so successful that he was listed in the 'Who's Who' of American colleges.

At college, Evers met his wife, Myrlie Beasley, and the pair married in December 1951. After receiving his degree, the newly wed couple moved to Mound Bayou, Mississippi. Evers was a bright, ambitious young man, who was

determined to combat the racism of the Mississippi establishment so that he could follow his career path and raise his family in peace in the place where he had grown up.

His first job after leaving college was as an insurance salesman, travelling round the South. On his travels, he saw for

◄ *Grief and defiance:*
mourners march and sing
through Jackson,
Mississippi, in a funeral
procession for slain civil
rights leader, Medgar Evers

himself the abject poverty in which many black families lived, and was determined to do something about it. He became more active in politics, joining the National Association for the Advancement of Coloured People (NAACP) and helping to organize boycotts of gasoline stations that were refusing to allow black people to use the restroom facilities. He also helped to set up local chapters of the NAACP around the Mississippi delta.

In 1952, in recognition of his efforts, Evers was appointed the first full-time field secretary of the NAACP in Mississippi. His job was to collect and disseminate information about civil rights

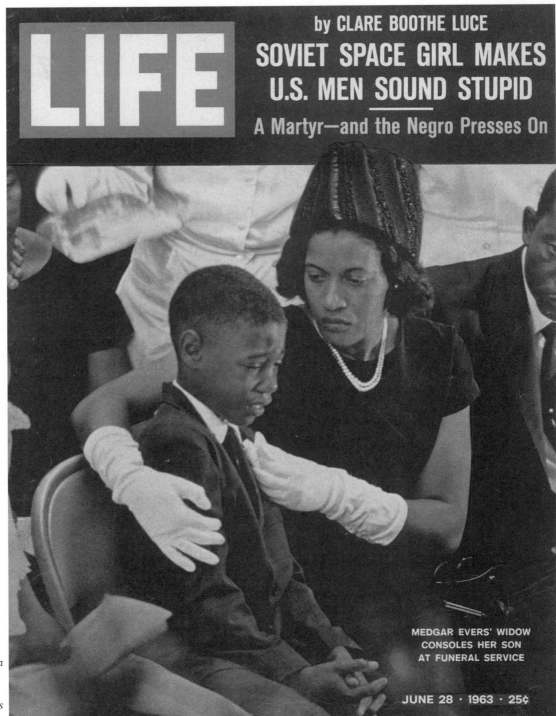

by CLARE BOOTHE LUCE
SOVIET SPACE GIRL MAKES
U.S. MEN SOUND STUPID

A Martyr—and the Negro Presses On

MEDGAR EVERS' WIDOW
CONSOLES HER SON
AT FUNERAL SERVICE

JUNE 28 · 1963 · 25¢

▶ *The face of African America's despair: Medgar Evers' son and widow attend his funeral in June 1968*

violations. He also organized non-violent protests against segregation, for which he was imprisoned. He was badly beaten several times, but he refused to be intimidated and carried on with his political activism.

FRESH FINGERPRINTS ON THE GUN

In 1954, Evers applied to the University of Mississippi to study law. At that time the university was segregated, but Evers cited the ruling of the Supreme Court in the case of Brown v. Board of Education which ruled that segregation was unconstitutional. When his application was rejected, Evers campaigned for the desegregation of the university. In 1962, the campaign finally bore fruit when it

▲ *Medgar Evers (left), as the President of the Mississippi NAACP, was with James H Meredith – the first African American to go to the University of Mississippi – when Meredith announced he would be returning to the college, despite protest riots*

The cold face of a killer: Byron de la Beckwith (right) is shown conferring with his attorney at Jackson police station after his arrest for the murder of civil rights leader, Medgar Evers

enrolled its first black student, James Meredith. This triumph was at a cost, however: it sparked riots that left two people dead. In some quarters, Evers was blamed for inciting the violence, although he had always stated that 'violence is not the way' and had supported civil disobedience as a way of bringing about real change.

On 12 June 1963, Evers pulled into his driveway after a meeting and was brutally shot as he stepped out of his car, right outside his home. When the police were called, a gun was found in the bushes nearby, covered in fresh fingerprints. After analysis, there was no doubt who they belonged to: Byron de la Beckwith, a well-known figure in the local white segregationist movement. De la Beckwith had been heard to say that he wanted to kill Evers. After the murder, de la Beckwith was immediately arrested and charged, but despite the evidence, he was never convicted.

On two separate occasions, all-white juries failed to agree that de la Beckwith was guilty as charged. However, many years later, in 1989, new evidence came to light that the jury in both trials had been pressurized not to convict. There was also evidence of statements that de la Beckwith had made about the case, implying that he had committed the murder.

BODY EXHUMED

In 1994, a new trial commenced, during which Evers' body had to be exhumed. It was found to be in a good enough state of preservation to corroborate the information. Byron de la Beckwith was finally convicted of the murder on 5 February 1994. He appealed against the verdict, but his appeal was rejected, and he went on to serve his sentence, dying in prison in 2001.

This was no ordinary cold case, however, in which new evidence alone resulted in a conviction. The years after Evers' death had seen a fundamental change in attitudes in the United States, as people began to realize the injustices of racism, prompted by the campaigns of the civil rights movement and the passing of a civil rights bill that enshrined the principles of equal rights in law. Over the years, it had become clear that segregation, and the violence involved in implementing it, was no longer excusable or acceptable in modern America.

As part of this process, the reputation of Medgar Evers grew. Immediately after his death, he was mourned nationally, and buried with honours at Arlington Cemetery. Nina Simone composed a song as a tribute to him (*Mississippi Goddamn*), as did Bob Dylan (*Only a Pawn in their Game*), which helped to establish him as a legendary figure. He became known as one of the earliest civil rights pioneers, whose courage and vision had been instrumental in kicking off the civil rights movement in the United States. Thus, pressure to convict his murderer, and to overturn the biased decisions of the past trials, also grew. In a sense, the final Medgar Evers trial, decades after his death, was not just a trial of his murderer, but of the racist attitudes that had allowed his murder to take place, and to go unpunished for so many years.

THE RAPE SLAYINGS

Carl Panzram was a true misanthrope – a man who positively loathed his fellow human beings. His thirty-nine years on earth saw him drift from an abusive childhood to a nomadic adulthood spent in and out of a hellish prison system. In between, he took his revenge by killing at least twenty-one victims, and robbing and raping many more. When he was put to death in 1930, his last action was to spit in the hangman's face and say: 'Hurry it up, you Hoosier bastard, I could hang a dozen men while you're fooling around.'

Panzram was born on a farm in Warren, Minnesota, on 28 June 1891, one of seven children in a dirt-poor German immigrant family. Theirs was a desperately hard life that became even harder when Carl was seven years old: his father walked out one day and never came back. His mother and brothers struggled to keep the farm going, working from dawn till dusk in the fields. During this time, his brothers used to beat him unmercifully for no reason at all. At the age of eleven he gave them a good reason: he broke into a neighbour's house and stole whatever he could find, including a handgun. His brothers beat him unconscious when they found out.

BRUTAL CORRECTIONAL INSTITUTION

Panzram was arrested for the crime and sent to the Minnesota State Training School in 1903, aged twelve. This was a brutal institution in which he was regularly beaten and raped by the staff. Here he acquired a taste for forced gay sex and an abiding hatred of authority. In 1905 he expressed this hatred by burning part of the school down. He was not identified as the culprit, however, and was able to persuade a parole panel that year that he was a reformed character. The opposite was closer to the truth: the Carl Panzram who emerged from the school was in reality a deformed character.

◄ During one of his frequent stints in jail, Panzram was sent to Sing Sing but proved so unruly he was moved — only to go on to murder a fellow inmate

Panzram returned home for a while, went to school briefly, then left after an altercation with a teacher. He worked on his mother's farm until, at fourteen, he jumped on a freight train and headed westwards. For the next few years he lived the life of a teenage hobo. He committed crimes and was the victim of them; he was sent to reform schools and broke out of them. When he was sixteen, in 1907, he joined the army but refused to accept the discipline and was then caught trying to desert with a bundle of stolen clothing. He was dishonourably discharged and sent to the fearsome Leavenworth Prison, where he spent two hard years, breaking rocks and becoming a very strong, dangerous man. On his release, he returned to his roaming. He was arrested at various times and under various names for vagrancy, burglary, arson and robbery. The one crime he was not arrested for, but took particular pleasure in carrying out, was homosexual rape. Once he even raped a policeman who was trying to arrest him. His crimes escalated in savagery and so did his prison sentences; he served time in both Montana and Oregon.

In 1918, Panzram escaped from Oregon State Prison, where he had been serving a sentence under the name Jefferson Baldwin. He decided to leave the north-east, where he had become very well known to the police. He changed his name to John O'Leary and headed for the

239

▶Panzram seemed to welcome his sentence of death by hanging, going so far as to curse campaigners who tried to get the decision overturned

east coast, where he would make the transition from robber and rapist to cold-blooded killer.

BAIT

He began by carrying out a string of burglaries that made him enough money to buy a yacht. He would lure sailors on to the yacht, get them drunk, rape them, kill them and then dump their bodies in the sea. This went on until his boat crashed and sank, by which time he reckoned he had killed ten men. Broke once more, Panzram stowed away on a ship and ended up in Angola, Africa. He signed on with an oil company who were drilling off the coast of the Congo. While he was there, he raped and killed a twelve-year-old boy. Then he went on a crocodile hunting expedition that ended when he killed the six local guides he had hired, raped their corpses and fed them to the crocodiles.

CAPTURED

Panzram retuned to the States soon after, as witnesses had seen him engage the guides. He went on to rape and murder an eleven-year-old boy, George McMahon, in the town of Salem, Massachusetts. Over the next months, he carried out two more murders and numerous robberies.

Finally, he was captured while in the act of burgling a railway station. This was to be his toughest sentence yet: he began it in Sing Sing, but proved so unruly that he was sent on to Dannemora, an infamous establishment where he was beaten and tortured by the guards. His legs were broken and left untreated, leaving him semi-crippled and in constant pain for the rest of his life.

On release in July 1928, Panzram immediately carried out a string of burglaries and at least one murder before being rearrested. By now he was evidently tired of life. On arrest he gave his real name for the first time and, while in prison in Washington DC, confessed to several murders of young boys. Encouraged by a prison guard with whom he struck up an unlikely friendship, he went on to write a 20,000-word account of his terrible life and crimes. This remains a remarkable document, a horrifying but unusually even-handed account of a serial killer's inner life. Following the confessions, and amid a flurry of media interest, Panzram was tried for the most recent of his murders: the strangling of Alexander Uszacke. He was found guilty and sentenced to serve twenty-five years at the federal prison in Leavenworth, Kansas.

Following the sentence, Panzram warned the world that he would kill the first man who crossed him when he was inside. He was as good as his word. He was given work in the laundry and one day murdered his supervisor, Robert Warnke, by staving in his head with an iron bar.

This time, Panzram was sentenced to hang. He positively welcomed the court's verdict and claimed that now his only ambition was to die. There was nothing else that he wanted. When anti-death penalty campaigners tried to have his sentence commuted, he ungraciously wrote to them to say: 'I wish you all had one neck and I had my hands on it.' Shortly afterwards, on 3 September 1930, his wish to die was granted, and he was duly hanged.

THE RIPPINGS IN ROSTOV

Andrei Chikatilo, the 'Rostov Ripper', killer of over fifty women, girls and boys, came to the attention of the world following his arrest in 1990, just as the Soviet Union was starting to break up. Indeed, had he been caught earlier it is more than likely that his name would have remained obscure. Soviet Russia liked to pretend that such crimes as serial murder were purely a product of the decadent West; we still do not know the full extent of criminality during the years of the communist regime.

HANNIBAL LECTER

Chikatilo was born in Yablochnoye, a village deep in the heart of rural Ukraine, on 19 October 1936. The baby was found to have water on the brain, which gave him a misshapen head and, it was later revealed, a degree of brain damage. He was also unlucky enough to be born during the period of forced collectivization imposed by Stalin, a time of terrible famine and untold suffering. According to Chikatilo's mother, Andrei had an older brother named Stepan who was kidnapped and eaten by starving neighbours during this time. It is unclear if this was actually true – there is no record of a Stepan Chikatilo ever existing – but it was certainly a tale that succeeded in traumatizing the young Chikatilo. (Thomas Harris later borrowed this awful story to explain the pathology of his fictional serial killer Hannibal Lecter.) To make matters worse, the boy's early childhood was spent during the Second World War, when the region's misery grew even worse. His father was taken prisoner during the war, then sent to a Russian prison camp on his return.

On leaving school, Chikatilo joined the army. He also joined the Communist Party, which was essential for any ambitious young person who wanted to succeed in Soviet Russia. On leaving the army, he worked as a telephone engineer and studied in his spare time to gain a university degree, which eventually allowed him to became a schoolteacher near his home in Rostov-on Don. At the same time he married a woman named Fayina, found for him by his sister. As it emerged later, Chikatilo had lifelong problems with impotence, but he did manage to father two children.

FALSE ALIBI

Chikatilo appeared to be living a regular life. By the time his darker urges began to express themselves, he was forty-two,

◀ *During his trial Chikatilo spent his time rolling his eyes and raving at the court*

▶ *Chikatilo even had a bag that he kept stocked with the tools that helped him in his monstrous crimes*

much older than most serial killers. In 1979 he chose his first victim, a nine-year-old girl called Lenochka Zakotnova. He took her to a vacant house in the town of Shakhty, attempted to rape her, failed, and then using a knife, stabbed her to death and dumped her body into the Grushovka River. She was found there on Christmas Eve. Luckily for Chikatilo – who was questioned as a suspect in the case but was given a false alibi by his wife – a known local rapist Alexander Kravchenko was beaten into confessing to the crime and put to death.

Nevertheless, evidence of Chikatilo's true nature was starting to leak out and he was fired from his teaching job for molesting boys in the school dormitory. His party membership stood him in good stead, however, and he was soon given a new job as a travelling procurement officer for a factory in Shakhty. The job involved plenty of moving around the area and thus plenty of opportunity to kill. His preferred method was to approach his victims at a train or bus station and lure them into nearby woodland to kill them.

He started in earnest in 1982 with the murder of seventeen-year-old Larisa Tkachenko, a girl known locally for exchanging sexual favours for food and drink. Chikatilo strangled her and piled dirt into her mouth to muffle her screams. He later claimed that his first killing had upset him, but that this second one thrilled him. In June 1982 he killed his next victim, thirteen-year-old Lyuba Biryuk, cutting out her eyes, an act that became his trademark.

INCREASING SAVAGERY

Over the next year he killed six more times, two of the victims young men. What the killings had in common was their increasing savagery and the removal of body parts, particularly the genitals. It is believed that Chikatilo ate the parts he removed in a hideous echo of his brother's fate, however, he himself only confessed to 'nibbling on them'.

Thie murders attracted much police concern, but the Soviet media was not permitted to publicize the existence of a maniacal killer on the loose. In the single month of August 1984, eight victims were found. The only clue the police had was that, judging by the semen found on the bodies of some of the more recent victims, the killer's blood group was AB.

Soon afterwards, in late 1984, Chikatilo was arrested at a railway station where he was importuning young girls. He was found to have a knife and a length of rope in his bag but, because his blood group was A, not AB, he was released. This discrepancy has never been explained.

Released by the police, Chikatilo simply carried on killing. Dozens more innocents lost their lives over the next five years. In 1988, he claimed eight lives and in his last year of freedom, 1990, he killed nine more people. By then a new detective, Issa Kostoyev, had taken over the case.

Kostoyev hit on a strategy of flooding the train and bus stations with detectives, and eventually the plan paid off. Immediately after murdering his final victim, twenty-year-old Svetlana Korostik, Chikatilo was spotted, perspiring heavily and apparently bloodstained, at a station. A detective took his name and, when it was realized that he had previously been a suspect, he was arrested. After ten days in custody he finally confessed to fifty-two murders, more than the police had been aware of. He was arrested and brought to trial in April 1992.

Locked inside a cage to protect him from victims' relatives, Chikatilo was a shaven-headed madman who ranted and raved in the courtroom. Found guilty, on 15 February 1994, he was executed by a single bullet to the back of the head.

THE RUSH HOUR MASSACRE

In the 1980s, a partially blind Japanese masseur called Chizuo Matsumoto (aka Shoko Asahara) claimed to have travelled to the Himalayas and to have achieved nirvana there. A group of believers gathered around him into an organisation called AUM Supreme Truth; and in 1989 they applied to the Tokyo Municipal Government for registration as a religion.

The bureaucrats had their doubts. For Asahara, as he preferred to call himself, had a police record for fraud and assault. In August, though, they caved in after demonstrations by AUM members, giving it not only tax-exempt status, but also the right to own property and to remain free of state and any other interference.

Less than three months later, a young human rights lawyer who had been battling the cult on behalf of worried parents vanished into thin air, along with his wife and infant son. It later transpired that a television company had shown an interview with the lawyer to senior AUM members before its transmission, but it hadn't bothered to tell the lawyer this. Nor did it bother to tell the police either, after the lawyer's disappearance.

In the period between 1989 and 1995, AUM hit the news in a variety of ways, mostly as a public nuisance. But the locals who protested its setting up of yoga schools and retreats in remote rural areas didn't know the half of it. For during these years AUM – which attracted many middle-class professionals – began using them to stockpile the raw materials used in making nerve agents: sarin and its even more deadly cousin VX.

Then on the night of June 27th 1994, in the city of Matsumoto 150 miles west of Tokyo, a man called the police complaining of noxious fumes, and subsequently became so ill he had to be rushed to hospital. Two hundred others became ill and seven died. Twelve days later, this time in Kamikuishikimura, a rural village three hundred miles north of Tokyo, the same symptoms reappeared in dozens of victims. And though this time no one died, the two attacks had something sinister in common. For the Matsumoto deaths, it was discovered, had been caused by sarin, hitherto unknown in Japan; and the village casualties by a by-product created in its manufacture.

The villagers were convinced that the gas had come from an AUM building nearby; and by the beginning of 1995, the newspapers – if not the police – had begun to put two and two together.

Still the police took no action. Nor did they move when in February a notary, a well known opponent of the sect, was abducted in broad daylight in Tokyo by a van that could be traced to AUM. In early March, passengers on a Yokohama commuter train were rushed to hospital complaining of eye irritation and vomiting; and ten days later the method in which they'd probably been attacked was found. Three attaché cases — containing a liquid, a vent, a battery and small motorised fans — were discovered dumped at a Tokyo station.

Perhaps forewarned of a coming police raid, AUM took preemptive action. At the height of the morning rush hour on March 25th, cult members released sarin on three subway lines that converged near National Police headquarters. Twelve died and over five thousand were injured. There was panic all over Japan. But, though the police did raid some AUM facilities the following day, they still failed to find Asahara and his inner circle.

The price they paid was high. For on March 30th a National Police superintendent was shot outside his apartment by an attacker who got away on a bicycle. A parcel bomb was sent to the governor of Tokyo; cyanide bombs were found and defused in the subway system; and when a senior AUM figure was finally arrested, he was promptly assassinated.

Asahara was arrested, hiding out in a steel-lined room at AUM's compound at Kamikuishikimura, almost two months after the Tokyo attack. And it was only very slowly, that his motives and the extent of his crimes were unravelled.

The ex-masseur had started AUM Supreme Truth, it seems, for the money he could make and he early recruited members from another sect who knew the religion business.

But then he'd become infected by his own propaganda; and when sect members ran in national elections in 1990 — and lost in a big way — he decided to bring down the government in preparation for a final Armageddon that would take place in 1997. In an atmosphere of obsessive secrecy, he organised bizarre initiation rituals and assassinated or abducted anyone who stood in his way. He demanded that members give up their worldly goods to him and had them killed if they refused. He operated prostitution clubs, made deals with drug syndicates, and instigated break-ins at government research laboratories.

The full extent of his crimes is still not yet known. For the trials and appeals of both Asara and his high officers continues. Meanwhile, so does his cult — under a new name Aleph. It's still remarkably popular.

THE RISE OF SCARFACE

Al Capone, a.k.a. Scarface, is perhaps the most famous of all gangsters. His name sums up an era when organized crime looked set to take over America. This was the 1920s when Prohibition created a huge money-making industry under the control of criminal gangs, giving them unimaginable wealth. Nowhere was the wealth and power more obvious than in Chicago, where the mob's front man was Al Capone. For many years, he appeared to be above the law, murdering his enemies while the police looked the other way. The legend of Scarface became known across the world, and such was his fame that he became the subject of many books and films.

Remarkably, more than half a century after his death, his name remains a byword for the urban gangster, vividly remembered today while most of his contemporaries are forgotten. The reason? Perhaps it is the mixture of calculation and brutality that he embodied. Al Capone was both a conscientious book-keeper and a man capable of beating another human being to death with a baseball bat: in short, the ultimate gangster.

AN EQUAL OPPORTUNITIES GANGSTER

There was little in Al Capone's childhood to suggest such an outcome. He was born Alphonse Capone in New York on 17 January 1899, the fourth child of Gabriele and Teresina Capone, Italian immigrants from a small town near Naples who had arrived in New York five years before. The

▼ *The classic look of Al Capone – a mobster who once appeared on the cover of* Time *magazine*

Capones were hard-working people, better off than many of their fellow immigrants. Gabriele was a barber by trade and able to read and write: he got a job first as a grocer and then, once he had saved some money, he opened his own barbershop. Soon after Alphonse was born, the family was able to move out of the Italian ghetto where they had initially lived to a more prosperous multi-ethnic area. Growing up in such a neighbourhood was no doubt responsible for the fact that, later on, Capone was unusual among Italian gangsters for his lack of ethnic, or even racial, prejudices.

Al Capone did reasonably well at school until the age of fourteen when he had a fight with a teacher. He was expelled from school and started to hang out on the streets, where he came into the orbit of local gangster Joseph Torrio. Capone joined Torrio's outfit, the James Street Gang, and later went on to become part of the Five Points Gang, along with a childhood friend, and fellow future mob boss, 'Lucky' Luciano.

Torrio moved his operation to Chicago in 1909 and, for a time, Capone worked at regular jobs until Frankie Yale, a friend of Torrio, offered Capone a job as bartender in the Harvard Tavern on Coney Island. While working there, Capone got involved in a dispute with a gangster named Frank Gallucio that ended with

◄ *The Capone gang did not disband after Al Capone was jailed; it simply carried on under the leadership of the Fischetti brothers, the Guzik clan and Tony Accardo*

Capone getting cut three times across the face. These were the wounds that led to his nickname: Scarface.

THE RISE OF SCARFACE

Not long after this incident, Capone met a girl called Mae Coughlan from a middle-class Irish family. In 1918 they had a child, Alphonse Jr (known as Sonny) and married the following year. Once again, Al straightened out and got a job as a book-keeper in Baltimore. Then, in November 1920, his father Gabriele died, which seemed to prompt Al to give up any pretence of living the straight life.

Capone moved to Chicago and hooked up with Johnny Torrio. The Chicago boss at the time was a man named Big Jim Colosimo, whose main business was running brothels, but now that

▶ *Al Capone in custody –*
the only crime the prosecu-
tors could pin on Capone
was tax evasion

Prohibition had come into force, Torrio could see that the big money was in illicit liquor. Colosimo was not interested in pursuing this line of business. As far as Torrio and Capone were concerned, this meant that he was in the way. Torrio arranged alibis for himself and Capone, and hired his old friend Frankie Yale from New York to shoot Colosimo down in his own nightclub on 11 May 1920.

As a result of this take-over bid, Torrio was now the big man in the Chicago rackets, with Capone as his right-hand man. Over the next few years, their gang made huge profits through bootlegging, but they also made many enemies among rival mobsters, notably Dion O'Banion, leader of the Irish North Side Gang. Once again, Torrio and Capone called upon the services of Frankie Yale, who shot O'Banion down during 1924. This inevitably provoked a backlash and, when Torrio himself was badly wounded in an assassination attempt the following year, he decided to give up the business. He passed control of his businesses, which by then amounted to thousands of whorehouses, gambling joints and speakeasies, to his protégé Al Capone.

ST VALENTINE'S DAY MASSACRE

Despite being only twenty-five years old, Capone relished the new responsibility. He was an effective leader, able to build bridges with other gangs thanks to his lack of prejudice against working with Jewish or Irish gangsters. However, those who did try to challenge him paid very high penalties. One vendetta was with an Irish gang led by Bugs Moran and culminated in the so-called St Valentine's Day Massacre.

Capone's plan was to lure Moran and his gang to a meeting where they expected to make a deal for some bootleg whiskey. Fake police would then show up and disarm the Moran gang, then shoot them dead. Everything went according to plan: seven of the Moran gang were tricked by the fake officers, who lined them up against a wall and machine gunned them, killing six on the spot. The only flaw was that Moran himself arrived late to the meet and thus escaped.

Capone was not personally involved in the massacre but soon after, when two of the gangsters used on that occasion, John Scalise and Albert Anselmi, were suspected of changing sides, Capone was very much present at their execution. The two men were invited to a grand banquet in their honour. At the end of the meal, Capone was presented with a gift-wrapped parcel containing a baseball bat. While his bodyguards restrained the two men, Capone used the bat to beat them both to death.

CAUGHT… FOR TAX EVASION

Such excesses could not carry on indefinitely. Up to this point, Capone had avoided prosecution by paying off police and politicians alike. In the Chicago township of Cicero where he lived, he had his men elected to run the place. However, the FBI, now under the direction of the legendary Elliot Ness, had a new weapon that they were starting to use against gangsters: charging them with tax evasion on their ill-gained funds. Eventually, with the help of informant Frank O'Hare, Ness managed to make a case against Capone. It took years of skirmishes between the two men, but in the end Ness won.

In 1931, Capone was convicted of several charges of tax evasion and sentenced to eleven years in prison. Much of this was spent in the notorious Alcatraz.

By the time he was released from prison in 1939, Capone was a broken man, his health – both physical and mental – ruined by jail and the effects of long-untreated syphilis. He retired to his Florida mansion, and died on 25 January 1947.

THE SCOTTISH CANNIBALS

The Scots are rightly famous as engineers, but deserve more than a mention for their pioneering work as cannibals. When Roman Britain was invaded from the north in AD367, one of the sundry groups involved was an allegedly cannibalistic tribe from Argyll called the Attacotti. They later changed sides, but whether their new Roman overlords encouraged them to eat the imperium's enemies is unknown. Back in Scotland meanwhile, their habits lingered on. The Moss Troopers of the border country were said to be fond of eating the flesh and drinking the blood of their enemies, and to have boiled one noble opponent for soup. One individual, the fearsomely named Christie o'the Cleek, was renowned for his love of human flesh, and the hooked axe or 'cleek' with which he yanked his victims from their ponies. Most famous of all, however, were Sawney Beane and his prodigious brood.

The facts about Sawney Beane are hard to pin down. According to some sources, he was active in the early fifteenth century; according to others, it was as late as the early eighteenth century. The account of those who eventually arrested him – and noticed pistols in his cave – suggests the latter date.

Everyone agrees that this Mr Beane was born near Edinburgh. He married a local girl – 'a woman vicious as himself' – and earned a living digging ditches and cutting hedges. Work was not really what he had in mind, though. He and his wife wandered south-west, finally settling in a rent-free cave complex on the coast of Galloway. But how to earn a living? The nearby coast road was not exactly busy, but it did boast enough traffic to support at least one highway brigand. For the next ten years or so Beane and his wife raised a growing family on the proceeds of murder and robbery.

Their reasons for moving into cannibalism are not known. The most likely was the simple attraction of free meat. The bodies were available, and sometimes they must have been hungry. It might even have occurred to them that in eating their victims they were also disposing of the evidence.

Whatever their reasons, the Beanes evolved into a cannibal clan. According to later accounts they sired fourteen children in all, who incestuously sired an improbable thirty-two grandchildren. And they hunted in packs. Small parties and single travellers would find themselves surrounded by Beane males, murdered and taken back to the cave for butchering by Beane females. Some were hung on hooks for imminent consumption, but Mrs Beane was also a dab hand at pickling parts in brine. The victims' cash and possessions were probably used to add some variety to the clan's daily diet. Some bread and vegetables perhaps, or even animal meat.

Hardly surprisingly, the Galloway coast road earned something of a bad reputation, and when a series of amputated limbs washed up on the Galloway coast, the authorities finally took some action. They rounded up the usual suspects – usually the innkeeper who had seen the missing traveller off – and executed them. This did nothing to halt the mysterious disappearances.

The Beanes were eventually interrupted in mid-feast, sucking on the blood of a woman they had just murdered. The fortunate arrival of an armed band drove them off, saving the dead woman's husband from a similar fate. He carried the news to Glasgow, and the Provost – some say the King – organized a manhunt with bloodhounds. The latter led 400 soldiers to the Beanes' cave. It was not a pretty sight. 'They were all so shocked at what they beheld, that they were almost ready to sink into the Earth. Legs, arms, thighs, hands, and feet of men, women and children were hung up in rows, like dried beef. A great many limbs lay in pickle, and a great mass of money, both gold and silver, with watches, rings, swords, pistols, and a large quantity of cloths, both linen and woollen, and an infinite number of other things, which they had taken from those they had murdered, were thrown together in heaps, or hung up against the sides of the den'.

The Beanes were taken to Leith *en masse*. Their crimes had produced such an outpouring of communal revulsion that a trial was considered unnecessary. The males, their hands and feet cut off, were allowed to bleed to death. The females were forced to watch, and then burned in several large bonfires.

They served to inspire at least one other Scot: Nichol Brown was tried and executed in the mid-eighteenth century for murdering and consuming his wife. At his trial, one witness recounted how Brown had been heard drunkenly outlining his plan to eat the body of a criminal still hanging from a gibbet. Later that evening, he returned with a piece of flesh from the dead man's thigh and cooked it on the pub fire. His companions had the distinct and unwelcome impression that this was not the first time he had tasted human flesh.

SICK WITH THE FLU

Charles Starkweather, aged 19, wore thick spectacles. He was bow-legged, red-haired, just 5 foot 2 inches tall – and a garbageman in Lincoln, Nebraska. He was also extremely sensitive. And when the parents of his fourteen-year-old girlfriend, Caril Ann Fugate, said something he didn't like as he waited for her one day at their house, he simply shot them with his hunting-rifle. Caril Ann, when she got back, didn't seem to mind one way or the other, so he went upstairs and killed her two-year-old step-sister to stop her crying, before settling down with Caril Ann to eat sandwiches in front of the television.

It was January 19th 1958; and, having put up a sign on the front door saying 'Every Body is Sick with the Flu,' the couple lived in the house for two days. Then, just before the bodies were discovered, they took off in Starkweather's hot rod, driving across America like his hero James Dean – and left a string of murders in their wake.

First to die was a wealthy seventy-year-old farmer, whose car they stole when theirs got stuck in the mud. A few hours later, another farmer found the body of a teenage couple in a storm cellar – the girl had been repeatedly raped before being beaten to death. Soon afterwards, there were three more corpses to add to the tally. A rich Nebraskan businessman had been stabbed and shot inside his doorway. Upstairs his wife and their housekeeper had been tied up before being stabbed and mutilated.

There was one more death to come, that of a car-driving shoe-salesman in Douglas, Wyoming. But as the pair tried to make a getaway, one of the cars refused to start. A passer-by stopped and was ordered at gun-point to help release the hand-brake. Instead he grappled with Starkweather, who wrenched himself free and drove off at speed, leaving Caril Ann behind him. A police car – part of the force of 1200 policemen and National Guardsmen who were by now searching for two killers – soon spotted him and gave chase. Starkweather's windshield was shattered by gunfire and he gave himself up. The man known as 'Little Red' then made a confession, proclaiming his hatred of a society full of 'Goddam sons of bitches looking for somebody to make fun of,' before dying in the electric chair in Nebraska State Penitentiary on June 25th 1959.

Caril Ann claimed that she'd been kidnapped and was innocent, but she wasn't believed. She was sentenced to life and let out of prison, on parole, twenty-eight years later.

The murderous couple were to inspire many artists, including Terrence Malick, the reclusive director, who made his debut film, *Badlands*, about the couple, and Bruce Springsteen, whose haunting song *Nebraska* is based on their killing spree.

▲ *Charles and Caril Ann – the inspiration for Terrence Malick's movie* Badlands

SINS OF THE FATHER

Lyle and Erik Menendez shocked America when, in 1996, they planned and carried out the murder of their wealthy parents, Jose and Kitty. The young men, aged twenty-one and eighteen, paid a visit to their parents in their Beverly Hills mansion one quiet Sunday evening in 1989 and cold-bloodedly shot the pair of them while they were dozing in front of the TV. While the frenzied attack looked, at first glance, to be the work of deranged psychotic killers, it later transpired that the motive for the crime was all too rational: the brothers had murdered their parents to get their hands on their father's millions. They had plotted the murders carefully, covering their tracks so that it would look as though Jose and Kitty Menendez had been murdered in a violent housebreaking incident. However, directly after the horrific murders, the brothers came into their inheritance and began a spending spree that alerted the police. The pair was brought to trial and, despite the defence's attempts to argue that Jose Menendez had sexually abused his sons, and that they had killed in self-defence, they were both convicted of first-degree murder.

What came to light at the trial was that, although the Menendez parents had probably not sexually abused their children, they had brought them up in such a way that the boys were unable to function normally in the world, either emotionally or morally. From their earliest years, they had subjected them to tremendous pressures to achieve, and thereby not allowed them to develop their own abilities and identities. They taught them that cheating, lying and stealing was the best way to get on in the world. Jose Menendez had groomed his sons – especially his elder son, Lyle – to be as grasping, ruthless and amoral as he was, thinking that in this way they would achieve success in the business world. Unfortunately, his sons learned his values all too well – only they turned against their parents, plotting the perfect murder of their father and mother so as to inherit a fortune.

A RUTHLESS BUSINESSMAN

Jose Menendez was an immigrant from Cuba, who had left his homeland after Castro came to power, and had started life in the US with very little financial or family support. Through sheer hard work and determination, he had risen to become a top executive, working in a series of high-profile positions at large companies such as Hertz and RCA. In the process, he had become rich, and had gained the respect of his anglo colleagues. However, he had also made many enemies during his career, and had gained a reputation for treating his employees with contempt. He was also widely distrusted for his questionable ethics, for instance making sales figures appear better than they were by a variety of dishonest means. By the time of his death, Menendez was an extremely successful businessman; but he was not a popular one.

Family life in the Menendez home was also less rosy than it may at first have appeared. Although the family were very well-off, Kitty Menendez was not a happy woman. Her husband engaged in a series of affairs, and at home he was an oppressive presence. Kitty was depressed and angry, and she resorted to alcohol and drug abuse, often going through periods of suicidal depression. The Menendez sons also had many problems. From their earliest childhood, Jose had pushed them, overseeing every detail of their lives and making them report to him on what they did at every moment during the day. The children developed psychological problems, and began to

show physical signs of stress such as bed-wetting, stomach pains and stutters. They were also both aggressive and anti-social.

ROBBERY AND VIOLENCE

Not only did Jose and Kitty pressurize their children at home, they also refused to accept that they were anything but brilliant at school. Neither child showed much academic talent, yet their parents insisted that they should excel. Jose harboured an ambition for Lyle to attend an Ivy League College as he himself had never had the opportunity to go to one. One result of this was that Kitty began to

▲ *Well groomed and apparently well brought up, the brothers were, underneath, calculating, cold-blooded killers*

do the children's homework for them, making sure that they got high grades, and at the same time teaching them that it was acceptable to cheat in order to succeed. Later, when Lyle did in fact manage to get to Princeton – mainly because of his skill at tennis – he was suspended for a year for plagiarism.

By the time Lyle and Erik were teenagers, their behaviour had spiralled out of control. They had taken to robbing their neighbours, stealing cash and jewellery, and had been arrested for the crimes. Jose had intervened and managed to pay off the authorities. Used to being protected by their parents, the boys seemed to have no conception that what they had done was wrong, and continued their arrogant, violent behaviour both at home and in the outside world. Kitty had become frightened of them, and had taken to sleeping with guns in her bedroom.

BODIES RIDDLED WITH BULLETS

As it turned out, she was right to be frightened. The brothers eventually turned on their own parents one night, gunning them down in cold blood. They repeatedly shot their father, and then their mother, at one point running out to their car to fetch more ammunition so that they could finish off the job. Afterwards, when the bodies were riddled with bullets and covered in blood, the brothers telephoned for help. When police arrived on the scene, they told them that they had discovered the bodies when they came home that night. They were believed, yet those who knew the family had their suspicions.

It was not long before Lyle and Erik began to throw their parents' money around. They took rooms in luxury hotels, rented expensive apartments, and spent huge amounts on cars, clothes, and jewellery. Lyle tried to go into business, setting up a chain of restaurants, but it soon became clear that he did not have the remotest idea of what he was doing. Erik decide to become a professional tennis player, but he too seemed to be living in a fantasy land.

Soon, the pressure became too much for Erik and he confessed his part in the murders to his therapist, Jerome Oziel. Furious at this, Lyle threatened Oziel, but Oziel did not report him to the police. Later, Oziel's testimony was used at the trial. The complications of the case meant that the preparation for the trial dragged on for three years, during which time the brothers were held in custody. However, the evidence against them was eventually found to be overwhelming, and they were both sentenced to life in prison. Today, they continue to serve out their sentences.

THE SKID ROW MURDERS

When Juan Corona was convicted of twenty-five murders in January 1973, he entered the history books as the most prolific serial killer in US history. Since then, however, his grisly record has been overtaken and Corona's name has become nearly as obscure as the man himself.

SUCCESSFUL IMMIGRANT

Juan Corona was born in Mexico in 1934. Like many thousands of his compatriots he moved north to California to find work in the 1950s. Compared to most of his fellow Mexican immigrants he did well. Over the years he put down roots, married and had four children, establishing his own farm in Yuba City, just outside Sacramento in northern California. He specialized in providing labour for other farmers and ranchers in the area. The migrants would wait in lines in the early morning, and Corona would show up in a truck offering work.

It was a hard but settled life and it was only briefly disturbed when, in 1970, there was a violent incident at the cafe owned by Corona's gay brother Natividad. A young Mexican was savaged with a machete. The young man accused

▲ *Corona's appearance as a successful businessman masked a hideous reality*

Natividad of being the attacker. Natividad promptly fled back to Mexico, and the case was soon forgotten.

Forgotten, that is, until the following year when, on 19 May 1971, one of Juan Corona's neighbours, a Japanese-American farmer who had hired some workers from Corona, noticed a hole that had been dug on his land. Suspicious, he asked police to investigate. On excavating the hole they found a body, which proved to be that of a drifter called Kenneth Whitacre. Whitacre had been stabbed in the chest and his head almost split in two by blows from a machete or similar cleaving instrument. Gay literature was

THE SKID ROW MURDERS

259

found on the body, leading the police to suspect a sexual motive.

Four days later, workers on a nearby ranch discovered a second body, a drifter called Charles Fleming. At this point, the police started searching the area in earnest. Over the next nine days they discovered a total of twenty-five bodies, mostly in an orchard on Corona's land. They had all been killed by knives or machetes: a deep stab wound to the chest and two gashes across the back of the head in the shape of a cross. In some, but not all, cases there was evidence of homosexual activity.

FRENZIED KILLING RATE

What was overwhelming was not just the number of victims, but the fact that none of the bodies had been in the ground for longer than six weeks. Whoever had killed them had been in the midst of an extraordinary orgy of murder, killing at a rate of more than one every two days. None of the dead had been reported as missing; indeed, four of them were never identified at all; the rest were migrant workers, drifters and bums.

The police quickly came up with a suspect: Juan Corona. To start with, all the bodies were buried on or near Corona's land. Secondly, two victims had bank receipts with Juan Corona's name on them in their pockets.

It was no more than circumstantial evidence, but the extraordinary scale of the crimes was enough to persuade the police to act, and Juan Corona was duly arrested and charged with the murders. His defence team tried to pin the blame on his brother Natividad, but failed to prove that Natividad was even in the country at the time.

Overall, Corona's defence was incompetent. They failed to mention that Juan had been diagnosed schizophrenic in 1956, which prevented them from mounting a defence of insanity. Even so, the lack of direct evidence meant that the jury deliberated for forty-five hours before finding Corona guilty. He was sentenced to twenty-five terms of life imprisonment.

Juan Corona continued to protest his innocence and he was allowed a retrial in 1978 on the grounds that his previous defence had been incompetent. Even with competent defence, however, Corona was again found guilty. While in prison he was the victim of an attack by a fellow inmate, in which he lost an eye. He is currently held in Corcoran State Prison along with Charles Manson. However, while Manson remains the focus of a gruesome following, Corona is ignored, and can be seen mumbling to himself in the prison courtyard – like his victims, another forgotten man.

SLAUGHTER OF THE INNOCENTS

In recent years, cold cases have been solved in different ways. Most often, it has been DNA profiling that has provided the concrete evidence needed to convict suspected killers, sometimes decades after the event.

In other cases, it has been dogged police work that, in the long run, has yielded results – tracking down the culprit through following up the slightest of leads, such as a name in a diary, or a watermark on an envelope. Then there are the cases where the perseverance of journalists, politicians, even friends and family, has pressurized the police and legal authorities to open the file and re-investigate the case once more.

But perhaps the most fascinating of all cold cases are the ones where witnesses have changed their minds and come forward to tell their story – people who saw or heard about a murder, but were unable or unwilling, for reasons of their own, to report it at the time; people whose consciences have continued to trouble them over the years, sometimes for decades.

In some cases, their relationship with the murderer may have changed so that they now feel free to speak: if they were once married to the murderer, they may now be divorced; if the murderer was their lover or friend, there may have been a falling out. In others, witnesses may be pressurized by the police or the law courts to tell their story; this applies especially to prisoners, who are often offered lighter sentences or other privileges if they assist the police with their enquiries. And, of course, once the culprit is safely in police custody, witnesses usually feel less frightened to speak; indeed, once the threat of retribution has been removed, they are often keen to relieve themselves of the burden of their knowledge. For it remains a fact that most people, however corrupt or depraved, consider murder – especially, as in this case, the murder of innocent children – a crime that cannot be forgotten or forgiven.

NAKED, BOUND BODIES

In October 1955, the brutal killing of three young boys who were on their way home from a trip to the cinema shocked the citizens of Chicago. Today, it might be thought unwise to let three ten-year-olds travel to the cinema and back by themselves in the big, bustling city of Chicago, but at that time, the area on the north-west side of the city was more or less crime-free, and it was

▲ Collapsed in grief: Mrs Schuessler is carried into church to attend the double funeral of her murdered sons, John, 13, and Anton, 11

a common enough practice to let children walk the streets on their own during the daytime. Accordingly, John and Anton Schuessler and their friend Bobby Peterson set out from their homes with their parents' permission, to watch a matinee at the cinema in the Loop downtown. Unfortunately, they did not come straight back home after the show ended, but stayed around in town to enjoy themselves for a while.

At six o'clock that evening, they were seen in the lobby of the Garland Building at number 111, North

Wabash. It was unclear why they were there. The only known link they had to the building was that Bobby Peterson had visited an eye doctor there, but that did not seem a reason for visiting the building on a Sunday.

The lobby was known at the time as a hang-out for gay men and prostitutes, and it is possible that they may have been there to meet an older boy, John Wayne Gacy. Gacy, who later became one of America's most notorious killers of all time, was known to frequent the building at that period. He also lived not far from John and Anton's family home. However, there is no record that the boys met up, and the theory remains speculative. Whatever the reason they went to the lobby, they did not stay for very long, and continued on their way to a bowling alley on West Montrose called the Monte Cristo.

Witnesses later reported that a man of around fifty was seen hanging around the many young boys playing in the bowling alley and eating in the restaurant. It was unclear whether the three boys spoke to the man. After that, they hitched a ride at the intersection of Lawrence and Milwaukee Avenue. Again, this was not an uncommon practice at the time. However, by now the boys had spent the four dollars their parents had given them for the trip, and it was getting late. When they did not return by nine o'clock that night, their parents began to get worried about them, and contacted the police.

BEATEN AND STRANGLED

The police conducted a search, but could not find the three boys. It was only when a salesman stopped to eat his lunch, two days later, that he saw the bodies of three children lying in a ditch not far from the river at Robinson Woods Indian Burial Grounds. The bodies were naked, bound up, and their eyes were covered with adhesive tape. There was evidence to show that they had been beaten and strangled. The coroner pronounced that their deaths had been caused through 'asphyxiation by suffocation', and a murder investigation was launched.

The crime deeply shocked the police officers, who described it as the worst murder scene they had ever witnessed. When news of the murders hit the headlines, the citizens of Chicago were horrified. As the father of one of the boys remarked, 'When you get to the point that children cannot go to the movies in the afternoon and get home safely, something is wrong with this country.'

THE CASE GOES COLD

The murder investigation began in Robinson Woods, with teams of officers searching the area to look for any clues such as items of clothing, footprints, or murder weapons. However, it appeared that the murderer had been very careful to cover up his traces. It was difficult to find fingerprints anywhere. Further examination of the bodies showed that they had probably been thrown from a car. Whoever had killed the boys had been an accomplished criminal, who was adept at escaping detection.

In retrospect it seems that, in the panic to find the killer, the police may have missed or misplaced vital clues. There were several different teams on the job,

▼ *Fathers of the boys: Malcom Peterson and Anton Schuessler at the inquest into the brutal slayings of their sons*

some of them from the central police department, and others from suburban forces. Perhaps for this reason, nothing of any significance was turned up; as it was, lack of co-ordination between the different teams, and the general prevailing air of confusion and shock, meant that little came out of the investigation – much to the disappointment of the officers concerned, and the public at large.

Out of respect for the three young victims, the Schuessler-Peterson case, as it became known, remained open. However, as the years went by, it became clear that no initiatives were being taken to move the investigation on. It was not until 1977, however, when the police were investigating the disappearance of candy heiress Helen Brach, that new and very promising information came to light – information that was to lead, through witnesses, to the boys' killer.

THE MURDERER FOUND

During the investigation, police talked to an informant named William Wemette who mentioned in passing that a man named Kenneth Hansen was known in some circles to have committed the murders. At the time of the murders, Hansen was twenty-two years old. He was working as a stable hand for a violent fraudster named Silas Jayne, who was notorious in the racing world as a cold-blooded killer. Jayne had actually been convicted of murdering his own brother, and had served a prison sentence for the crime.

Police investigators then talked to a number of other witnesses who, up to that time, had remained quiet about the stories involving Hansen and the three children. Apparently, Hansen had bragged to several men that he had lured the boys to his stables, telling them that he wanted to show them some special horses there. Once they were at the stables, he had sexually assaulted the boys, and had then strangled them. Shockingly, his employer Jayne had known of the killings, and had burned down the stables so as to destroy any clues. Not only that, but Jayne had actually collected insurance money on the buildings.

In August 1994, Hansen was arrested and charged with the murders. The following year, he was brought to trial. At the trial, the prosecution produced four witnesses who had been young men at the time of the murders. They were all now serving prison sentences in jail. The witnesses told how Hansen had promised them work in return for sex, and how he had threatened to kill them – as he had the three young boys – if they should ever speak of what he had

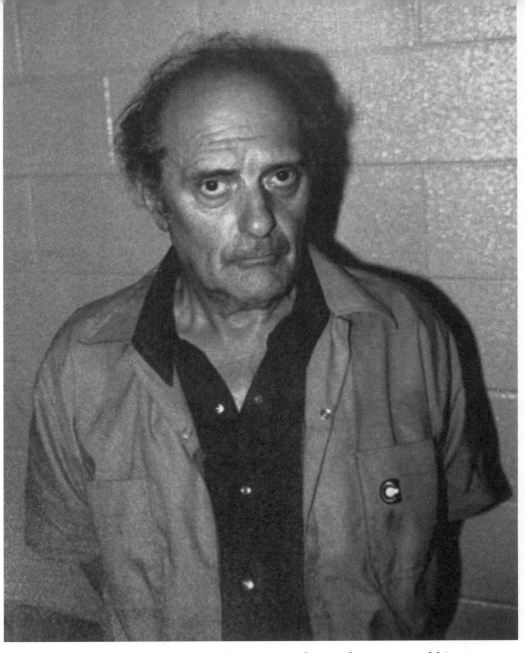

▶ *Justice is served: Kenneth Hansen on the day of his sentence in October 1995, a full 40 years after he beat and strangled three boys to death*

done. For more than forty years, they had lived with the knowledge of the child murders, but now they were able to come forward and bear witness to what had happened.

Kenneth Hansen was convicted of the three murders in September 1995. The presiding judge sentenced him to a term of two to three hundred years – in effect, life imprisonment. It had taken decades to find the boys' killer, but eventually, through the testimony of the witnesses, he was finally put in the place where he belonged – behind bars.

THE SON OF SAM KILLINGS

For just over a year the killer known as the 'Son of Sam' terrorized New York City. He was a lone gunman who killed without warning or apparent reason; his victims were young women and couples, shot dead as they sat in their cars or walked down the street. The terror intensified when the killer began to leave notes for the police and to write to the newspapers – strange, rambling letters in which he referred to himself as the 'Son of Sam'. For a while this killer achieved demonic status in the popular imagination, but when he was finally caught he turned out to be a seemingly ordinary individual named David Berkowitz, a twenty-three-year old native New Yorker.

For the first twenty or so years of his life, David Berkowitz was not someone people took a lot of notice of. He was born on 1 June 1953 and was immediately given up for adoption by his birth mother, Betty Falco. His adoptive parents, Nathan and Pearl Berkowitz, were quiet people who kept to themselves. David grew into a big, awkward boy who found it hard to make friends. His adoptive mother

tragically died of pancreatic cancer when David was fourteen.

MOTHER'S DEATH

His mother's death deeply affected him and his previously good grades in school started to slip. Then his father married again, to a woman who did not take to David. In 1971, his father and stepmother moved to a retirement community in Florida, leaving David in New York. He responded by joining the army, where he remained for three years, learning to become an expert marksman along the way. It was also during this time that David, who was extremely awkward with women, had his only sexual experience, with a Korean prostitute who left him with a venereal disease.

VIOLENT FANTASIES

Berkowitz left the army in 1974, returned to New York and got a job as a security guard. Meanwhile, he was starting to nurse increasingly violent fantasies about women and his overall mental state was declining rapidly. He evidently had some awareness of this, as he wrote to his father in November 1975 that: 'The world is getting dark now. I can feel it more and more. The people, they are developing a hatred for me. You would not believe how much some people hate me. Many of them want to kill me. I do not even know these

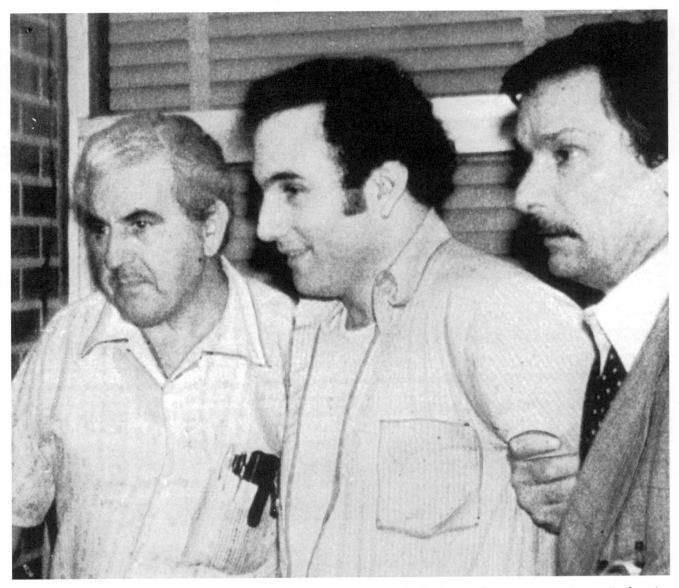

▲ *The apparently mild David Berkowitz is led to trial for a gruesome spate of killings*

people, but still they hate me. Most of them are young. I walk down the street and they spit and kick at me. The girls call me ugly and they bother me the most. The guys just laugh. Anyhow, things will soon change for the better.'

With hindsight this was part cry for help and part warning. Berkowitz believed he was surrounded by demons urging him to kill, and he felt increasingly powerless to resist them. Finally, he snapped. At Christmas he went out armed with a knife and stabbed two young women. Both survived.

Next time the demons spoke to him he was armed with a gun. In July 1976, two young women, Jody Valenti and Donna Lauria, were sitting in a car in Queens, New York when an unseen assailant approached and shot them both through the windscreen. Lauria was killed, Valenti survived.

There was not a huge reaction immediately: it was just another New York horror story. Then, three months later, in October, Berkowitz struck again. Carl Denaro and Rosemary Keenan were also sitting in a parked car when a shot rang out, hitting Denaro. The pair survived. The bullet matched the one that had killed Lauria.

A month later, Berkowitz shot his next victims, Donna DeMasi and Joanna Lomino, outside a house in Queens. Both survived, though DeMasi was left paralysed as the bullet had struck her spine. By now, police and public alike were aware that a deranged gunman was on the loose.

Berkowitz waited until the New Year before killing again. In January 1977 he shot Christine Freund dead as she sat in a car with her boyfriend John Diel. Next, in March, he shot Virginia Voskerichian dead as she walked home. A month later, he went for a couple again. This time, both Valentina Suriani and her boyfriend Alexander Esau were killed instantly. A note was found at the scene, addressed to the policeman leading the investigation:

'Dear Captain Joseph Borrelli, I am deeply hurt by your calling me a wemon (sic) hater. I am not. But I am a monster. I am the "Son of Sam". I am a little brat. When father Sam gets drunk he gets mean. He beats his family. Sometimes he ties me up to the back of the house. Other times he locks me in the garage. Sam loves to drink blood. "Go out and kill," commands father Sam.'

The note was leaked to the press in early June and public anxiety mounted. Then, in June, Berkowitz struck again, shooting Salvatore Lupo and Judy Placido as they sat in their car. Fortunately, both survived.

More letters from the 'Son of Sam' followed, both to the police and to the press. It was a boiling hot summer but New Yorkers, especially those living in Queens, were afraid to go out. The police investigation was drowning in too much information, too little of it concrete. Among the leads they did not have time to follow up was a tip from Yonkers resident Sam Carr, who had been receiving anonymous letters about his dog, followed by his dog being shot. Carr had come up with a suspect, a neighbour called David Berkowitz.

The police did not act in time to prevent Berkowitz from striking again. In

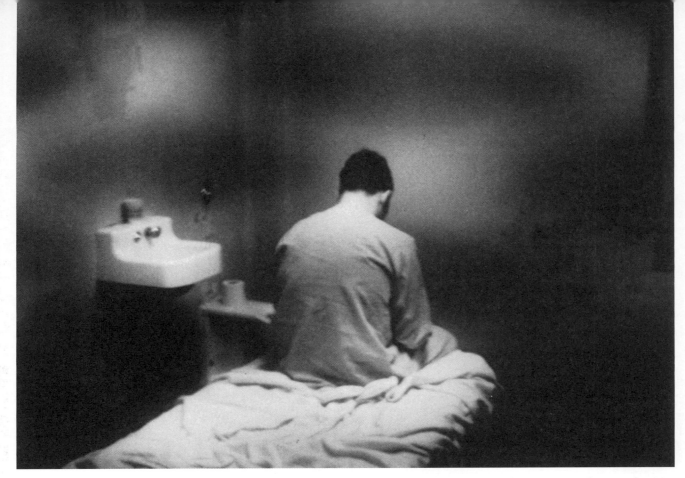

▲ *Berkowitz waits on death row*

July, Robert Violante and Stacy Moskowitz parked their car, feeling safe because they were in Brooklyn, not Queens. Berkowitz shot them both, killing Moskowitz and blinding Violante.

Following this assault, the police were told that a man had been seen fleeing the scene in a car that had received a parking ticket. A check on parking tickets produced the name of David Berkowitz, among others. Cross-referencing this with the tip from Sam Carr, the police were confident they had found their man.

They staked out Berkowitz's house and found his car parked outside with a rifle lying on the front seat. When Berkowitz emerged they arrested him and he immediately confessed. Though evidently a paranoid schizophrenic, he was found sane and guilty and sentenced to 365 years in prison, a sentence he is still serving.

While in prison he has become an evangelical Christian and his church maintains a website on which Berkowitz publishes his, mostly religious, thoughts. In recent years, the Spike Lee film *Summer of Sam* has reminded New York of the time when one paranoid loner held the entire city to ransom.

STRAIGHT A FOR MURDER

Charlie Whitman was to all appearances a straight-A American. At one time he'd been the youngest Eagle Scout in the World. He'd graduated seventh in his class at a Catholic School in Lake Worth, Florida; and he'd won a Navy and Marine Corps scholarship to the University of Texas in Austin. Yet in one morning, on August 1st 1966, this 6-foot-tall, twenty-five-year-old killed fifteen people and wounded another twenty-eight in the bloodiest single rampage within living memory.

What exactly was in his mind when he took the service elevator up to the observation-deck on the clock tower next to the University of Texas's administration-building, we will never know. But he was carrying six rifles and pistols with more than 700 rounds of ammunition, not to mention three hunting knives, a machete and a hatchet.

He had already stabbed to death first his mother and then his wife, leaving notes beside their bodies saying how much he loved them. He also said that he hated his father and that life was no longer worth living.

He meant, then, to die. But first there was business to attend to. So at the entrance to the observation deck he killed the receptionist and two visitors. Then he went out onto the deck itself and, protected by 4-foot high stone parapets, he started shooting anyone he could see. One of the people he hit was crossing a street 500 yards away.

When the police arrived they knew there was little they could do from the ground. While a police marksman in a light aircraft distracted Whitman, an team of police and volunteers entered the tower unseen and then climb up to the deck. Whitman fought back, but died in a hail of shotgun fire, just an hour and a half after he'd arrived.

A TASTE FOR FLESH

The most infamous white cannibal of the American West was Alferd [sic] G. Packer. Famous '60s folk-singer Phil Ochs wrote a song about him, and Colorado University students named their dining room in his honour. He was also the recipient of a wonderful comic epitaph: 'There were only seven Democrats in Hinsdale County,' his trial judge told him, 'and you ate five of them, you depraved Republican son of a bitch!'.

In the autumn of 1873, Packer agreed to guide a party of nineteen gold prospectors into the San Juan Mountains of western Colorado. He was in his mid-twenties, already a veteran of the Union Army, and supposedly knew the area inside out. If so, his decision to leave for the high country in autumn seems rather strange.

For several weeks the party headed south-eastwards from their Salt Lake City starting point. They found no gold, but did manage to lose some of their supplies in a botched river-crossing. Winter was fast approaching, and the whole party was close to starvation when they stumbled, by luck, into Chief Ouray's Gunnison Valley camp. Ouray gave Packer and his party all they could spare, and earnestly entreated them to give up their folly while they still could. Ten listened, and headed back to Salt Lake City. The nine who refused to abandon their gold fixation were advised to follow the course of the Gunnison River.

Packer had other ideas. The party's intended destination was near the source of the Rio Grande, and he claimed he knew a short cut across the mountains. Four of his nine followers decided they should stick with Ouray's advice, but five took the fatal decision to follow Packer. They only had two days' worth of food, and a blizzard soon brought them to a hungry halt. For a while they lived on rosebuds and pine gum, which probably taste worse than they sound. Either way, they were not enough to live on.

Of the four who followed Ouray's advice, two died of starvation. The other two reached the Los Pinos Indian Agency in February 1874. The Agent Charles Adams supervised their recovery before sending them back down to civilization. Packer showed up a month later, alone. He also pleaded for food, but he did not look that hungry. When Adams asked him what had happened to his companions, he said they had deserted him. Adams was suspicious, but he had no way of disproving the story. He fed Packer and let him go.

The evidence Adams needed trickled in over the next two months. Packer himself was one witness. He failed to discard guns and knives which were later recognized as belonging to the other members of his group, and he let slip a stream of interesting details while drunk in public.

This was enough for Adams to have him arrested, but a second piece of evidence was provided by Indians. Just before reaching the Agency, they noticed some pieces of what looked like strips of human flesh. Adams put two and two together – Packer had dumped his supply before coming in. Adams confronted Packer with the pieces of flesh.

Packer may not have been the brightest person ever, but he had had plenty of time to work out a story. The other five had indeed been killed, he said, but he had only killed one of them, and that in self defence. The first man, Swan, had been killed while he, Packer, was out gathering wood, and was already being cut up for consumption when he returned. The food had not lasted long, and Packer himself had suggested that another man, the corpulent Miller, should be next. One of the others had split his skull with a hatchet. Two more men had gone the same way, leaving only Packer and a man named Bell. 'One day Bell said: "I can stand it no longer!" and he rushed at me like a famished tiger, at the same time attempting to strike me with his gun. I killed him with a hatchet'.

It seemed like a good story until a painter named Reynolds came across the five bodies during a search for picturesque slices of wilderness. Five of them were lined up in a row. Four of the men had been shot in the back of the head; the fifth, Miller, had had his skull smashed in with a rifle butt. Packer's story had been a tissue of lies.

He escaped before charges could be brought, and spent at least some of the next nine years living the outlaw life in Wyoming. He was eventually recognized by another gold prospector, arrested, and brought back to Lake City, Colorado for trial. His story had been rearranged to accommodate the known facts, but he still insisted that he had only killed the one man, and that in self-defence. The jury found him less than credible, and voted for the death penalty, but Packer was not finished yet.

An appeal was granted, the execution stayed, a retrial ordered. This time he was sentenced to forty years on five counts of manslaughter, but only served seventeen. He always swore he was innocent, but when forensic scientists re-examined the skeletal remains in 1989, they found that the four men had all been shot with the same gun – Packer's.

THIS CHARMING MAN

Everyone liked Theodore Bundy. Even the judge at his Miami trial in July 1979 took to him. After sentencing Bundy to death, he said:

'Take care of yourself, young man. I say that to you sincerely. It's a tragedy to this court to see such a total waste of humanity. You're a bright young man. You'd have made a good lawyer.'

But Bundy's good looks and intelligence were murderous. For between January 1974 and January 1978, when he was finally arrested in Pensacola, Florida, he brutalised and killed perhaps as many as thirty-six girls and young women in four states.

The first of these states was Washington, where the disappearances began in the Seattle area at the beginning of 1974. One after another, within six months, seven young women vanished, seemingly into thin air. One of them had been abducted from a rented room; another had left a bar with a man at two in the morning. But the others had simply been out for a walk or on their way somewhere: a cinema or a concert or home. Except for bloodstains in the rented room, they left no trace at all.

In the summer of that year, there were more disappearances, including two in one day from a Washington lakeside resort. But there were also, for the first time, clues. For a good looking young man with his arm in a sling – and introducing himself as Ted – had been going around the resort asking young women if they could help him load a sailboat onto the roof of his car; and one of the disappeared had been seen going off with him. The scattered remains of both women – and of yet another unknown victim – were found by hunters a few miles away two months later.

A massive manhunt began, producing huge numbers of calls from the public and more than 2,000 potential suspects – among them, thanks to a woman's call, Theodore (Ted) Bundy. But by that time he'd moved to Salt Lake City in Utah to study law; and it was there that the disappearances resumed.

There were three in October 1974; one the teenage daughter of a local police chief, who was later found – raped, strangled and buried – in the Wassatch Mountains. Then, at the beginning of November, one of his Salt Lake City victims – whom 'a good-looking man' posing as a police officer had lured into his car and had then attacked with a crowbar – managed to

escape and to give a description to the police.

Bundy was lucky this time for she failed to recognise him in a photograph the police later showed her. But after one last abduction and murder in Salt Lake City, he from then on began to operate only out-of state, over the border in Colorado. Between January and July, five more young women disappeared, this time two of the bodies were discovered quickly. One, had been beaten to death with a rock. The other had been raped and then bludgeoned.

Bundy, in the end, was picked up by accident, as a possible burglary suspect.

▲ *Even the judge liked Ted Bundy, a 'charming and personable young man'*

275

▶Bundy always protested his innocence, right up to his execution

But police at the scene found a crowbar, an ice-pick and a ski-mask in his trunk; and in his apartment, maps and brochures of Colorado. Hairs from the interior of the car were found to match those of the police-chief's dead daughter. He was extradited to Colorado to stand trial; but then he escaped – twice.

The first time he was quickly found hiding out in the mountains. But the second time it took police more than forty days to catch him, and by then – this time in Florida – another three young women were dead, one of them with teeth marks on her body; three other women had been savagely beaten but survived.

The subsequent trial did little to uncover Bundy's reasons for killing – for the sheer viciousness and voracity of his sexual attacks. But in an interview with a detective after his arrest, he remarked:

'Sometimes I feel like a vampire'

and later, on Death Row, though never confessing to the murders, he speculated to two writers about an early career as a Peeping Tom and a massive consumer of pornography. He also talked about an 'entity' inside him that drove him to rape and murder.

It was the marks of his teeth – experts confirmed his identity from these– on the body of a Tallahassee student killed when Bundy was on the run that finally undid Bundy. After numerous, lengthy appeals, he was electrocuted on 24 January 1989, protesting his innocence.

TRAIL OF DESTRUCTION

Every serial killer leaves a trail of destruction, not only of victims whose lives are destroyed, but also of whole networks of families, friends and loved ones. In the case of the Belgian serial killer Marc Dutroux, however, the havoc he wrought had even wider repercussions. His crimes traumatized the entire nation, provoked the biggest demonstrations ever seen in the country and caused the resignations of several government ministers. For not only was Dutroux a paedophile and a murderer, but he was linked to a paedophile ring that included many people in positions of authority.

HOMOSEXUAL PROSTITUTE

Marc Dutroux was born in Brussels, Belgium's capital city, on 6 November 1956. He was the eldest of six children born to Victor and Jeanine Dutroux. Both parents were teachers; Marc later claimed that they frequently beat him. However, Dutroux's statements on this or any other matter must be regarded with extreme caution. What we do know is that the couple split in 1971, when Dutroux was fifteen. Soon afterwards he left home, drifted into petty crime and, according to some press accounts, became a homosexual prostitute.

By the time he was twenty, Dutroux had found a trade as an electrician. He had married his first wife and had two children with her, before she divorced him on the grounds of infidelity and violence. One of the women with whom he had had extra-marital affairs was Michele Martin, who later became his second wife. She evidently shared his darker sexual predilections.

In 1989, the pair were both convicted of child abuse, jointly abducting five girls for Dutroux to rape. Dutroux was sentenced to thirteen years in prison but was released for good behaviour after serving only three years inside. This was despite Dutroux's mother writing to the prison authorities at the time to say that, during supervised outings from prison to visit his grandmother, Dutroux had terrified the old lady by making an inventory of her possessions. The prison authorities had never replied to Madame Dutroux's letters.

Prior to going to prison, Dutroux had become involved in various criminal enterprises ranging from mugging to drug dealing. On his release, he made no effort to find work; instead, the first thing he did was to build a dungeon underneath a house in

▲ *Dutroux wears a bullet proof vest at his trial to guard against revenge attacks*

As with so many serial killers, it is quite possible that Dutroux is guilty of more crimes than we are aware of. It seems unlikely that his dungeon was unused for three years. However, the first atrocity we know of took place on 24 June 1995 when two eight-year-old girls, Julie Lejeune and Melissa Russo, were abducted from near their homes in Liege, Belgium. They were taken to Dutroux's dungeon, where they were kept as sexual playthings and almost certainly abused by the members of a paedophile ring.

Two months later, Dutroux and an accomplice Bernard Weinstein abducted two teenage girls, An Marchal and Eefje Lambreks, from the seaside town of Ostend. They were taken to Weinstein's house and raped by both men. At some point both girls were killed, and then for unknown reasons Dutroux also killed Weinstein. He buried all three bodies under a shed in the garden.

STARVED TO DEATH

Meanwhile the two children were still alive in the Charleroi dungeon. The police received a tip-off about Dutroux, and called at the house; however, during their search they failed to notice the dungeon, even though they had been specifically told of its existence. Then, in December 1995, Dutroux was

the town of Charleroi, one of several houses he had bought with his criminal gains. The dungeon was to be used not only for the abuse of children but also to film that abuse; the videos would be sold to paedophiles who would pay vast sums of money for this material.

sentenced to four months in prison for car theft. When he left for prison he told Michele Martin to feed the two girls. Almost unbelievably, she failed to do this. Even though she visited the house regularly to feed Dutroux's dogs, she claimed to have been too scared to go down into the cellar to feed the girls. They starved to death.

When Dutroux came out of prison he found their dead bodies, put them in a freezer for a while, and then buried them in the garden of another of his houses, in Sars-la-Buissiere. On 28 May, he kidnapped Sabine Dardenne, aged fourteen, and took her to the dungeon. He told her that he was rescuing her from a paedophile gang that was responsible for kidnapping her and was awaiting a ransom from her family. As she recorded in her diary, he then raped her around twenty times. After seventy-two days in the dungeon, on 9 August, she was joined by Dutroux's latest victim, Laetitia Delhez, aged twelve.

This time, however, a witness noticed a suspicious car close to where Delhez was abducted. The car belonged to Dutroux and, on 13 August the police arrested Dutroux and Martin at the house in Sars-la-Buissiere. Two days later, they raided the Charleroi house and found the dungeon. They brought out Dardenne and Delhez alive. Over the next few weeks, Dutroux insisted that he was merely a pawn in a much wider conspiracy. As the nation looked on in horror, he led the police to the bodies of his five victims.

That horror turned to anger as the prosecution of the case dragged on endlessly, fuelling speculation that it was being deliberately sabotaged by paedophiles in the higher echelons of Belgian society. The lead prosecutor in the case was then suddenly removed from his job. The Belgian people responded by mounting a huge demonstration, complaining at the authorities' corruption.

Two years later, Dutroux briefly escaped custody, further angering the public. This episode forced the resignation of two government ministers. Even so, it was another six years before the case at last came to trial, in March 2004. Dutroux tried to blame his accomplices for everything, but the testimony of the surviving victims, particularly Sabine Dardenne, incriminated him utterly.

In June 2004 Dutroux was found guilty of murder and sentenced to life in prison without the possibility of parole. Michele Martin was sentenced to thirty years for her unspeakable cruelty in abetting Dutroux and letting the two girls starve to death.

THE UNABOMBER

Ted Kaczynski, also known as 'The Unabomber', was a highly intelligent, educated man who nevertheless organized a series of crude bombings that killed and maimed a number of people. He apparently carried out the crimes in the belief that he was helping to cause the downfall of civilized society and halt the progress of technology; but it also emerged that, although he had a brilliant academic mind, he was mentally unbalanced.

He was born Theodore John Kaczynski in Chicago on 22 May 1942. He grew up in Evergreen Park, a working-class area in the suburbs of Chicago. While still a baby, he had a strong allergic reaction to some medicine he was given, and had to be taken to hospital. He was kept there for several weeks, separated from his parents, who were only allowed to visit occasionally.

His mother attests that, having been a happy baby before the incident, he then became withdrawn and turned away from human contact. It is thought that this separation may have caused him mental health problems later in life.

MATHEMATICS GENIUS

Despite this early setback, Ted showed very high intelligence as a young child, and was clearly very gifted. However, he entirely lacked social skills, and was disinclined to play with other children or to engage with adults. He did well academically, graduating from high school early after skipping several grades. He went on to study mathematics at Harvard, earning his degree there, and then gaining a master's degree and a Ph.D. from Ann Arbor University, Michigan.

He astounded his professors with his ability to solve problems they could not, and in a short time reached a level in the subject that only a handful of people in the country would have been able to comprehend. Not surprisingly, he was offered a fellowship and teaching work, and spent three years as a lecturer in Michigan. He went on to publish a number of papers on mathematics in several learned journals.

Kaczynski was then offered a post at the University of California, Berkeley. He spent two years there as an assistant professor in mathematics, before abruptly resigning from the job in 1969. It was unclear why such a brilliant mathematician, who could have reached the top of his profession in a very short time, suddenly quit the academic scene.

KILLER MAIL BOMBS

Kaczynski no longer had a source of income, other than the occasional odd jobs he did locally. His family also helped him out, lending him money. However, he was now very poor, and lived in a cabin in the countryside, isolated from the community and becoming more and more eccentric.

In the late 1970s, Kaczynski began to send bombs through the mail. His first target was a university professor who became suspicious and had the package opened by a campus police officer. It exploded, but fortunately the officer was only slightly injured. Next, Kaczynski began to target airlines, sending bombs designed to explode in airports and on aeroplanes. The bombs were home-made, and not very efficient, so initially little damage was done.

However, Kaczynski then stepped up his campaign with bombs that, while still primitive, were now lethal. In 1985, he sent one to the University of California, which resulted in a student losing four of his fingers and the sight in one eye. In the same year, Kaczynski began to target computer stores, leaving nail bombs in the parking lots outside these stores. In one case, the store owner was killed outright.

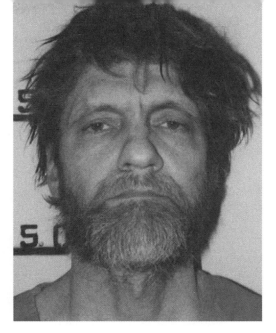

◀ *When put beside those of suave mobsters or white-collar fraudsters, Ted Kaczynski's plans were crude, yet effective*

THE UNABOMBER MANIFESTO

After this atrocity, Kaczynski's activities ceased for a while. However, in 1993 his next target was a computer science professor at Yale University, David Gelernter, who survived the bomb Kaczynski mailed to him. Another academic, geneticist Charles Epstein, was not so lucky. He was maimed by one of Kaczynski's bombs in the same year. In 1994, Kaczynski targeted an advertising executive, and the year after, the president of the California Forestry Association.

Kaczynski now began to write letters to the papers, and in some cases to his former victims, claiming responsibility for the attacks, on behalf of his 'anarchist group' Freedom Club (FC). He demanded that a manifesto he had written be printed in one of the US's major newspapers and claimed that he would then end his bombing campaign. In order to try to resolve the situation, *The New York Times* printed it, which became known as 'The Unabomber Manifesto'. A great deal of controversy surrounded this decision; in some quarters, it was felt that this was pandering to the murderer. However, the newspaper argued that printing the manifesto might help to solve the mystery of who the Unabomber was, and track the culprit down.

The manifesto was a rant, though at times an intelligent and informed one, against the evils of modern technology. It argued that human beings suffer from the 'progress' of technology, which harms the majority of people on the planet and causes immense environmental damage. Its author believed that the only way forward was through halting technological progress, and returning to the simple life, living close to nature. Kaczynski also criticized 'leftists' for allowing an advanced, complex society to develop to the detriment of humanity.

CLOSING IN ON KACZYNSKI

When the manifesto was published, Kaczynski's brother David recognized it as putting forward Ted's ideas in the writing style he knew only too well. At one time, David had admired his brother greatly, and followed his ideas. In fact, he had bought a plot of land with Ted outside Lincoln in western Montana. Ted now lived there, in a 10 x 12-foot cabin without electricity or running water. He led a reclusive life, rarely going out, as his neighbours later reported, except to buy food that he could not grow in his garden.

David had baled out from this way of life early on and decided to join the mainstream. When he realized that his brother must be responsible for the bombings, he contacted the police and told them where Ted could be found. Officers arrested Ted Kaczynski at his cabin in Montana in April 1996.

The FBI had assured David that they would not tell his brother who had turned him in, but unfortunately, his identity was later leaked. David used the reward money he received to pay his brother's legal expenses, but also to recompense the families of his brother's victims.

When the case came to trial, the most obvious defence for Ted Kaczynski was insanity, but Kaczynski rejected this. Instead, he was diagnosed fit to stand trial, though suffering from schizophrenia. Kaczynski pleaded guilty to the bombings, but later withdrew his plea. The withdrawal was not accepted, and Kaczynski was given a life sentence with no parole. Today, he continues to serve out his sentence in Florence, Colorado.

THE UNLIKELY COUPLE

Doug Clark and Carol Bundy appeared to make an unlikely couple. Doug was a good-looking man from a well-to-do family, a thirty-two-year-old charmer with a string of girlfriends pining after him. Carol was a divorcee with thick glasses and a weight problem. Five years older than Clark, she had recently split from an abusive husband and was working as a nurse. Underneath, however, the pair had a great deal in common: both were sexually driven, both lacked a moral compass and together they embarked on a rampage of sexually motivated murder.

'KING OF THE ONE NIGHT STAND'
Douglas Daniel Clark was born in 1948, the son of a Naval Intelligence officer, Franklin Clark. The family moved repeatedly during Doug's childhood, due to his father's work. He later claimed to have lived in thirty-seven countries. In 1958, his father left the navy to take up a civilian position as an engineer with the Transport Company of Texas: some sources suggest that this was in fact merely a cover for continuing intelligence

◄ *The plain Carol seemed an unlikely mate for attractive Doug, but they shared a passion for murder*

activities. Either way, it did not put a stop to the family's nomadic lifestyle. They lived in the Marshall Islands for a time, moved back to San Francisco, and then moved again to India. For a while Doug was sent to an exclusive international school in Geneva. Later, he attended the prestigious Culver Military Academy while his father continued to move around the world. When he graduated in 1967, Doug naturally enough enlisted in the air force.

At this point, however, Clark's life began to unravel. He was discharged from the air force and for the next decade he drifted around, often working as a mechanic, but really concentrating on his vocation as a sexual athlete: 'the king of the one night stand' as he called himself. The 70s was the decade when casual sex first became a widespread, socially acceptable phenomenon – at least in the

▲ Clark was always the picture of a charming and confident man in court

big cities – and Doug Clark, a smooth-talking, well-educated young man, was well placed to take advantage of this change in the nation's morals.

Nowhere was this lifestyle more prevalent than Los Angeles, and eventually Doug Clark moved there, taking a job in a factory in Burbank. One of the bars he liked to frequent and pick up women was a place in North Hollywood called Little Nashville, where, in 1980, he met Carol Bundy.

Bundy was thirty-seven years old. She had had a troubled childhood: her mother had died when she was young, and her father had abused her. Then, when her father remarried, he had put her in various foster homes. At the age of seventeen, Bundy had married a fifty-six-year-old man; by the time she met Clark she had recently escaped a third marriage to an abusive man, by whom she had had two young sons. Most recently, she had begun an affair with her apartment block manager, a part-time country singer called John Murray. She had even attempted to bribe Murray's wife to leave him. Murray's wife was not pleased at this and had told her husband to have Bundy evicted from the block. However, this had not ended the infatuation and Bundy continued to show up regularly at venues where Murray was singing. One of these was Little Nashville.

Clark, an experienced manipulator of women, quickly saw the potential in seducing the overweight and transparently needy Bundy. He turned on the charm and won her over immediately. Before long, he moved into her apartment and soon discovered that this was a woman with whom he could share his increasingly dark sexual fantasies.

PROSTITUTES

He started bringing prostitutes back to the flat to have sex with them both. Then he began to take an interest in an eleven-year-old girl who was a neighbour. Carol helped lure the girl into sexual games and posing for sexual photographs. Even breaking the paedophile taboo was not enough for Clark, however. He started to talk about how much he would like to kill a girl during sex and persuaded Carol to go out and buy two automatic pistols for him to use.

The killing began in earnest during June 1980. In June, Clark came home and told Bundy about the two teenagers he had picked up on the Sunset Strip that day and subsequently murdered. He had ordered them to perform fellatio on him and then shot them both in the head before taking them to a garage and raping their dead bodies. He had then dumped the bodies beside the Ventura freeway, where they were found the next day. Carol was sufficiently shocked by this news to make a phone call to the police admitting to some knowledge of the murders but refusing to give any clues as to the identity of the murderer.

REFRIDGERATED REMAINS

Twelve days later, when Clark killed again, Bundy had clearly got over her qualms. The victims were two prostitutes, Karen Jones and Exxie Wilson. Once again, Clark had picked them up, shot them and dumped the bodies in plain view, but this time he had decided to take a trophy: Exxie Wilson's head. He took the head back to Bundy's house and surprised her by producing it from her fridge. Almost unbelievably, she then put make-up on the head before Clark used it for another bout of necrophilia. Two days later, they put the freshly scrubbed head in a box and dumped it in an alleyway. Three days after this, another body was found in the woods in the San Fernando Valley. The victim was a runaway called Marnette Comer, who appeared to have been killed three weeks previously, making her Clark's first known victim.

▶ *Clark reportedly waits out his days on death row playing bridge with fellow inmates and serial killers Lawrence Bittaker and William Bonin*

Clark waited a month before killing again. Meanwhile Bundy was still infatuated with John Murray. She would go to see him singing in Little Nashville, and after a few drinks her conversation would turn to the kind of things she and Clark got up to. These hints alarmed Murray, who implied he might tell the police. To avert this, Bundy lured Murray into his van after a show to have sex. Once they were inside the van, she shot him dead and decapitated him. However, she had left a trail of clues behind her: Bundy and Murray had been seen in the bar together and she had left shell casings in the van.

Bundy herself was unable to take the pressure. Two days later, she confessed to her horrified co-workers that she had killed Murray. They promptly called the police and Bundy began to give them a full and frank confession about her and Clark's crimes.

Clark was immediately arrested and the guns found hidden at his work. Bundy was charged with two murders: Murray and the unknown victim whose killing she confessed to having been present at. Clark was charged with six murders. At his trial he represented himself and tried to blame Bundy for everything, portraying himself as an innocent dupe.

The jury did not believe him, and he was sentenced to the death penalty, while Bundy received life imprisonment. Ironically enough, it was Bundy who met her end first, dying in prison on 9 December 2003 at the age of sixty-one. Clark, meanwhile, continues to fight his conviction.

THE VATICAN FRAUD

Martin Frankel conducted one of the most far-reaching series of frauds in the history of the US financial world. With no formal qualifications and a string of failed business ventures behind him, he managed to pose as an investment specialist and persuade several skilled, intelligent people to part with their money and involve themselves in his scams. He showed no moral scruples whatsoever, and for many years got away with his crimes. However, his insecurity and paranoia finally got the better of him, and he was eventually brought to justice when his trail of lies was uncovered.

Born in Toledo, Ohio, in 1954, Frankel's father was a well-respected Lucas County judge, Leon Frankel. Martin was the second child of the family. He was a bright pupil at school and did well at his studies, but socially he was a misfit. After leaving high school, he went on to study at the University of Toledo, but dropped out of his course before finishing it. He had developed a crippling fear of taking tests, and was also completely unable to discipline himself to work. It seems that his early success at school had been achieved without trying very hard, and he had later become anxious about any situation in which he had to make an effort, or in which there was a chance of being seen to fail.

After dropping out of college, Frankel began to take an interest in the world of finance. He believed that by researching and playing the securities market, he could earn a great deal of money very quickly – which, fortunately, proved to be the case. Unfortunately, however, he did not also take into account that he could also lose it just as quickly, especially if he had gained it under false pretences.

FEAR OF FAILURE

Frankel took to hanging around brokerage houses, learning as much as he could about the finance business. He took a particular interest in big fraud cases, such as that of Robert Vesco, who had masterminded one of the largest swindles in US history. He met many business people, befriending a couple named John and Sonia Schulte, who owned a securities business affiliated to the New York company of Dominick & Dominick. Frankel impressed the couple with his extensive knowledge of the market and with a scheme that he said could help him predict which stocks

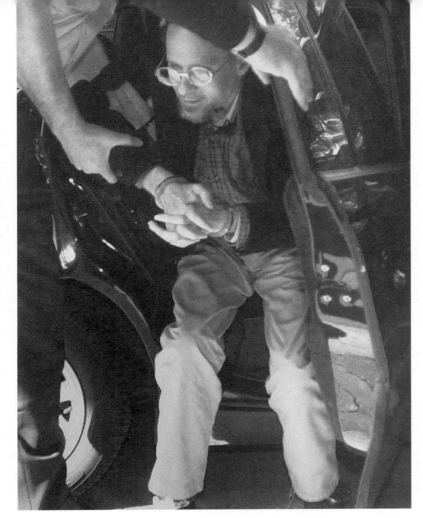

▲ *Martin Frankel is helped out of a car on the way to his trial in Hamburg. Having had the potential for a glittering future, his choice to go down the path of criminality was a particularly poor one*

would yield a great deal of money in future.

Sonia Schulte persuaded her husband to take Frankel on as a consultant analyst, but it was not long before John Schulte regretted his decision. Frankel was not a good employee. He refused to conform to the company's dress code, turning up for work in jeans rather than a suit and tie. His money-making scheme was also failing to yield any good results. One of the problems was that, although Frankel knew how to analyze the market, he did not actually have the confidence to trade.

As with taking tests at school, he feared that he would be seen to fail.

The final straw for Schulte was when Frankel posed as an agent working for the larger affiliated firm of Dominick & Dominick, a move that could have put his boss out of business. Schulte lost patience with his new employee and fired him. However, that was by no means the end of his relationship with Frankel: for, by this time, Frankel had become Sonia's lover.

THE VATICAN FRAUD

Now unemployed and living at his parents' house, Frankel set up his own bogus investment business, which he named Winthrop Capital. He advertised in the yellow pages, and gained the trust of several clients, telling all sorts of lies to do so. However, his investments were not sound, and he lost a great deal of money on his clients' behalf. Not deterred, he set up another business, Creative Partners Fund LP. He was joined by Sonia Schulte, who by this time had left her husband. Together, the pair set up another company, Thunor Trust, and began buying failing insurance companies, doing shady deals to fund their ever more lavish lifestyle.

Frankel's next, and most bizarre, scam was to mastermind a fraudulent charity scheme with links to the Vatican. Posing as a wealthy philanthropist, he set up a body called the St Francis of Assisi Foundation, and made several important contacts: with Thomas Bolan, founder of the Conservative Party of New York; and with two well-known New York priests, Peter Jacobs and Emilio Colagiovanni. It was a complicated fraud, involving the buying and selling of insurance companies with funds certified to belong to the Vatican, but the lure for all parties was a simple one: money.

SADOMASOCHISTIC ORGIES

By 1998, Frankel's assets were over four million dollars. He and Sonia moved to a large mansion in Greenwich, Connecticut, together with Sonia's two daughters. However, the new family home was not a happy one. Frankel began to show a greedy sexual appetite and a cruel streak, surrounding himself with young women and hosting sadomasochistic orgies in the house. Sonia soon left with her daughters. In 1997, one of the young women living in the house, who had apparently been rejected by Frankel, hanged herself there.

By 1999, Frankel's many nefarious dealings were finally attracting the attention of the authorities. His companies were put under state supervision, and it seemed only a matter of time before his rackets would be revealed for what they were. Frankel became extremely anxious and decided to make a run for it. He assumed several false identities and hired a private jet to fly him to Europe, taking with him millions of dollars' worth of diamonds. He also took with him two of his girlfriends, who later baled out and were replaced as companions by an employee called Cynthia Allison. He hid out until he was finally found, along with Cynthia, in one of the most luxurious hotels in Hamburg, Germany. He was immediately arrested.

INDICTED FOR FRAUD

Frankel was indicted by the US federal government for frauds worth over two million dollars. The German authorities also accused him of using a false passport and smuggling diamonds into the country. He pleaded guilty to the German charges, but came up with several far-fetched excuses, including the claim that he had smuggled in the diamonds so that he could feed the poor and hungry of the world. Not surprisingly, the German courts were not impressed with this story, and at his trial Frankel received a three-year sentence. While serving out his sentence, he attempted to escape from prison, but failed. In 2002, Frankel was charged with twenty-four federal counts of fraud and racketeering in the US, and finally sentenced to more than sixteen years in prison.

THE VOODOO KILLINGS

One of the most horrifying cult murderers of modern times was Adolfo Constanzo. Constanzo's speciality was ritually torturing and killing his victims: he ripped out their hearts and brains, boiled them and then ate the result. According to Constanzo's perverted logic, this ritual slaughter – which was derived from the Santeria and Voodoo religious practices his mother had taught him as a child – was intended to ensure him success in his career as a drug dealer. As it happened, he did prosper for some years and became a rich man, but in the end he met his fate as violently as had his unfortunate victims.

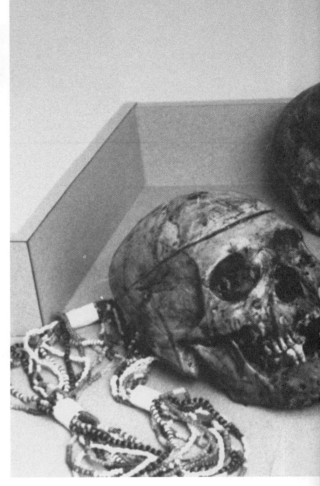

SORCERER'S APPRENTICE

Adolfo de Jesus Constanzo was born in 1962 to a teenage Cuban mother, and grew up in Puerto Rico and Miami. As a child, he served as an altar boy in the Roman Catholic religion, and also accompanied his mother on trips to Haiti to learn about Voodoo. As a teenager, he became apprenticed to a local sorcerer, and he began to practise the occult African religion of Palo Mayombe, which involves animal sacrifice. Later, as an adult, he moved to Mexico City and met the men who were to become his first followers: Martin Quintana, Jorge Montes and Omar Orea. He set up a homosexual ménage a trois with Quintana and Orea (calling one his 'man' and the other his 'woman') and began to run a profitable business casting spells to bring good luck, which involved expensive ritual sacrifices of chickens, goats, snakes, zebras and even lion cubs. Many of his

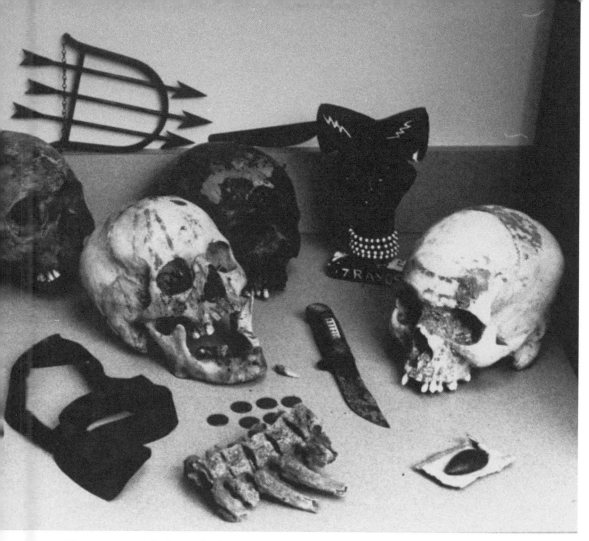

clients were rich drug dealers and hitmen who enjoyed the violence of Constanzo's 'magical' displays. He also attracted other rich members of Mexican society, including several high-ranking, corrupt policemen, who introduced him to the city's powerful narcotics cartels.

At this time, Constanzo started to raid graveyards for human bones to put in his *nganga* or cauldron, but he did not stop at that: before long, live human beings were being sacrificed. Over twenty victims, whose mutilated bodies were found in and around Mexico City, are thought to have met their end in this way. Constanzo began to believe that his magic spells were responsible for the success of the cartels, and demanded to become a full partner with one of the most powerful families, the Calzadas. When he was rejected, seven family members disappeared; their bodies were found with fingers, toes, ears, brains and even – in one case – the spine missing.

Not surprisingly, relations soon cooled with the Calzadas, so Constanzo made friends with a new cartel, the Hernandez brothers. He also took up with a young woman named Sara Aldrete, who became the high priestess of the cult. In 1988, he moved to Rancho Santa Elena, a house in the desert, where he carried out ever more sadistic ritual murders, sometimes of strangers, and sometimes – killing two birds with one stone, as it were – of rival drug dealers. He also used the ranch to store huge shipments of cocaine and marijuana.

However, on 13 March 1989, he made a fatal mistake. Looking for fresh meat to put in the pot, his henchmen abducted a student, Mark Kilroy, from outside a Mexican bar and took him back to the ranch. There Constanzo brutally murdered him. This time, however, the victim was no drug runner, petty crook or local peasant; he was a young man from a respectable Texan family that was determined to bring their son's killer to justice.

Under pressure from Texan politicians, police initially picked up four of Constanzo's followers, including two of the Hernandez brothers. They interrogated the men, eliciting horrifying tales of occult magic and ritual human sacrifice. Officers then raided the ranch, discovering Constanzo's cauldron, which contained various items such as a dead black cat and a human brain. Fifteen mutilated corpses were then dug up at the ranch, one of them Mark Kilroy's.

DEATH PACT

Constanzo meanwhile had fled to Mexico City. He was discovered only when police were called to his apartment because of a dispute taking place there. As the officers approached, Constanzo opened fire with a machine gun, but he soon realized that he was surrounded.

He handed the gun to a follower, Alvaro de Leon, who was a professional hitman, and ordered Leon to open fire on him and his lover, Martin Quintana. By the time police reached the apartment, Constanzo and Quintana were dead, locked in a ghoulish embrace. De Leon, known as 'El Duby', and Sara Aldrete, Constanzo's female companion, were immediately arrested.

A total of fourteen cult members were charged with a range of crimes, from murder and drug running to obstructing the course of justice. Sara Aldrete, Elio Hernandez and Serafin Hernandez were convicted of multiple murders and were ordered to serve prison sentences of over sixty years each; El Duby was given a thirty-year term. The reign of Adolfo de Jesus Constanzo, high-society sorcerer and maniacal murderer, was over.

THE WILDERNESS KILLINGS

It sounds like the stuff of pulp fiction – a serial killer who abducted his victims, set them loose in the Alaskan wilderness, then hunted them down with knife and rifle. Robert Hansen made it a nightmare reality for the dozen or more women he plucked from the sleazy Tenderloin district of Anchorage, Alaska, between 1973 and 1983. Hansen appears to have been motivated to kill by little more than a desire to get back at the world in general, and women in particular.

RESENTMENT

Born in Pocahontas, Idaho, on 13 February 1939, Hansen's father, Christian, was a Danish immigrant who ran his own bakery. A strict disciplinarian, he soon had his son working in the bakery at all hours. This did not help Robert's social life as a teenager; neither did the young man's acne, or his stammer.

After Robert left school he carried on working for his father, while also signing up for the army reserves. In 1960, he married a local girl. Shortly afterward he burnt down part of the local high school. He was arrested, found guilty and sentenced to three years in prison. His wife responded to discovering this unsuspected side of her new husband by divorcing him.

NEW START

Shortly after his release from prison, Hansen remarried and in 1967, the couple decided to make a new start, and headed for America's last frontier: Alaska. They settled in the main town of Anchorage and, for the first time, Hansen seemed to find a place where he could fit in. He had used his time in the army reserves to become an expert marksman and was now able to put these skills to use, gaining a reputation as an outdoorsman.

Somewhere along the way, though, killing wild animals failed to fulfil Hansen's need for revenge. The year after the last of his record-breaking animal kills, he was arrested for the attempted rape of a housewife and the actual rape of a prostitute. The rape of prostitutes not being taken too seriously, he served only six months in prison.

According to his own confession, from 1973 onwards Hansen developed a routine whereby he would pick up prostitutes and topless dancers from Anchorage's Tenderloin district, fly them out into the wilderness and rape them. If they submitted to his sexual whims, he let them live, taking them back to Anchorage with the threat that if they reported what had happened they would be in big trouble. He murdered those who did not comply; setting them loose in the wilderness, giving them a head start, then hunting and killing them. His activities went on unnoticed Anchorage, during the 1970s oil boom, was a wild town, where people came and went all the time.

In 1980, however, the bodies of two young women did come to light. One has never been identified. The second was a topless dancer named Joanna Messina. Two years later the body of another topless dancer called Sherry Morrow was found by hunters near the Knik River. By now, the police suspected they were dealing with a serial killer.

RESPECTED CITIZEN

Far from being a suspected murderer, Hansen had by now become a well-to-do respected citizen. He had his own bakery, lived in a pleasant house with his wife and two children, and even had his own small private plane.

In June 1983, all that changed. A trucker picked up a prostitute running down the road with a pair of handcuffs trailing from one wrist. He took her to the police station, where she explained that she had been picked up by a client who had taken her to his house, raped and brutalized her, then taken her to his private plane. She had managed to escape at the last minute, and was convinced that, if she had not run, the man would certainly have killed her since he had made no attempt to hide his face. She led the police to the house and then to the light aircraft from which she had escaped. Both belonged to Robert Hansen.

Hansen denied everything. He produced an alibi, claiming to have spent the evening in question with two friends. With no more evidence than the unsupported word of a prostitute, the police decided not to press charges.

Three months later, another body was found, that of Paula Golding. The police task force called in FBI serial-killer expert John Douglas, and they decided to have another look at Hansen. Hansen's friends admitted that the alibi was false. Hansen's house was searched and the police found weapons used in the murders, plus IDs taken from the dead girls.

Hansen made a deal whereby he would be charged with four murders, and would serve his time in a federal prison. In return for this he confessed to many other murders, for which he was never charged. He took state troopers on a tour of the wilderness, in the course of which they were able to recover eleven bodies, several of which remain unidentified.

On 18 February 1984, Hansen was convicted of murder and sentenced to life plus 461 years.

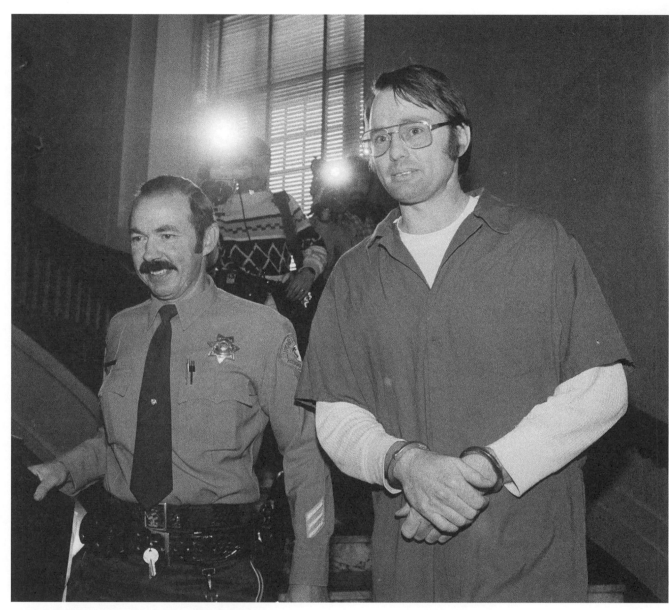

THE WOMAN IN A BOX

The 'Woman In A Box' refers to a case so traumatic to its victim that the media have universally protected her anonymity to this very day, twenty years after her case finally came to trial. Even today, she is referred to simply as 'Carol Smith' (or sometimes 'Colleen Stan').

▲ *Looking surprisingly relaxed: Cameron Hooker, mid trial. Who knows how long he may have kept Carol locked up, if his wife had not turned him in*

295

Twenty-year-old Carol was living in Eugene, Oregon, when she left one May morning in 1977 to visit her friend in Westwood, California, to wish her a happy birthday. It was a four-hundred mile trip, but this was the 1970s, and Carol shared the free-wheeling spirit of her times. She walked on down to Interstate 5 to hitch a ride with someone kind enough to give her a lift – but tragically chose the wrong car.

After four days with no news of Carol, her friends back in Eugene rang her family, but they had not heard from her either. When they found out she had never arrived in Westwood, alarm bells started ring: Carol had always been the sort of person who kept in touch with those close to her, and now nobody knew where she was. Her friends in Eugene filed a missing persons report with the local police department.

MIRACLE RETURN

The first suspect was Carol's ex-husband (Carol had married when she was seventeen), but he was easily ruled out. Time passed, still with no sign of the young woman, and hope faded. Jenise, her sister, was the first to believe that she had been murdered, and as time went by, her case grew cold.

Then came an amazing development: more than two years after she disappeared, her sisters received a letter from her. It was full of affection, but short on detail: she had settled down somewhere with a man, 'Michael', and they were not to worry. She was sorry she could not be in touch more. Carol's family breathed a sigh of relief. Three years later, they finally got to see her again. She did not divulge much about her own life, but she was visibly overjoyed at seeing her family again. They were curious, of course, about what she had really been up to all that time, but they felt that they must have somehow offended her for her to go off like that, and they did not want to risk offending her again. They did not press her on her personal life but it might have been much better if they had, because Carol's life had turned into a living nightmare.

HEAD IN A BOX

Carol had hitch-hiked all the way down to Red Bluff on the day she had left Eugene, back in 1977, and she only had another fifty miles to go when a blue Dodge Colt pulled over with a young family inside. She climbed in without hesitation, but however clean-cut the young couple and their baby appeared to be, she began to feel increasingly uncomfortable. The Hooker family seemed amiable enough, but deep down she felt something was wrong. When they stopped at a gas station

◀ *Cameron Hooker listens as he is sentenced to 104 years in prison*

she very nearly did not get back in the car, but when she did they were so nice to her she felt ashamed of herself. Then they made a detour to look at some ice caves. When they pulled off the road the man held a knife to her throat, and asked her if she was going to do whatever he said.

'Yes,' said Carol, desperately afraid. One word: yes. It destroyed her life, but it also saved it. She was then bound, blindfolded, and gagged. The man took a heavy soundproofed plywood box and fastened it to her head, which nearly suffocated her. Then she could feel them putting her into a sleeping bag.

DAILY TORTURE

When they got her back to their home she was kept in a large wooden box in the cellar, although Hooker would often take her out to torture her, or leave her dangling by her wrists from the ceiling. At other times she would be left in the box for days on end, with a bedpan. Initially she was fed a single meal every other day, but when her health began to seriously deteriorate Hooker and his wife began to feed her once a day. Hooker made her sign a contract which appeared to give their master-slave relationship some legal status. He told her she was registered with the Slave Company, who saw everything, and who would kill Carol's family if she ever ran away. Over the years, Carol's mind gave way and she came to believe it all.

After that, Carol's life got marginally easier. She was given handiwork to perform in a cage under the stairs. She was allowed out into the yard on weekends (neighbours believed she was a nanny). She was allowed to go jogging and to write home, albeit letters that were heavily censored. Janice Hooker took her out for a night's drinking, and Cameron Hooker escorted her for that single visit home, from whence she returned, for another three and a half years in captivity. Their hold on her was total.

THE JEALOUS WIFE

Jealousy was the key to Carol's freedom. Cameron had begun to have sex with Carol, and his wife was jealous. She confessed to her pastor, and he phoned the police. When the police came, she showed them the remains of an earlier victim who had not been as pliant as Carol, and who had been shot in the belly.

Janice Hooker plea bargained and was set free. Cameron Hooker was sentenced to life imprisonment. Even at the trial it was a close run thing, with the victim showing no signs of hostility towards her former captor of seven years. Some say it was only the physical scars of her torture that swung the jury, but whatever the truth, after so many years of horrifying cruelty, justice was finally done.

THE YORKSHIRE RIPPER

Peter Sutcliffe, the Yorkshire Ripper, was a hen-pecked husband who had difficulty in getting or maintaining an erection. He only had sex with one of his thirteen female victims, and on the night he was caught – January 2nd 1981 – he was again having difficulties with a prostitute called Ava Reivers, who would have become his fourteenth. Impotence, in fact, may have driven him to murder in the first place; and killing may have been his sinister way of finding its solution and cure. For at some time in the late-1960s, he'd been publicly humiliated by a prostitute for his inadequacy. So he took his revenge: he began to rape them, not with his penis, but with a knife, a hammer, a sharpened screwdriver – any tool that came to hand.

The first mutilated body was found on playing fields in Leeds on October 30th 1975; the second, less than three months later, in an alleyway nearby. Thirteen months after that a third victim was discovered, stabbed to death, in the same general area, though this time in a suburban park. Though the police took

▲ *Sutcliffe was found guilty of 13 murders and 7 attempted murders*

action in all three cases – and the name 'Yorkshire Ripper' was coined in a national newspaper – the respectable folk of the city were not particularly concerned. For all three women, however brutally murdered, had been streetwalkers, sinners, and the killings had been centered on the red-light district of Chapeltown.

With the next two killings, though, the respectable folk of Yorkshire learned to fear. For the Ripper now moved around and might attack any woman. On 24 April 1977, he killed a fourth prostitute in another Yorkshire city, Bradford; and then, back in Leeds again, an ordinary sixteen-year-old who was involved in nothing more sinister than walking home after an evening out dancing.

The photos are labelled: JEAN ROYLE, JAYNE MACDONALD, JOSEPHINE WHITAKER, BARBARA LEACH, HELEN RYTKA

▶ What drove Sutcliffe to murder so many young women? He has never revealed his motivation to commit murder

With this fifth murder, especially, the people of Yorkshire, indeed of the whole country, began to wake up. The police were inundated with telephone calls, tips, information, supposition – and began to sink under the burden. By this time they had only two pieces of information that firmly linked the murders together: the savagery of the killer's attacks and identical shoeprints that had been found near the bodies of two of the victims. But then, when with the next two attacks really important clues were offered, they clearly failed to see them.

The first, again in Bradford, was on another prostitute who, this time, was savagely beaten but not killed, as if the Ripper had been interrupted. When she recovered from surgery, she told police that her attacker had been blond and had driven a white Ford Cortina. The second was much further afield, in Manchester in

Lancashire; and the victim, again a prostitute, had actually been attacked and mutilated twice, the second time eight days after her death. The police, who found her body a day after the second attack, also found her handbag nearby; and in it was a brand-new £5 note, which turned out to have been issued by a bank in Shipley, Yorkshire. It had formed part of the payroll at the engineering and haulage works where Peter Sutcliffe worked as a truck-driver.

The friendly, unassuming Sutcliffe was interviewed – he was actually interviewed eight times in all during the enquiry. But, though he drove a Ford Cortina, he was not blond, so he was on this occasion eliminated. Apparently the police didn't pay much attention to the handwritten placard this neatly-dressed, diffident man had put up in the cab of his truck:

'In this truck is a man whose latent genius, if unleashed, would rock the nation, whose dynamic energy would overpower those around him. Better let him sleep.'

Sutcliffe seems to have been unfazed by this, his first brush with the law. In short order after this, he battered and mutilated three more prostitutes, in Bradford, Huddersfield and again Manchester; and then killed a nineteen-year-old building-society clerk as she took a short cut through a park in Halifax. Whatever suspicions the police might have had of him were, in any case, soon dismissed. For the investigating squad at this point received an audio-tape with a taunting message from 'the Ripper,' which seemed to contain inside information about the crimes. But the accent 'the Ripper' spoke in wasn't from Yorkshire, as Sutcliffe's was. It was Geordie, said phoneticists – i.e. from the area around Newcastle.

The whole investigation, then, went off at a highly-publicised tangent; and Sutcliffe was free to strike again. In September 1978, he killed a nineteen-year-old university student in the centre of Bradford; and the following August, a respectable forty-seven-year-old civil servant on her way home from the Department of Education in Pudsey. He went on to attack, first a doctor in Leeds and then a sixteen-year-old girl in Huddersfield – though both survived, the first because he seems to have changed his mind and stopped, and the second, because her screams brought people running and scared him away. His final onslaught came more than a year later when a twenty-year old student at Leeds University got off a bus in a middle-class suburb and started walking towards her hall of residence. Sutcliffe got out of his car and beat her about the head with a

▲ *Sutcliffe photographed on his way to court*

the weapons in the back of the car, but both he and Reivers were taken back to a police-station and the weapons were later recovered. After a while, the man who'd given his name as Peter Williams confessed to being the Yorkshire Ripper.

There's been endless speculation about what drove Peter Sutcliffe to murder. Was it because of his worship of his mother and his shyness with girls as a boy? Or because of the time he spent as a young man working first in a graveyard and then in a morgue? Or was it because of the prostitute who'd mocked him in public or the wife who continually nagged him? Was the whole killing spree triggered by his discovery in 1972 that his adored mother was only too human after all — and had long been having a love affair?

Whatever the cause or the trigger, though, Peter Sutcliffe was found guilty of thirteen murders and seven attempted murders. He was sentenced to life imprisonment on each count, with the recommendation that he not be released for at least thirty years.

The man with the Geordie accent who sent the police the hoax tape — and caused indirectly the deaths of three women – was tracked down 20 years later. In 2005 John Humble was arrested after DNA evidence tied him to the envelopes. He confessed to perverting the course of justice in 2006 and was jailed for eight years.

hammer, before dragging her across the road into some bushes. He undressed her and stabbed her repeatedly, once straight through the eye, with a sharpened screwdriver because —

'she seemed to be staring at me'

— he said later.

He was finally picked up in Sheffield on January 2nd 1981, while sitting in his car with Ava Reivers in a well-known trysting-place for prostitutes and their johns. Police stopped by for a routine check, and wondered why Reivers' client's car seemed to have false number plates. Sutcliffe did his best to get rid of

INDEX

PICTURE CREDITS

PICTURE CREDITS

Page 2, Yale Center for British Art, Paul Mellon Collection; p.12, By courtesy of The Mercers' Company/photo: Nicholas Turpin; p.15, Courtesy of the Dean and Chapter of Ely Cathedral/photo: Eileen Tweedy; p.18 &19, Courtesy Wenhaston St. Peter Church/photo: Eileen Tweedy; p.20, Courtesy Ranworth St. Helen's Church/photo: Eileen Tweedy; p.22-3, By courtesy of The Mercers' Company/photo: Nicholas Turpin; p.25, Courtesy of Cullompton Church, Devon/photo: Nick Tilly; p.26-7, © Joe Rock; p.28-9, Courtesy St. Mary's Church, Abergavenny/photo: Eileen Tweedy; p.31, Courtesy Exeter Cathedral/photo: Eileen Tweedy; p.33, Courtesy St. Mary Magdalene Church, Withersdale/photo: Eileen Tweedy; p.37, Courtesy St. Cuthbert's Church, Wells/photo: Eileen Tweedy; p.40-41, Reproduced by courtesy of the Trustees, The National Gallery, London; p.43, Jewish Museum/Art Resource, New York. © ARS, NY and DACS, London 1999; p.44, Courtesy Merthyr Issui Church, Patrishow/photo: Eileen Tweedy; p.46, photo: Eileen Tweedy; p.50, © Country Life Picture Library; p.52-3, National Trust Picture Library/photo: John Hammond; p.56, By courtesy of the Board of Trustees of the Victoria & Albert Museum/photo: Sarah Hodges; p.57, Courtesy of the Marquess of Salisbury; p.60, Reproduced by courtesy of the Trustees, The National Gallery, London; p.61, The Royal Collection, © Her Majesty the Queen; p.62, Museo Thyssen-Bornemisza, Madrid; p.64, The Royal Collection, © Her Majesty the Queen; p.65, Reproduced by kind permission of His Grace the Duke of Marlborough; p.68

& 72, The Royal Collection, © Her Majesty the Queen; p.73, Devonshire Collection, Chatsworth/Photographic Survey Courtauld Institute of Art; p.76, In the collection of the Duke of Buccleuch & Queensberry KT; p.77, Collections/photo: John Miller; p.78, ©1986 Malcolm Crowthers; p.80, © The Sir Alfred Munnings Art Museum, Dedham, Essex; p.84, National Gallery of Scotland; p.85, Yale Center for British Art, Paul Mellon Collection; p.92-3, National Trust Photographic Library/photo: Jerry Harpur; p.96-7, Courtauld Institute Galleries, London; p.101, Reproduced by courtesy of the Trustees, The National Gallery, London; p.102, © The British Museum; p.105, The Tate Gallery, London; p.107, Yale Center for British Art, Paul Mellon Collection; p.109, Private Collection/photo: The Royal Academy of Arts, London; p.112-13, Reproduced by courtesy of the Trustees of the National Gallery, London; p.114, © The Frick Collection, New York; p.115, The Royal Collection, © Her Majesty The Queen; p.116-17, National Trust Photographic Library; p.120, Private Collection; p.121, Yale Center for British Art, Paul Mellon Collection; p.124, The Turner Collection, Tate Gallery, London; p.128 & 129, Courtesy Royal Society of Arts, London/photo: A.C.Cooper Ltd.; p.132, By courtesy of the Board of Trustees of the Victoria & Albert Museum; p.133, Tate Gallery, London; p.134, Birmingham Museums & Art Gallery; p.139, Sir John Soane Museum/photo: Ole Woldbye; p.141, By courtesy of the Board of Trustees of the Victoria & Albert Museum; p.142, Reproduced by courtesy of the Trustees, The National Gallery, London; p.144-5, By courtesy of the Board of Trustees of the Victoria & Albert Museum; p.149, 152-3 & 156-7, The Turner Collection, Tate Gallery, London; p.160, Holloway Collection, Royal Holloway College; p.163, Reproduced by courtesy of the Trustees, The National Gallery, London; p.167, Birmingham Museums and Art Gallery; p.171, photo:

Jeremy Cockayne/ARCAID; p.174, The Board of Trustees of the National Museums & Galleries on Merseyside; p.177, © Ashmolean Museum, Oxford; p.179, The Board of Trustees of the National Museums & Galleries on Merseyside; p.182, © Manchester City Art Galleries; p.183, Tate Gallery, London; p.184 & 186, © Manchester City Art Galleries; p.187, Tate Gallery, London; p.189, Delaware Art Museum. Samuel and Mary R. Bancroft Memorial; p.190-91, The Faringdon Collection Trust, Buscot Park; p.194, John Birdsall Photography; p.197, © BBC Worldwide; p.198, Courtesy Artangel and Karsten Schubert, London/photo: Nicholas Turpin; p.203, National Gallery of Scotland; p.207, Tate Gallery, London/© Wyndham Lewis and the estate of Mrs. G. A.Wyndham Lewis, by kind permission of the Wyndham Lewis Memorial Trust; p.210, Reproduced by kind permission of the President and Council of the Royal College of Surgeons of England/Crown Copyright. Reproduced with the permission of the Controller of HMSO; p.213, photo: Chris Gascoigne 1990/ARCAID; p.215, Fitzwilliam Museum, Cambridge/© Estate of Stanley Spencer 1999. All rights reserved DACS; p.217, © The Henry Moore Foundation; p.219, City of Nottingham Museums; Castle Museum and Art Gallery/© Henry Lessore; p. 221, Tate Gallery, London; p.222-3, Staatsgalerie moderner Kunst, Munich/Andreas Freytag, Artothek; p.227, The Museum of Modern Art, New York. Philip Johnson Fund/Courtesy Bridget Riley (Karsten Schubert, London); p.228, Kunsthalle Tübingen, Sammlung G.F. Zundel/© Richard Hamilton 1999 All rights reserved DACS; p.229, Arts Council Collection/© David Hockney, 1961; p.232, Collection Michael D. Abrams/© Patrick Caulfield 1999 All rights reserved DACS; p.233, Private Collection, Mexico. Courtesy Anthony d'Offay Gallery; p.238-9, Originally commissioned and shown at Matt's Gallery, London, 1987/Saatchi Collection, London/photo: Anthony Oliver.